AF247577

READY FOR BUSINESS "OVER THERE"

SOLDIERS OF THE SEA

The Story of the United States Marine Corps

by

WILLIS J. ABBOT

ILLUSTRATED

The Scholar's Bookshelf

**Soldiers of the Sea: The Story of the
United States Marine Corps**
by Willis J. Abbot

First Published in 1918

This edition published 2005 by

The Scholar's Bookshelf

110 Melrich Road
Cranbury NJ USA 08512
www.scholarsbookshelf.com

ISBN: 0-945726-97-X
Library of Congress Control Number:
2005936672

Printed in the United States of America

FOREWORD

I BELIEVE Mr. Abbot has produced a worthy and important addition to the military history of our country in this volume, which follows the present day U. S. Marines throughout their experiences, to the Bahamas, the burning deserts of Africa, to Tripoli, Fiji Islands, Japan, China, Philippine Islands, the Arctics, the South Seas, Nicaragua, Haiti—and wherever duty has raised her hand, and, pointing, said " Go."

Until now one could search the public libraries almost in vain for works pertaining to the U. S. Marine Corps, as such, and Mr. Abbot has rendered a notable service in bringing out a work which will, in thrilling narrative and excitement, resemble the imaginings of a Dumas or a Jules Verne, but which deviates not one jot from historical truth.

T. G. STERRETT,
Major, U. S. Marines.

CONTENTS

ILLUSTRATIONS

SOLDIERS OF THE SEA

SOLDIERS OF THE SEA

CHAPTER I

Antiquity of the Marine Corps.—Jests at the Expense of
Marines.—Early Uniforms and Qualifications.—The Marines in the Revolution.—The *Bon Homme Richard* and
the *Serapis.*—The Descent on New Providence.

THE MARINES

By James J. Montague

Who Were Then Doing Police Duty at Santiago.

There is just a handful of 'em; little scraps is what they're for.
They're a lot too shy in numbers for a reg'lar big league war.
But you set 'em down in Cuba, or some other messy spot,
Where there's something being started, and the fuss is getting hot;
Where there's wild-eyed riot rampant and the shots are flying
    thick,
And there'll be an end of trouble mighty quick.

They don't ask for even chances; all they want to have in sight
Is their equal weight in wildcats and they'll sail right in and fight.
Show 'em any bunch of scrappers that must needs be pacified
An' it won't be many seconds 'fore the rough-house will subside.
Just police work is their business, show 'em what there is to do,
And it never takes 'em long to put it through.

Killed and wounded? Yes, a plenty, though their jobs are al-
    ways small
That don't make a bit less deadly a careerin' rifle ball.
In a war or in a scrimmage half an ounce of flying lead
Is as dangerous to soldiers, and will kill 'em just as dead.
They may not be splendid figures in historic battle scenes,
But they're able-bodied fighters—those Marines.

AMPHIBIOUS? Yes, more than that. No one word can fully express the multifarious activities of the members of the United States Marine Corps. Equally at home on land and sea they deserve the title of Amphibians. But the members of their highly skilled flying corps ride the aerial currents as confidently as their fellows ride the waves. Once the world laughed at the idea of " horse-marines," but it is nearly a century since our marines made a record-breaking march across the North African deserts astride of camels.

And as for fighting! The adversaries of our marines have been as multi-colored as Joseph's coat, as varied in skin, language and habitat as the exhibits in the ethnological department of a great world's fair. They have fought savages in the Libyan desert, Chinese at the walls of Pekin, South Sea Islanders at Nukahiva, Mongols in Corea, American Indians in Alabama and Florida, and pirates of every race in Quallah-Batoo. And as for their services against men of their own color—well, let us read a little later of what they have been doing on the fields of France.

Both romance and jest hang about the word marines. Innumerable are the stories told at their expense, growing largely out of the dislike of sailors for the men who exercised police supervision over them. In the British navy a century ago the marines were called " empty bottles " by the bluejackets, the implication being that they were useless. It is said that a marine officer was dining at a mess table with the then Duke of York when the latter in a stentorian voice called to the servant, " Here, take away those empty bottles ! "

Deeming himself insulted the marine officer demanded an explanation.

" I merely meant," said the Duke suavely, " that they had done their duty once well and are prepared to do it again."

The common phrase, " Tell that to the marines," had its origin in a sailors' jest which depicted the sea soldiers as capable of swallowing any yarn however egregious.   Byron put it into poetry:

> " But, whatsoe'er betide, ah, Neuha! now
> Unman me not; the hour will not allow
> A tear: ' I'm thine whatever intervenes!'
> ' Right,' quoth Ben, ' that will do for the marines.' "

But earlier far than Byron, the gossipy Mr. Pepys, himself a figure in the British navy in the days of Charles II, gave this account of the origin of the phrase:

" I had speech yesterday at Deptford," said Mr. Pepys, " with the captain of the Defyance, who hath but lately returned from the Indies and who told me the two most wonderful things that ever I think I did hear in my life." Among the stories told were those of fish flying in the air.

" Fish flying in the air! " exclaimed his Majesty, " Ha Ha, a quaint conceit which 'twere too good to spoil with keeping. What, Sir—" (he turned and beckoned to the Colonel, Sir William Killigrew of the newly raised maritime regiment on foot, who was following in close conversation with the Duke of York)—" we would discourse with you on a matter touching your element. What say you, Colonel, to a man who swears he hath seen fishes flying in the air?"

"I should say, Sire," returned the sea soldier simply, "that the man hath sailed in Southern seas. For when your Majesty's business carried me thither of late I did frequently observe more flying fish in one hour than the hairs of my head in number."

Old Rowley glanced narrowly at the Colonel's frank weatherbeaten face. Then with a laugh he turned to the secretary and said, "Mr. Pepys, from the very nature of their calling, no class of our subjects can have so wide a knowledge of seas and lands as the officers and men of our loyal maritime regiment. Henceforth whenever we cast doubt upon a tale that lacketh likelihood we will tell it to the Marines—if they believe it, it is safe to say it is true."

The most cruel witticism at the expense of the marine corps flourished in the United States up to a decade ago, when it languished and died, killed by the rapid development of the corps in efficiency and the marked improvement in its personnel. It had long been the practice of men prominent in American public service, military, naval or political, who had sons who were wild, and had no liking for the curriculum of either West Point or Annapolis, to get these youths commissions in the Marine Corps. As a result there sprang up a cynical reading of the initials of the official designation of that organization—U. S. M. C., "Useless Sons Made Comfortable."

To-day, when the standard of admission to the Marine Corps is perhaps higher than of any other branch of the armed service, this rather sardonic pleasantry is forgotten.

The marine corps is no mere modern upstart among the military and naval organizations of the United States. Its origin runs back to the earliest days of the nation and even earlier. It is one of our antiquities—as antiquity runs in this most modern of nations. As early as 1740, when the American colonies still yielded cheerful allegiance to the British crown, three regiments of American marines were raised for service in the British navy on this side of the Atlantic. Their regimental officers were appointed by the crown, and it is notable that the first commander was Colonel Spotiswood, of Virginia, a name notable in the history of that colony. Their uniform was camlet coats, brown linen waistcoats and canvas trousers—a rather tropical outfit it would seem. Lest " camlet " be a word not readily understandable in these days it may be explained that it was a durable and almost water-proof cloth, much used before the days of rubber or cravenetted fabrics.

What these earlier American marines in the days before American independence may have done is lost in the mists of time. It was a period when the chief service of the British navy on this side of the water was in the suppression of West Indian pirates, and the marines may well have taken an active part in that. But along toward 1775 the British found other things than sporadic piracy to trouble them. A half-imbecile German king on the English throne, and a ministry void of the principles of liberty and justice for which the English people have ever valiantly fought, oppressed the American colonies and they rose in revolt. What might be called the British-American marines disappeared in the welter, and on the 10th of November, 1775, the true United States marine corps was created by the following resolution of the Continental Congress:

Resolved, That two battalions of marines be raised consisting of one colonel, two lieutenant-colonels, two majors, and other officers, as usual in other regiments; that they consist of an equal number of privates with other battalions; that particular care be taken that no persons be appointed to offices, or enlisted into said battalions, but such as are good seamen, or so acquainted with maritime affairs as to be able to serve to advantage by sea when required; that they be enlisted and commissioned to serve for and during the present war with Great Britain and the colonies, unless dismissed by order of Congress; that they be distinguished by the names of the First and Second Battalions of American Marines.

Not until a month later, when Congress commissioned several small war vessels did the American navy have its true beginnings. Wherefore the marines find a certain proud satisfaction in pointing out that their organization antedates that of the navy itself.

It will be noted that the resolution creating the marine corps specified that the men enlisted must be " good seamen." That is a qualification long since discarded. Though " soldiers and sailors too," as Kipling wrote of Her Majesty's marines, the members of the corps never took part in working the ships, although they at times have served certain of the ship's guns. Their battle service in the old navy in the days of yardarm to yardarm conflicts was mainly to board the adversary or to repel boarders, and with their muskets to keep up a constant fire on the decks of the enemy picking off so far as possible the conspicuous officers.

Always the marines have been the police of a man-of-war, serving as the captain's orderlies, mounting guard at gangways and maintaining order among the crew. In the early days of the British navy when seamen were largely obtained through the methods of the press-gang and served but sulkily at their unsought posts the marines, musket or pistol in hand, were often posted about each gun to keep the bluejackets up to their duty. Out of this task, and the less offensive but more irritating incidents of daily police duties, sprang a pronounced antagonism between sailors and marines, which in many ships was fostered by the commanders, who thought that it added to the police efficiency of the latter. It never developed to any extent in the American navy, which has happily, since its earliest days, been able to man its ships without recourse to press-gangs, and has not needed armed guards to see that the bluejackets fought their best in the moment of action.

In telling the early history of the marines the historian is handicapped by the fact that the chroniclers of those days drew no sharp distinction between the sailors and the marines. The part played by the latter in ship actions is not distinctly described, and a joint expedition or landing party of the two forces is commonly credited to the blue-jackets alone. But we know that when in December, 1775, Congress authorized the building of thirteen ships of war and appointed Esek Hopkins commander-in-chief, the marine corps of two battalions was fully organized, and was able to put a detachment on each ship as soon as it went into commission. It was in that year and month that Paul Jones first took the sea in the *Alfred*, flying the first flag of the colonies, showing a pine tree with a rattlesnake about to strike, with the motto, " Don't tread on me! "

Early in 1776 Commodore Hopkins began a cruise in southern waters with a squadron made up of the *Alfred, Columbus, Doria, Cabot, Providence, Hornet, Wasp* and *Fly*. The last was a dispatch boat; the other two insects small sloops of war. The whole expedition could have been annihilated by one of our modern destroyers. Yet it was strong enough to make a descent upon a British navy base at New Providence, in the Bahamas, where a large body of stores had been collected. All the marines in the little fleet, numbering in all about 200, together with some sailors, were landed under command of Captain Nichols. The affrighted populace made no effort to oppose the landing, and the small fort, which represented British power on the island, was too distant from the point of debarkation to make any resistance to it. After a brief delay

Nichols formed his marines into a storming party and carried the fort gallantly by assault. After holding the town for a day the marines retired, taking with them 40 cannon, 15 brass mortars, and a large quantity of munitions, as well as the governor and several prominent citizens to be held as hostages. It might have been the occasion—though it was not—for the first employment of the famous dispatch:

"*The marines have landed and have the situation well in hand.*"

During the year 1776 there were a score or more actions between the little brigs and barks then forming the United States navy, and the armed ships of King George. Though there is no historical record of the services of the marines during the year, the fact that in every action officers and privates of that corps were reported killed shows that they were pretty widely distributed among the ships. Eleven suffered in the action between the *Albert* and *Cabot* and the British 20-gun frigate *Glasgow;* four when the *Lexington,* Captain Richard Barry, captured the *Edward.*

Toward the end of this year Congress, in the course of some naval legislation, changed the style of the uniforms for marines, directing that they should wear " a green coat faced with white, round cuffs, slashed sleeves and pockets with buttons around the cuffs, a silver epaulet on the right shoulder, skirts turned back, buttons to suit the facings, white waistcoat and breeches edged with green, black gaiters and garters." Furthermore, the men were to wear green shirts "if they can be procured."

Some different costume this to the simple and business-like khaki of the service uniforms in the war year of 1918. But explicit as were the directions for the marine's garb, some commanders took liberties with them. In 1799 John Adams, our envoy to France, being in Port Louis L'Orient, fell in with Captain Paul Jones, who was fitting out a squadron in that port. He writes in his diary:

"After dinner walked out with Captain Jones and Landais to see Jones's marines dressed in the English uniform, red and white; a number of very active and clever sergeants and corporals are employed to teach them the exercises and maneuvers and marches, etc.; after which Jones came on board our ship. This is the most ambitious and intriguing officer in the American navy. Jones has art and secrecy, and aspires very high. You see the character of the men in his uniform, and that of his officers and marines *variant* from the uniform established by Congress,— golden buttons for himself, two epaulets; marines in red and white instead of green. Eccentricities and irregularities are to be expected from him. They are in his character, they are visible in his eyes. His voice is soft and still and small; his eye has keenness and mildness and softness in it."

The extent to which marines participated in the exploits of Paul Jones, beginning in 1777, and continuing with practically uninterrupted glory for two years must be somewhat a matter of conjecture. We know that Jones was a stickler for naval etiquette, form and organization, and was a man little likely to let his ships be destitute of a force which was found on every enemy vessel. He had, after two years or more of service as a privateersman, or in command of small commissioned vessels, been summoned by Congress to advise as to the organization and development of the navy, and it was at this period that the marine corps received its greatest encouragement and impetus.

In 1777 Jones received his commission to command his first frigate, the *Ranger*, of 18 guns. It happened that on the day he took command Congress adopted the Stars and Stripes as the design for the national flag. Jones had one made immediately and raised it on the *Ranger*—the first of the starry flags to float over an American warship. He had likewise been the first to raise the pine-tree flag over a colonial cruiser.

In the first action of the *Ranger*, in which the British sloop of war *Drake* was taken, Lieutenant Wallingford of the marines was killed. It is difficult to tell how many marines were assigned to this or other ships in the early days of the history of the corps. An old requisition for uniforms for marines on the frigate *Boston* enumerating "forty green coats faced with white; forty white waistcoats and forty white breeches" indicates pretty clearly how many were on that ship. Jones's report of the battle between the *Bon Homme Richard* and the

Serapis indicates that on the former ship were 149 marines. But it is only by inference from such isolated data that we can guess the extent of the marine forces on our early ships of war.

Much of the dashing work of Paul Jones was of a character which would naturally engage the activities of the marines in his ship's company. His descent, for example, upon Whitehaven, where he personally led one landing party which set the torch to British vessels in the harbor engaged most of the marines on his ship. Lieutenant Wallingford led one of the landing parties. Later in the famous raid on the estate of Lord Selkirk, with the purpose of carrying that nobleman off into captivity, the marines took a prominent part.

In the famous action between the *Bon Homme Richard* and the *Serapis* the American ship carried a force of 149 marines, of whom 49 were killed or wounded. The nature of the battle was such as to give especial importance to the work of the marines, as the two ships were never more than a half-pistol shot from each other, and much of the time locked yardarm to yardarm, thus making the fire of the marines' rifles most effective. The battle was one of the most sanguinary in all naval history. The ships at times were so close together that the gunners on one, in loading their guns, would thrust the ends of their ramrods into the portholes of the ship opposite. Both ships were on fire much of the time. Repeatedly each side strove to board but was repulsed by the bluejackets and marines of the other. Indeed the incident that closed the battle was one that could only occur in the close quarters of hand-to-hand battle.

So close were the ships that the marines of the *Richard* were supplied with hand grenades and sent into the upper works and tops of the ship to throw them. One man, with cool daring, clambered far out on the yardarm of the *Richard* and dropped his grenade straight down the open hatch of the *Serapis*. Exploding between decks it set fire to some loose powder that lay strewn upon the decks, by which the cartridges piled near the guns were touched off. Guns were overthrown, men blown to bits; some of them so dreadfully burned that nothing but their collars and wristbands of their shirts and the waistbands of their trousers were left of their clothing.

In a closely fought battle of this character the part played by the marines is necessarily one of the utmost importance. Twice, it is related, the British strove to board the *Bon Homme Richard* but were driven back by the fierceness of the fire from the American tops which were manned by the marines. The same fire kept the enemy closely penned between decks, rendering their main-deck guns almost useless. The ultimate glorious triumph of the Americans was in no slight degree attributable to the valor of the members of the marine corps.

It is not my purpose to tell here in detail the story of the naval events of the Revolution, or for that matter of any of the other wars in which the United States has been engaged. Rather is it my endeavor to disentangle from the maze of early records such portions as indicate the part played by the marine corps that our people may judge how great has been the contribution to American independence and power of this body of fighters so little recognized in our historical literature. In our earlier wars, though the marines did valiant service they received but scant credit at the hands of the historians.

In the spring of 1779 the British established a military post at Castine on the coast of Maine, near the mouth of the Penobscot River. At this time Maine was a district of the colony of Massachusetts where the spirit of revolution was rife. The post was one of some military strength, and three British men-of-war were anchored in the bay under Captain Mowat, notorious for having burned the town of Falmouth, later named Portland, to the ground earlier in the Revolution. Massachusetts was aroused by the news that this officer was again on her coasts. Her legislature vowed that no British post should be established on her soil, and accordingly a joint naval and military expedition was fitted out to proceed against the works at Castine. Great enthusiasm marked the work of outfitting. It is even reported that the ship *Vengeance* carried as common sailors 30 former masters of merchantmen who waived considerations of rank to take part in this adventure. Nine hundred militiamen accompanied the fleet and

300 marines under command of Captain Osborne were scattered among the vessels, of which 44 in all made up the fleet. It was the first naval expedition of any considerable proportions set under way by the colonies and expectation of a very considerable victory ran high. The fleet reached the mouth of the Penobscot without accident. Here they found the banks of the river high and precipitous, and perched on the crest the enemy's batteries, while a considerable fort frowned from the summit of a steep hill that commanded the surrounding terrain. In the river were anchored Mowat's four ships.

Just why the Americans with their marked superiority afloat did not at first dispose of these ships is not explained in any of the contemporaneous accounts of the battle. Instead immediate preparations were made for landing, and a force of about 300 marines and 900 militia were put ashore, covered by a spirited cannonade from the flagship, *Warren*, and her supporting sloops of war. Once landed they found they had to meet about an equal number of Scotch regulars, well drilled and veterans of European service. But the marines and the Massachusetts men dashed forward in the charge with unexampled gallantry. The defenders of the batteries turned and fled to the fort, followed by the eager Americans. But here the assailants found themselves checked. The fort was powerful for defense, with heavy bastions, and a deep moat. More than 100 men had already been put out of action in the American lines, and they hesitated to sacrifice more. So a siege was determined upon, and, digging trenches and mounting in them the guns of the enemy's captured batteries, the Americans sat down to starve out the foe.

It was a fatal decision. Indeed, at no time was the leadership of this expedition at all worthy of the enthusiasm which animated the rank and file. The siege had been in progress three weeks, during which time the marines had twice vainly sought permission to storm the works, when the scout schooner *Tyrannicide* was seen beating up the river with signals flying that indicated the possession of news of importance. Scarcely was her anchor down when a boat put off and made for the flagship *Warren*.

A breathless lieutenant clambered over the flagship's side and saluted Commodore Saltonstall on the quarter deck.

" Captain Cathcart's compliments, sir," he said, " and five British men-of-war are just entering the bay. The first one appears to be the *Raisonnable*, 64."

The news was stunning. The American fleet, though superior in numbers, was far inferior in weight of metal. To oppose the *Raisonnable* with her 64 guns was the *Warren* with 32. Most of the American ships were small privateers, or schooners used as transports. The ships of the regular American service mounted 58 guns, as against 204 guns in the newly arrived fleet. Moreover, the four

British vessels in the river, which should have been destroyed immediately on the arrival of the American flotilla, were still intact, and mounted 54 guns more.

There was nothing for it but flight. Signals notified the marines and troops on shore of the disaster, and the torch was applied to the American vessels. Three fell into the hands of the British. The rest blazed along the river's banks. More than 2,000 men were now left in the midst of almost a trackless wilderness which they must traverse in order to find their way back to friendly shelter. Escape by water was cut off by the British fleet. Separating into parties, they plodded homeward, half starved, with torn and rain-soaked garments, until, footsore and almost perishing, they reached the border settlements and were aided on their way to Boston.

It is recorded that the marines alone retained their military organization and discipline throughout the course of this long and painful retreat.

At one time a United States ambassador to France armed himself and stood shoulder to shoulder with the marines on a war vessel about to go into battle. It was in 1778 when John Adams was being carried to France on the frigate *Boston*—the same ship whose captain, as we have seen, needed 40 pair of white breeches for his marines. A heavily armed ship was sighted in the offing, and the captain of the *Boston*, Samuel Tucker, a fine type of fighting seaman, ordered a chase. As they came up with the quarry, and the roll of the drums calling the ship's company to quarters resounded through the vessel, Mr. Adams seized a gun and took his station with the marines. But he was not long permitted to maintain that militant stand, for Captain Tucker, seeing him in the ranks, requested him to go below. When the envoy demurred the captain put his hand on his shoulder and in a tone of authority said:

" Mr. Adams, I am commanded by the Continental Congress to deliver you safe in France and you must go below."

The envoy smilingly complied.

A good fighter was Tucker and a man of infinite humor. Many are the anecdotes told of him. On this particular occasion the *Boston* for a long time made no response to the continued fire of the ship that it was chasing. Though the guns of the *Boston* were shotted, and the gunners stood at their posts with smoking match-stocks, the captain gave no order but seemed intent upon the maneuvers of the two vessels. The bluejackets at the guns began to murmur, and the undertone of oaths and questions rose so that Tucker could no longer ignore it. Leaning over the taffrail of the quarter deck, he shouted out:

" Hold on, my men! I want to save that egg without breaking the shell."

Not long after he brought his broadside to bear on the stern of the fleeing ship and she struck her colors without awaiting the raking fire.

In 1778 the island of New Providence, which had years before experienced a touch of American valor, had new occasion to judge how United States marines could fight. At that time the British colony numbered about 1,000 souls, and was defended by Fort Nassau, a work of no mean power.

In the neighborhood of New Providence was cruising the United States sloop of war *Providence,* Captain Rathburne, mounting 12 four-pounders, and carrying a crew of 50 men, with about 25 marines. Rathburne determined to make an effort to take New Providence. In addition to the fort, the place was always defended by at least one British armed vessel lying in the harbor, and indeed on this occasion one privateer of 16 guns was there. To those who asked how he would overcome the odds against him Rathburne answered confidently, " By dash and daring."

Anchoring by night on the 27th of January, 1778, in a sheltered cove, Rathburne put a landing party, including his marines, ashore. Luckily they found a small body of American prisoners on the island, and thus reënforced made a night attack on Fort Nassau. The sleepy sentries were speedily overcome, and rockets announced the news of the capture to the *Providence,* which entered the harbor and anchored silently under cover of the darkness. In the morning her crew saw a large 16-gun ship lying near them. She looked suspiciously like a privateer, while five other vessels near by had the general air of being captured American merchantmen. So quietly had the conquest of the night before been effected that the crew of the privateer had no reason to suspect that the fort had changed hands, until "by dawn's early light" they saw flung out from the flagstaff, not the scarlet ensign of Great Britain, but the little known Stars and Stripes. Then a boat put off from the *Providence* and an American lieutenant clambered over the rail of the privateer. He told the captain that the heavy guns of Fort Nassau were trained on his ship, while the *Providence* was ready to attack her unless she surrendered instantly. The Englishman gave in. His crew were taken ashore and deposited in the dungeons of the fort which had lately held American prisoners. Meanwhile, the marines had taken possession of the town, overawed the populace, spiked the guns of a fort on the other side of the harbor, and seized a great quantity of powder and other munitions of war.

But Captain Rathburne had no landing force adequate to hold the town against its people, and the certainty that almost any day some British man-of-war might drop in and overpower the small American force compelled quick action. So, after holding possession for three days, he spiked the guns, carried all the ammunition to his ship and with the American prisoners he had rescued sailed triumphantly away.

In later actions between the U. S. S. *Trumbull*, Captain Nicholson, and the British ship *Watt*, the

LANDING THE MARINES

U. S. S. *Alliance*, Captain Barry, and the British ship *Alert*, the *Congress* and British sloop of war *Savage*, and the Pennsylvania ship *Hyder Ally* and the British *General Monk*, all resulting in American victory, marines were present and served with distinction. A curious illustration of the lax organization of the marine corps at this early period is furnished by the fact that Captain Andrew Porter, who appears on the books of the *Trumbull* as commander of its detachment of marines, was in fact an army captain of artillery assigned for service on the *Trumbull* at his own request.

With the conclusion of the Revolutionary War the navy, and with it the marine corps, was disbanded in accordance with the theory, which it has taken 140 years to controvert in the American mind, that in time of peace we need *not* prepare for war.

While the records are but scanty and fragmentary, they amply show the presence on the principal ships of the infant American navy of a considerable body of marines. The law authorizing the creation of the corps provided for three regiments, presumably of 1,000 men each, and these were distributed among the ships in bodies ranging from a mere sergeant's guard of 12 or 15 up to a detachment of 60 men with two commissioned officers. All of the fighting ships that figured largely in the history of the war carried marines, and, while their captains do not discriminate in their reports between marines and seamen, it is fair to presume that both fought with equal gallantry and suffered with equal fortitude. The roll of officers killed, though short, is impressive in view of the small numbers of the corps at that time. When it was awakened to new life its proportions were greater, but the Revolution furnished it with its training and its baptism of fire.

CHAPTER II

AFTER the Revolution the colonies went through
that time of uncertainty, disorganization and chaos
which the eminent historian, John Fiske, has properly called " The Critical Period of American History." We were nominally at peace with Great
Britain, but her government nevertheless kept up an
insidious commercial war, excluding, for example,
our ships from all West Indian ports. The young
nation was practically bankrupt. The remaining
ships of the navy were sold for what they would
fetch, and their officers went into the merchant
service. There were mutterings of war in the air,
but no steps were taken to make ready for the conflict. The Algerian pirates preyed upon our commerce, and by the capture of our merchantmen threw
our sailors into slavery, but for a time the infant
United States saw no better course for the treatment
of these corsairs than to pay them for immunity as
did the greater part of the maritime nations.

But in 1793 an Algerian raiding fleet, composed of three Xebecs and a brig, captured 10

American ships in the Atlantic and threw 105 American citizens into slavery. The news filled the nation with wrath, and Congress, acting under the authority of the newly adopted constitution, ordered the construction of six frigates. These ships bulked so large in the ensuing naval history of the United States that it is worth while to give their names and rating here:

Constitution,	44 guns,	1,576 tons,	cost	$302,719
President,	44 "	1,576 "	"	220,910
United States,	44 "	1,576 "	"	299,336
Chesapeake,	36 "	1,244 "	"	220,678
Congress,	36 "	1,268 "	"	197,246
Constellation,	36 "	1,265 "	"	314,212

These were to be stout ships, outranking in weight of metal European vessels of the same rating, and such as were actually built—with the exception of the *Chesapeake,* which was an " unlucky ship "— gave a good account of themselves in subsequent naval wars.

At this time the infant navy was under command of the secretary of war. By the end of 1797 three vessels of the new fleet were launched, their officers having already been selected. We learn from the ancient records that a marine force was created under temporary legislation enacted by Congress, and that a lieutenant of marines was paid $26 a month and two rations. Later this was raised to $50 a month. In view of a vigorous controversy which has raged of late in the navy, it may be interesting to note that the lieutenant's rations included a pint of spirits, or two quarts of beer daily.

On the 30th of April, 1798, the first secretary of the navy was appointed, and the navy department formally organized. In July of the same year a law was passed establishing a permanent marine corps. Under this law the corps was to consist of a major, 4 captains, 16 first lieutenants, 12 second lieutenants, 48 sergeants, 48 corporals, 32 drums and fifes, and 720 privates—a total of 881 men. They were liable for duty by land or sea, enlisted for a term of three years, and the pay of the officers ranged from $25 and two rations for a lieutenant, to $50 and four rations for the major per month. It is pertinent to say that in proportion to purchasing power these wages were undoubtedly higher than those of to-day.

The first duty to confront the new navy was not, as might have been expected, the task of suppressing the Barbary pirates. Instead, a degrading treaty was made with Algiers, pledging the United States to pay to the Dey an annual tribute of $22,000. The time came when the last tribute was paid at the muzzle of our cannon, but meanwhile our navy's attention was turned from the Mediterranean corsairs to the depredations of French privateers.

The quasi-war with France, that ran its spluttering course on the ocean in the years 1798-1800, was one of the curious episodes of American history. The people of the two nations were on relations of the utmost amity. Franklin was not forgotten in France, nor Lafayette in the United States. Diplomatic relations were uninterrupted. And yet French and United States men-of-war fought pitched battles by sea, not infrequently ending in the victor's expressing polite regret for the occurrence.

It all grew out of the war between France and Great Britain, and the practice of the latter nation of impressing American seamen. France held that the United States should make to her the same concessions that she made to the British. True, those concessions were forced, but that made no difference. If three men were impressed by the British from an American ship, the French asserted their right to take three more. When Great Britain declared the ports of France in a state of blockade, France retorted with a similar proclamation affecting British ports. The American merchantman was a prey to the privateers of both nations, whatever the port to which he might be bound. So serious were these depredations that in 1794 Edmund Randolph charged France with having captured 38 American ships, though the two countries were at peace. In 1798 all treaties with France were declared abrogated and American cruisers and privateers were ordered to attack French vessels wherever found. Nevertheless, no formal declaration of war was promulgated.

As a result of these orders maritime hostilities raged between the two countries for two and a half years. How serious was the naval campaign, even though actual war was not declared, was shown by the final record of American achievement. In all, 84 French vessels had been captured, mostly privateers, mounting a total of over 500 guns. The captors were chiefly American naval cruisers, as we had but few privateers afloat. Of the captured ships eight had been released and one recaptured.

In practically all these actions the marines took a distinguished part. The American participants were ships of the regular navy, each carrying a considerable detachment of the men of the marine corps. In one action—that between the U. S. frigate *Constellation* and the French letter-of-marque *La Vengeance*—the marines suffered severely, their losses aggregating more than one-fourth of the entire loss on the American ship.

Though in effect a drawn battle, this was one of the most hotly fought actions of the war. The *Constellation,* under Commodore Truxton, was cruising off Guadaloupe when she sighted a strange ship which refused to respond to friendly signals. Perplexed by the mystery, the American gave chase, discovering, after 48 hours of hot pursuit, that the stranger was quite her equal in point of metal. When the ships came within hailing distance and Truxton mounted his taffrail and shouted through a speaking trumpet, "What ship is that?" the stranger answered with a shot from a stern port and the fight was opened.

It was a night battle, for darkness had fallen while the chase was still in progress. The tropic stars shone out from the clear heavens, and as the ships tore through the water the gleaming phosphorescent light of those latitudes lit up their parallel wakes extending far back into the blackness of the sea. Side by side the frigates plunged along before a fresh and favoring gale. The creaking of their cordage and the whistle of the wind through their rigging mingled with the deep reports of the guns, which were but slow and infrequent, since the chase was confined to her stern guns, while the *Constellation* could for a time use only her bow chasers. In time, however, the ships drew abreast, and the louder thunder of the broadsides told that the fight was growing fiercer.

Toward one in the morning it was seen that the enemy was drawing off, out of the fight. Swiftly the *Constellation* shifted her course in pursuit, but only to meet with sudden disaster which put her out of the chase. One officer discovered that in the fury of the fire all the shrouds and braces of the foremast had been cut away, and the spar was in grave danger of falling. Up in the foretop was Midshipman James C. Jarvis, with a group of marines and sailors, intent on picking off men from the enemy's decks. An old sailor warned the young officer that the mast was likely to fall.

"Ay, ay, my lad," was the response, "but our station is here; we must go with it."

Very shortly they did in fact go with it, for a sudden roll of the ship carried away the mast and threw the little company in the top far out into the black sea. Thus crippled, the *Constellation* could no longer continue the chase, and made for Jamaica to refit. Her adversary was later found to be the French frigate *La Vengeance,* mounting 52 guns, with a weight of broadside exceeding that of the *Constellation* by more than 300 pounds. She had been badly cut up in the fight. Of her crew of 330 the killed and wounded numbered 160. The *Constellation* lost 39 from her crew of 310. Of these more than one-fourth were marines.

The quasi-war with France was fought on the ocean for two and a half years, with a record of success almost wholly on the side of the young American navy. The treaty of February 3, 1801, ended hostilities, and since that time the relations of peace and amity between the two nations have been uninterrupted, being never warmer than to-day (1918), when American troops and American marines are fighting on the soil of France to preserve that nation and the world from the intolerable calamity of being subjected to the rule of the Hun.

The imbroglio with France was not ended when new encroachments upon the rights and liberties of American merchant ships on the high seas gave renewed proof that the United States must be a naval power whether it so desired or not.

Reference has already been made to the treaty with Algiers by which a war with that barbaric nation had been averted by the ignoble expedient of paying an annual tribute. In addition to the tribute, $59,496 had been paid for the ransom of American sailors seized and enslaved by the Algierians. Humiliating as the situation was, it was rendered somewhat less so by the fact that at this period all the leading powers of Europe were likewise paying tribute to Algiers, Tripoli and Tunis. Portugal for a time maintained a fight against the pirates, but suddenly ended it, at the incentive of England. Indeed the latter country rather encouraged the corsairs, believing that their depredations would discourage and handicap the smaller powers in their maritime enterprises, while England, with her huge fleet and her ability to pay tribute, would suffer but little.

In 1798, as a part of its tribute to Algiers, and partly as a penalty for delay in paying it, the United States sent as a gift to the Dey the frigate *Crescent*, with presents valued at $300,000. Twenty-six barrels of silver dollars formed part of the tribute which was in fact blackmail. This donation had a double effect. It awakened the cupidity of the other Barbary powers, who redoubled their demands, and it aroused the indignation of the people of the United States that their government should accede to such insulting exactions.

The Bashaw of Tripoli came to the front with a

complaint that " the Sahib-Tappa at Tunis had received more than $40,000 from the United States in cash, besides presents." The Bashaw protested that he himself had received little more, that he must not be put on an equality with so inferior a potentate, and that he would no longer be contented with flattering words but must have a speedy answer from the President. Presently thereafter he deposed the American consul at Tripoli and cut down the consulate flagpole. The Bey of Tunis joined in with similar complaints, demanded a gift of 40 cannon and 10,000 stands of arms, saying to the American consul, " Tell your government to send them without delay; peace depends upon compliance."

However, the covetousness and arrogance of the Barbary pirates defeated their own ends. In May, 1800, the frigate *George Washington,* Captain William Bainbridge, was sent to carry tribute to Algiers. Once there the commander was insultingly ordered by the Dey to make of his ship a messenger to carry an Algierian legation to Constantinople. Bainbridge at first refused.

" You pay me tribute," said the Dey. " That signifies that you are my slaves. I can order you to do whatever I like."

As his ship was unfortunately anchored under the guns of the castle, Bainbridge was compelled to yield. The mission was performed under conditions most galling to the Americans, and the commander wrote home, " I hope I may never again be sent to

Algiers with tribute, unless I am authorized to deliver it from the mouths of our cannon."

But the arrogance and the avarice of the corsairs grew with each new concession, and war could not long be averted. In 1801 a small expedition was dispatched to the Mediterranean. The ships of this squadron, and the marine officers attached to each were: *President,* Lieutenant John Heath; *Philadelphia,* Lieutenant William Osborne; *Essex,* Lieutenant Gamble; and *Enterprise,* Lieutenant E. S. Lane. The orders were to protect American shipping but to take no prizes. This order was overruled in the spirit, if not in the letter, by Captain Sterrett of the schooner *Enterprise* who, being fired upon by a Tripolitan ship, responded so fiercely that the foe soon struck. As he could not make her a prize he dismantled her, threw cannon, small arms and cutlasses into the sea, and sent her home to Tripoli with this message:

" Go tell the Bashaw of Tripoli, and the people of your country, that in future they may expect only a tribute of powder and ball from the sailors of the United States."

The luckless commander of the defeated ship, on reaching Tripoli, was bound, paraded through the streets on a donkey and severely bastinadoed. The American Congress warmly applauded the victors, voted a sword to Captain Sterrett and a month's extra pay to each of his officers, among whom was Lieutenant E. S. Lane of the marines.

But the message was of no effect. Tripoli, and the other nations of the Barbary coast, went on attacking American ships and enslaving American seamen until the patience of the young republic was exhausted, and in 1802 a real expedition was sent out to enforce peace by the stern methods of war. In this fleet were the *Chesapeake,* 38 guns; the *Constellation,* 38; *New York,* 36; *John Adams,* 28; and *Enterprise,* 12. All were under the command of Commodore Morris, who was later recalled, and Commodore Preble, with five additional vessels, sent in his place. Each one of these vessels carried a detachment of marines.

For a year the cruise of this squadron proceeded without notable incident. Then bad luck overtook it. In the fall of 1803 the *Philadelphia,* commanded by Captain Bainbridge, was pursuing a Tripolitan corsair which was making for Tripoli. At the very entrance to the harbor the frigate ran hard and fast aground on an uncharted rock. All efforts to lighten her sufficiently to escape failed, although most of her guns were cast overboard. Presently, the tide going out, she careened upon her beam ends so that had she still possessed her battery it would have been useless.

Thereupon, the Tripolitans came swarming out to their prey. In gunboats, Xebecs, feluccas and barges they flocked to the plunder. There was nothing to do but surrender, and the triumphant corsairs looted the ship, ransacking the pockets of officers, taking purses and watches and even ripping the gold braid from their uniforms. Then the whole ship's company was taken ashore and cast into dungeons.

Not for a month did news of this disaster reach Commodore Preble's squadron. Straitway with the *Constitution* and the *Enterprise* he repaired to Tripoli, where he found the *Philadelphia,* repaired and flying the Tripolitan ensign, floating at her moorings. Bainbridge, from his prison, had been allowed to write to Preble, and to his letters, which were of course examined by his jailors, had added postscripts written in lemon juice and legible when exposed to the heat, urging the destruction of the *Philadelphia.*

On her voyage the *Constitution* had captured a ketch, laden with female slaves—a gift from the Bashaw to the Sultan. The slaves, being rather embarrassing booty, had been released, but the ketch had been kept with the squadron. Stephen Decatur, a young lieutenant, now proposed that she be manned with volunteers and used in an effort to destroy the *Philadelphia.*

The plan was quickly put into effect. Sixty-two volunteered for the perilous service, among whom were the following members of the marine corps:

Sergeant Solomon Wren, Corporal Duncan, Privates James Noble, John Quinn, Isaac Compfield, Reuben O'Brian, William Pepper and J. Woolfrandoff.

The attempt was thoroughly successful. The

ketch, which had been named the *Intrepid,* made its way into the harbor by night and bore down on the *Philadelphia.* A hail from that ship warned her to keep off, whereupon she replied that she was a coaster from Malta, had lost her anchors in a gale, was badly injured in her rigging and besought permission to ride by the frigate for the night. Completely deceived, the Tripolitans sent out ropes to the ketch, by means of which she was pulled alongside, when her character was speedily discovered.

"Americanos! Americanos!" rang the alarm along the decks of the *Philadelphia.* But it was too late. Decatur, Midshipman Morris and their fellows were already over the bulwarks and rushing along the decks, cutlass and pistol in hand, driving the Tripolitans before them. Few of the enemy were armed. They plunged overboard, or threw up their hands in abject surrender. In ten minutes the assailants were in complete possession and the work of firing the ship was begun. So rapidly did the flames spread that the Yankees could scarcely make their escape to their ketch, while the shower of sparks that fell upon that vessel before it could be cast off threatened it for a time with the fate of the larger craft. As the little band of adventurers pulled away the shotted guns of the frigate were discharged in quick succession, one battery sending its iron messengers into the streets of Tripoli, while the guns on the other side bore upon Fort English across the harbor. The angry glare of the Tripolitan batteries and ships, which had now opened fire, lighted up the bay and exposed the gallant adventurers to destruction.

Nevertheless, the expedition returned to the *Constitution* without losing a man. The adventure became the talk of naval circles in every nation, and of it Lord Nelson, England's greatest admiral, said, "It was the most bold and daring act of the ages."

During the earlier part of the war the Americans confined their offensive to a mere blockade of Tripoli. Commodore Preble, however, was a fighting sailor, and this sort of work palled upon his mind. His gallant and favorite lieutenant, Decatur, was likewise a man of action. Betwixt them they planned a bombardment of Tripoli which it was hoped might bring the Bashaw to terms.

As a bombardment the effort was futile. Wooden ships and the old-style, smooth-bore, muzzle-loading cannon were no match for the stone walls of even the antiquated fortresses of the Bashaw. But in connection with the bombardment were some spirited actions between vessels in the harbor, in which the men of the marine corps participated with honor to themselves.

In one of these actions Lieutenant Stephen Decatur, followed by a band of bluejackets and marines, had boarded an enemy vessel. He had just heard that his brother, James Decatur, had been treacherously killed by the captain of a Tripolitan gunboat after she had struck her flag, and his rage and grief made him fight like an avenging spirit. One gunboat struck before his furious attack. Boarding a second, he found his party of but 10 men confronted by nearly 40 Tripolitans. The vessel was the one on which James Decatur had met his death, and Stephen singled out a huge man, with a bristly black beard and a scarlet skull cap who, he was convinced, was his brother's murderer. The foe was armed with a heavy boarding-pike, at which the American delivered a fierce stroke with his cutlass, hoping to cut it off. Instead, the cutlass itself broke off short at the hilt. With a yell of triumph the Turk lunged with the pike, the thrust being only partly avoided by Decatur, who suffered a slight wound in the breast. Then the men grappled in hand-to-hand conflict. In their struggles they fell to the deck, while their followers fought around them, trying to aid their respective commanders. A Tripolitan officer from a place of vantage aimed a blow of his cutlass at Decatur, who was powerless to guard himself. At this moment a marine from the *Enterprise,* who had parted in some way from his weapons, thrust his arm in the path of the descending blow. Decatur was saved, but the marine's arm dangled helpless from a strip of skin and bleeding flesh.

On gunboat 6, Lieutenant Trippe was likewise saved from death by the presence of mind and courage of a marine. The American officer was hotly engaged in a hand-to-hand struggle with the

Turkish commander when another Turk slipped up behind him and was about to strike him down with a cutlass, when Sergeant Meredith, of the marines, thrust a bayonet through the foeman's body.

During the course of the blockade of Tripoli a curious essay in Oriental intrigue gave the United States marines the unusual experience of marching across the sands of an African desert, and even taking the field on the backs of camels.

" Horse marines " has been in late years a term of ridicule, but a command that as early as 1803 achieved the distinction of being " camel-marines " has no reason to be sensitive.

The reigning Bashaw of Tripoli was a usurper, having overthrown his elder brother, Hamet. The latter, after escaping from captivity, sought refuge in Egypt, where he fell in with a certain General Eaton, who was at the moment United States consul at Tunis. Eaton conceived the idea of setting the two brothers at each other's throats and embroiling the people of Tripoli in a civil war. Managing to get official sanction for his plan, he secured the detachment of Lieutenant O'Bannon, one sergeant and six marines from an American ship and enlisted some 400 Mussulmen mercenaries. With this force he began the march from Alexandria to Derne. The route lay across the desert of Barca, and the means of locomotion consisted of 107 camels and a few donkeys. The reflections of the marines upon camel-back riding have not been preserved, and indeed as

their little squad of eight was expected to keep order
among the several hundred turbulent tribesmen from
the desert wastes they had little time to ponder on
the unusual circumstances of the service. Food grew
scarce. Water scarcer. Continually the caravan
seems to have been reënforced by Arabs whose pov-
erty was such that they welcomed a hard march,
and the certainty of fighting, if only there were a
prospect of loot at the end. At Donda, the **first**
seaport they reached, they found the place abandoned, and two dead men in the only cistern. Thirst,
however, triumphed over this discouragement.

While here the United States ships *Argus* and
Hornet put into port and supplied Eaton with provisions and a considerable reënforcement of marines.
The march was resumed, 10 to 15 miles a day being
covered over a mountainous and broken country.
Derne was reached after a march of about 50 days
and a summons sent to the Bashaw offering terms
of peace and amity in consideration of his surrender.
His response was brief and to the point—" My head
or yours ! "

Accordingly, an assault was ordered upon the
fortifications at Derne, the capital of the richest
province of Tripoli. The *Argus, Hornet* and *Nau-
tilus* ran into the harbor, landed more marines to
swell General Eaton's force and began the bombardment of the batteries. From the shore side the
assault was gallantly led by the marines—the Arab
mercenaries showing little stomach for fighting. The

enemy fought in the town, from houses and behind walls, defending his works with spirit. The fort, however, was stormed by the marines under command of Lieutenant O'Bannon and Mr. Mann, and was carried triumphantly. The Tripolitan ensign was hauled down and for the first time in the history of the young nation the American flag was hoisted over a fortress of the old world. The marines have raised it in many curious corners since.

The flag was the one in use at that time, with 15 stars and 15 stripes. Lieutenant O'Bannon himself carried it through the storm of pelting bullets, climbed the ramparts, planted the flagstaff upon the bastion and turned the guns of the fort upon the enemy. In his report of the battle General Eaton, who was himself wounded, said, " The details I have given of Mr. O'Bannon's conduct need no encomium, and it is believed the disposition of the government to encourage merit will be extended to this intrepid, judicious and enterprising officer."

Unhappily, Mr. O'Bannon resigned in discouragement two years later without even the reward of a brevet rank for his distinguished service.

The treaty of peace with Tripoli was signed June 3, 1805, after a four years' war. A few months later the Bey of Tunis, under naval compulsion, sent an envoy to the United States to negotiate a treaty. The ancient business of piracy, by which the Barbary rulers had so long subsisted, was on its last legs, and the *coup-de-grace* was admin-

ABOVE: MARINES AT PEKING DURING THE BOXER
REBELLION
BELOW: REVIEW OF MARINES AT SYDNEY, AUSTRALIA,
WHEN OUR FLEET WENT ROUND THE WORLD

istered not by one of the ancient and powerful seafaring nations of Europe, but by the youngest of all
nations building itself up on the far off coast of
America. In the war for the suppression of the
corsairs the United States marine corps played a
gallant part, but how great was its share in the
conflict no one can now tell with accuracy. For in
those early days no distinctive record was kept of
the achievements of the marines. The few incidents
that we have been able to cite of their valor have
been preserved chiefly because of the interesting circumstances attendant upon them. But we know that
the war with the Barbary powers was fought by
our regular navy and that all regular ships were
provided with detachments of marines. Moreover,
instances of individual action by members of that
corps crop out often enough in the insufficient annals
of the time to show that they were everywhere
present and always doing their duty.

CHAPTER III

FOR some years after the close of the war with the Barbary powers there was as much peace by sea as the persistent aggressions of Great Britain upon our merchant ships would permit. The navy, as usual, was permitted to go without attention or increase, but early in 1809 Congress, animated by some unusual forethought, did increase the marine corps by some 700 men, giving it a total of about 1,300 men when fully recruited. The increase was made in good season, for the United States was drifting fast, though unwillingly, into the second war with England—a war in which most of the glory for the Stars and Stripes was won upon the ocean.

The cause of the quarrel grew out of the British insistence upon the right to search American vessels on the high seas, and to take from them sailors who were British subjects, or suspected of being such, impressing them into service in the British navy. Protests from the United States were unavailing. The attitude of the British government was one of indifference, that of the commanders of the British men-of-war arrogant and at times brutal. Merchant seamen were usually the victims of this practice, but the time came when the British grew so overbearing that they actually sought to take men from a ship of the United States navy.

The affair of the U. S. S. *Chesapeake* and H. B. M. ship *Leopard* in Chesapeake Bay in 1807 was an incident which reflected little credit on the United States navy, yet was the final provocation to a war in which that navy won its most imperishable laurels.

The former vessel had been refitting in the Washington navy yard and was lying in the lower bay preparatory to going to sea when the British minister informed the government that three deserters from the crew of the British man-of-war *Melampus* had joined the *Chesapeake's* crew. He requested that they be surrendered. The request was made courteously, and would doubtless have been granted save that the men concerned proved that they were American citizens who had been impressed into the British service. Reporting this, Commodore Barron of the *Chesapeake* thought the incident closed.

But when, shortly after, the American ship put out to sea a British man-of-war, one of the four anchored in Lynn Haven Bay, hoisted sail and followed her. The pursuer was the more powerful craft of the two and soon overhauled the *Chesapeake,* signalling that she had a dispatch for Commodore Barron. The latter accordingly hove to at a distance of half-pistol shot. No suspicion of hostile design on the part of the Englishman seems to have entered the mind of Barron, whose ship was in a badly littered condition, and quite unfit for action. Some of the younger American officers noticed that the ports of the *Leopard*, the British ship, were open, and the tompions, or stoppers, removed from the muzzles of the guns.

When the messenger from the *Leopard* arrived he produced an order from the British admiral ordering that the American crew be mustered on deck and searched for British deserters. Commodore Barron, of course, indignantly refused. A signal from the *Leopard* recalled her boarding officer, and in a moment a voice shouted across the water, " Commodore Barron must be aware that the orders of the vice-admiral must be obeyed."

Now, for the first time, Commodore Barron noticed the exceedingly war-like appearance of his adversary. Her crew were at the guns, which were run out ready for action. On the American ship the crew was new, never exercised at the guns. On the gun deck lay great piles of heavy cables which the men had been coiling when called to quarters. The guns were loaded, but, hurrying to their stations, the gunners found no rammers, powder flasks, matches, wads nor gunlocks.

While all was confusion aboard the *Chesapeake*, a single round shot was fired from the *Leopard*, followed by a full broadside. Many men were wounded on the American frigate, from which came no response. Loaded though the guns were, there was no way of firing them. Matches, locks or loggerheads were not to be found. Mad with rage at the helpless condition in which they found themselves, the officers made every effort to fire at least one volley. Pokers were heated red-hot in the galley fire and rushed across decks to the guns, but cooled too quickly. The *Leopard* kept up her fire for nearly 18 minutes until the *Chesapeake* struck her flag. Just as it came fluttering down, Lieutenant Allen, crying, " I'll have one shot, anyway," ran to the galley, picked up a live coal in his bare fingers and carried it to the nearest gun, which was thus discharged, the only shot fired by the American ship during the affair—battle it cannot be called.

Three men had been killed and 18 wounded on the *Chesapeake*. A few moments after she struck the British boarding party returned to the ship and took away the four deserters. It may be noted here that long afterward the three who were able to prove that they were American citizens were returned to their native land with suitable apologies. But the practice of impressment was not abated. By 1812 the Washington authorities had listed over 12,000 cases of this abuse, while Lord Castlereagh, in a speech before parliament, admitted that " out of 145,000 seamen employed in the British service in January, 1811, the whole number claiming to be

American subjects amounted to no more than 3,300," —a very considerable number, nevertheless.

The nation went mad with wrath over this arrogant assault upon a frigate of the United States. Captain Barron was tried by court-martial, found guilty of " neglecting to clear his ship for action," and suspended from the service, without pay, for five years. The master commandant, and Captain Hall, of the marines, escaped with a slight reprimand, as it was held they had acted under command of a superior officer.

Attention was now turned to the development of the navy. It took a futile course. Instead of building frigates and sloops of war, small gunboats, serviceable for coast defense only, were built until the country had 257 vessels of this sort. They were a " fad " of President Thomas Jefferson, but in the war that was foreshadowed in his administration they rendered practically no service whatever. To a policy which denied to the navy its rightful development was added an embargo which kept all the merchant ships rotting at their wharves. The year 1807 was a sorry time for the United States on the ocean.

The British made no pretence of discontinuing their practice of impressment. Now and then some sporadic case of retaliation on the part of the United States is recorded, but for the most part the aggressors went unchallenged. But though official resentment was delayed, there grew up a feeling of hostility between officers of the two navies, and British and American ships could hardly meet on the ocean without a threat of battle. At last the younger nation could bear no more, and war was declared upon Great Britain on the 18th of June, 1812.

It was an audacious defiance. Without going further we may point out that at the moment of the declaration the American navy consisted of 17 ships, with a tonnage of 15,300 and a total complement of 5,025 men. The British had 1,048 ships of 860,990 tons and a force of 151,572 men. Notwithstanding these stunning odds American valor on the seas was such that the glory of the maritime actions was won almost wholly by ships under the Stars and Stripes.

It is not part of the plan of this book to tell the story of the naval war of 1812 in detail. That has been done under another title by the same author. But a rapid account of the battles—mostly single-ship actions—in which the marines took part will not be out of place.

In fact, in the very first engagement of the war, that between the *President* and the British frigate *Belvedere,* taking place only five days after the declaration of war, Lieutenant Heath of the marines was severely wounded.

Most notable among the single ship actions of the War of 1812 was that fought on the 19th of August by the United States frigate *Constitution,*

Captain Hull, and the British frigate *Guerriere*. The *Constitution* was then just beginning her glorious career which made her the pet ship of the navy, and won for her the name " Old Ironsides." Every American schoolboy will remember how in 1830, when she had long outlived her period of naval usefulness, and the navy department was about to sell her to the wreckers, to be broken up for junk, she was saved by the spirited poem of protest written by Oliver Wendell Holmes, beginning with the lines:

> " Aye, tear her tattered ensign down,
>   Long has it waved on high,
>   And many an eye has danced to see
>   That banner in the sky! "

In 1812 the *Constitution* was just beginning her career, and in August of that year was cruising along the New England coast when she fell in with the enemy frigate *Guerriere*. As not infrequently happens, the captains of the two hostile ships were personally the best of friends. Before the war Captain Dacres, of the British ship, had bet the American captain a hat that in the event of the two vessels meeting in battle the United States flag would fall in defeat. Probably no thought of that playful wager entered the mind of either captain as, on that August afternoon, the two ships drew rapidly together, making preparations for battle as they advanced. Toward five of the afternoon they came within hailing distance. On the English frigate was a Yankee sea captain from Marblehead whose vessel had been captured a few days before. Not recognizing the *Constitution*, Captain Dacres asked this man what he made of her.

" I soon saw," wrote the American sailor, " from the peculiarity of her sails and her general appearance that she was without doubt an American frigate and communicated the same to Captain Dacres. He immediately replied that he thought she came down too boldly for an American; but soon after added, ' The better he behaves the more credit we shall gain by taking him.' "

When the advancing stranger had come so close as to leave no doubt of her nationality and her hostile intent, Captain Dacres turned to his prisoner, saying, " Captain Orme, as I suppose you do not wish to fight against your own countrymen, you are at liberty to retire below the water line." It is worth while to chronicle here that at the same time Dacres, with a chivalric sense of justice not common in the navies of those days, allowed ten American sailors who had been impressed into service on his ship to leave their quarters and go below, rather than compel them to fight against their own countrymen.

The action that followed showed the usual characteristics of naval duels of the time. At a distance of two or three miles the two ships, plunging along before a fresh wind, fired steadily upon each other with solid shot, each in the hope that a lucky stroke might cripple the other. The *Constitution* was astern of the other and limited in action to her bow guns. But at last, coming abreast of the enemy, and within about half-pistol shot, the opportunity for a broadside presented itself. Hull, who up to that moment had suppressed any excitement he might have felt, now broke out.

"Now, boys, pour it into them!" he cried at the top of his lungs, gesticulating with such violence that the tight breeches of his naval uniform split down the side. His executive, Lieutenant Morris, joined in cheering the crew. "Hull her, boys! Hull her!" he shouted, and the crew took up the play upon their captain's name as they poured their broadsides into the hull of their enemy.

Deep down in the cockpit of the *Guerriere,* the American prisoner, Captain Orme, suddenly "heard a tremendous explosion from the opposing frigate. The effect of her shot seemed to make the *Guerriere* reel and tremble as though she had received the shock of an earthquake. Immediately after this I heard a tremendous shock on deck, and was told that the mizzen-mast was shot away. In a few moments afterward the cockpit was filled with wounded men."

From this moment the conflict became desperate, at times culminating in hand-to-hand struggles with cutlasses and pikes. Stripped to the waist and covered with the stains of blood and powder, the gunners tugged at their tackle and wielded their rammers with fierce energy. Only a few yards separated the shattered hulls. Sometimes they were in actual contact. They lay broadside to broadside when the Englishman's mizzen-mast was shot away, and fell over the side, throwing the men in the fighting top far out into the sea. As it fell it carried away the bulwarks of the side, and the Yankees, the marines leading as was their duty, made ready to board. But the sea was rolling heavily, and if the Americans, with their pikes and cutlasses, with heavy boarding caps or helmets protecting their heads, were ready enough to board so, too, the Englishmen, who rushed to the point menaced, were more than ready to receive them. So each party stuck to its own ship, though the fighting was at such close quarters as almost to warrant the term hand-to-hand. It was in such a struggle as this that the marines of the old navy were most serviceable. Armed with muskets, stationed on the poop, in the rigging, far up in the fighting tops wherever an unobstructed view of the enemy's deck might be had, and remote from the hand-to-hand struggle, they could take deliberate aim, and pick off the enemy's officers. Yet they were not at all times aloof from the utmost rigor of the fight. The ships drifting together again, Lieutenant Morris leaped upon the taffrail of the *Constitution* and shouted high above the din of the combat, " Boarders away! " The marines were quick to respond. Lieutenant Bush of their corps was first to reach the side of Morris. As he did so a volley of musketry rang out from the British marines drawn up on the enemy's deck. The three American officers, Lieutenant Morris, Lieutenant Bush and Mr. Alwyn, fell under the storm of lead, poor Bush dead with a bullet through his head.

At this moment, the ships again drifted apart, and the effort to board was for the second time abandoned. But there could no longer be any doubt as to the issue of the combat. The Englishman's mizzen-mast had been carried away early in the combat. Now the foremast was shot away, and in falling carried the mainmast with it, so that the dismasted hulk wallowed in the trough of the sea, without steerage way, unmanageable and helpless. Seeing Hull maneuvering to a raking position Captain Dacres struck his flag.

The execution done on the *Guerriere* was frightful. Captain Orme, coming on deck upon the cessation of the firing, describes it thus:

"I beheld a scene which it would be difficult to describe. All the *Guerriere's* masts were shot away; and as she had no sails to steady her, she was rolling like a log in the trough of the sea. Many of the men were employed in throwing the dead overboard. The decks were covered with blood and had the appearance of a ship's slaughterhouse. The gun-tackles were not made fast, and several of the guns got loose, and were swinging from one side to the other. Some of the petty officers and seamen got liquor, and were intoxicated; and what with the groans of the wounded, the noise and confusion of the enraged survivors on board the ill-fated ship, rendered the whole scene a perfect hell."

The *Guerriere* had lost 23 dead or mortally wounded, and 56 wounded, among whom were several officers. The boarding officer, Lieutenant Read, who went aboard to receive the surrender, was so impressed by the scene of carnage that he asked Captain Dacres if he would not like a surgeon or surgeon's mate from the *Constitution* to help care for the wounded.

"Well, I should suppose you would have business enough on board your own ship to occupy all your medical officers," said Dacres in surprise.

"Oh, no," responded Read. "We had only seven wounded, and they have been dressed long ago."

In dead, however, the American's loss was not light, amounting to seven killed, among whom was the marine officer, Lieutenant Bush, of whom Captain Hull said in his report, "In him the country has lost a valuable and brave officer."

The *Guerriere* was found to be in a sinking condition when boarded, and her people were removed in boats to the *Constitution*. When Dacres came over the side he was shown ceremoniously to Hull's cabin. Unclasping his sword from its place at his thigh, the defeated commander handed it silently to Captain Hull. The victor put his hand aside, saying:

"No, no, captain. I'll not take a sword from

one who knows so well how to use it. But I will trouble you for that hat."

Ignoring for the moment the sequence in the matter of dates of the actions of 1812, we may take up briefly the second battle of the *Constitution* in that year. Refitting after her fight with the *Guerriere* in Boston, she took the sea again in the fall under command of Captain Bainbridge, to whose service in the war with the Barbary powers we have already referred, and ran across the British 38-gun ship *Java*, Captain Lambert, the day after Christmas. Though outclassed in weight of metal by the American, Lambert was a fighting sailor and audaciously offered battle. In half an hour's combat the *Constitution* was seriously crippled by a round shot which carried away her wheel, and wounded Bainbridge by driving a small bolt into his thigh. Deprived of her steering gear the American ship drifted helplessly in the waters, while the enemy used all his ingenuity to secure a favorable position for delivering broadsides that would end the battle. But the Yankee captain was equal to the occasion. Tackle was rigged upon the rudder post between decks, and a crew of jackies detailed to work the improvised helm. The helmsmen were far out of earshot of the quarter deck, so a line of midshipmen was formed from the quarter deck to the spot where the sailors tugged at the steering lines.

"Hard-a-port!" Bainbridge would shout from his station on the quarter deck.

" Hard-a-port! " " Hard-a-port! " followed the echoing cry as the midshipmen passed the word along. And so the ship was steered, and notwithstanding the loss of her wheel, fairly outmaneuvered her antagonist.

The Englishman soon saw that in a duel of broadsides he was no match for the Yankee, so he determined to come to close quarters. Shifting his helm he bore down on the *Constitution,* striking her on the port quarter, his jib boom tearing its way through the forward rigging and sails of the American. But the guns of the latter had been making lively play the while, and as the ships met the *Java's* mizzen-mast fell, crashing through forecastle and main deck, crushing officers and men beneath it, and throwing its topmen far out into the sea to drown. Surging round the two ships lay yardarm to yardarm. A dense sulphurous smoke hung about the hulls of the vessels, hiding them often from each other. Once in a while a fresh puff of wind would lift the curtain, giving the jackies a glimpse of their adversaries, and showing fierce faces glaring from the open ports as the guns were run in for reloading. The marines on the quarter deck took advantage of every moment of clear vision to pick off some enemy with a musket shot. High up in the fighting tops of the *Constitution* were two small howitzers, with crews of topmen under command of midshipmen, raining charges of grapeshot down upon the crowded decks of the enemy. From the cavernous submarine depths of the cockpit and magazine to the tops of each ship not an idler was to be found— from chaplain to captain all fought.

Two hours the battle raged. An official historian of the marine corps, Major Richard S. Collum, writes of the battle: " The *Java* was literally picked to pieces by shot, spar following spar until she had not one left." In the course of the battle the British tried to board, but were repulsed by the Yankee bluejackets with pikes and cutlasses, and the marines, whose heavy musketry fire from poop and fighting tops worked havoc in the ranks of the boarders. In this effort Captain Lambert was mortally wounded, Lieutenant Chads badly hurt and the flag of the *Java* shot away. It was never replaced. Surrender soon after followed.

The *Constitution* in this action lost 12 killed and 20 wounded, the marines as usual suffering severely. The *Java* lost, in killed, her captain, five midshipmen—boys of from 12 to 16 years of age—and 42 members of her company. Her wounded numbered 105. The ship was too badly battered to save, so after taking aboard over 500 prisoners, the *Constitution* allowed her defeated adversary to sink to an honorable grave.

Before doing so the wheel of the *Java* was taken to replace the one on the *Constitution*, which had been shot away early in the action. And thereby hangs a tale. Years after, when peace had been restored, a British officer was shown over the *Con-stitution* in an American navy yard.

" She is one of the finest frigates, if not the very finest, I ever put my foot aboard of," said he when asked for his judgment on the ship, " but as I must find some fault, I'll just say that youɪ wheel is one of the clumsiest things I ever saw, and is unworthy of the vessel."

The American officer laughed.

" Well, you see," he said, " when the *Constitution* took the *Java* the former's wheel was shot out of her. The *Java's* wheel was fitted on the victorious frigate to steer by, and although we think it as ugly as you do, we keep it as a trophy."

In October, 1812, the *United States* and the *Macedonian* fought a savage battle, in which the Briton was defeated with terrible slaughter. Three American marines were killed in this combat, and in the official report of the battle the members of that corps were commended for their " good con-duct and utmost steadiness under fire." In the battle on Lake Ontario, in which the British vessels *Cale-donia* and *Detroit* were captured, the marines under command of Lieutenant William H. Truman, dis-tinguished themselves while in the duel between the *Wasp* and the British sloop *Frolic* two of the five wounded belonged to that corps. For the British the latter was one of the most sanguinary battles, in proportion to numbers engaged, ever known. When, the fire of the *Frolic* slackening, the American boarders piled onto her decks, they found none unhurt to oppose them—there was not even a man left capable of hauling down the flag.

In Perry's famous victory at Put-in-Bay on Lake Erie, considerable detachments of marines were on each of his vessels. On the flagship *Laurence* a lieutenant, a corporal and two privates were killed and five wounded. On the *Niagara,* to which the Commodore shifted his flag in the hottest moment of the conflict, a lieutenant, sergeant, corporal and six privates were wounded. And in the action on Lake Champlain, on the 11th of September, 1813—an action of high importance to the American cause—seven killed and eleven wounded was the measure of the marines' sacrifice in the American cause.

A single-ship action, which occurred in 1813 off Boston, gave to the United States navy its rallying cry of " Don't Give Up the Ship! " though in fact it ended in dire defeat for the American duellist.

In May of that year the British frigate *Shannon* sailed boldly up to the entrance of Boston Harbor, and by her actions challenged to combat the U. S. frigate *Chesapeake,* Captain Lawrence, which lay in port. The commander of the *Shannon* was Captain Philip Bowes Vere Broke, an officer of skill and devotion, who had made his ship one of the smartest and most effective in the British navy. Boys who read " Tom Brown at Rugby "—and what boy has not?—will recall how the youngsters of that English public school used to celebrate Broke, and the battle we are about to describe, in the roaring song:

> "Brave Broke he waved his sword
> And he cried 'Now lads, Aboard!
> And we'll stop their singing Yankee Doodle Dandy Oh!'"

The *Chesapeake* was unfit for battle, her refitting after a long and luckless cruise being still incomplete, and her crew ill-assorted and discontented. Nevertheless, the challenge was accepted, and on June 1st the ship started down the harbor for the fight. Great crowds of people in small boats followed her, while thousands more made their way along the shore to see the battle. No time was wasted in preliminaries. The ships bore down upon each other under topsails and jib, disdaining any long-distance fire, until they were abreast at about half-pistol shot. Then almost simultaneously the two broadsides were let fly. A heavy cloud of yellow smoke shut out from the eyes of the spectators the further details of the fight.

But under that gruesome canopy deadly work was being done, and fast. The first broadside of the *Shannon* so swept the decks of the American ship that of 150 men stationed on the upper deck not 50 were on their legs when the storm of shot had passed. The sailors in the British tops, looking down upon the decks of their enemy could discern nothing but a cloud of hammocks, splinters and wreckage of all kinds driven fiercely across the deck.

Two men stood at the wheel. Both fell dead. Swiftly the places thus vacated were refilled, and the *Chesapeake's* guns responded with spirit. The gunners had given names to their favorite pieces and loudly cheered the " Wilful Murder," " Spit- fire," " Raging Eagle " and " Mad Anthony." But the gun play was no match for that of the British. While the *Shannon* suffered in her masts and rigging, the *Chesapeake* was cruelly wounded in her men. They fell on every side. Officers in particular were the victims of the deadly fire of the enemy's marines.

The fresh breeze gradually drove the two ships together, and they fouled in such a position as to expose the *Chesapeake* to a raking fire, which beat in her sternposts and drove the gunners from her after guns. Lawrence, wounded in the leg, and propped up against the mast, ordered the boarders called away. Where was the bugler? No voice of command could be heard over the thunders of the cannonade and the shouts of the men at the guns. In vain little midshipmen ran about trying to call up the boarders by word of mouth. At last the negro bugler was found, skulking under the stern of the launch, and so paralyzed by fear that he could sound but a few feeble notes on his instrument. The moment for boarding was lost in the confusion and perplexity, and just at that instant Captain Law- rence was struck again—this time by a ball that inflicted a mortal wound. His officers rushed to his

U. S. MARINES HOISTING THE FLAG AT VERA CRUZ

side and were carrying him below when, with a firm voice, he cried:

" Tell the men to fire faster; and do not give up the ship. Fight her until she sinks."

But the *Chesapeake* was in fact already beaten. Captain Broke, from a position on the bow of the *Shannon,* could see that the decks of the American were in confusion and the men already flinching from their stations. Calling up his boarders, he himself led their attack. He encountered but little resistance save from a group of marines in one of the *Chesapeake's* tops, who made deadly play with their muskets. But a discharge from one of the *Shannon's* long nines, loaded with grape, swept this gallant squad away.

Broke was soon in control of the upper deck of the *Chesapeake.* But on the gun deck below, the Americans, ignorant of what was going on above them, were keeping up the battle with unflagging courage. When the news of the presence of the British on their ship reached them, Lieutenant Budd, calling upon the sailors and marines to follow him, rushed up to drive the invaders back to their own ship. Lieutenant Broom, commander of the marines, had been mortally wounded early in the battle. In the meantime Broke had summoned the marines of the *Shannon* to his aid, and a fierce battle followed on the *Chesapeake's* deck. Broke threw himself upon the Americans, cutting down the first man who attacked him, with his cutlass, and cheering on his men with fierce battle cries. The Americans fell fast and began to retreat before the onset of their foes. Up from the wardroom came Lieutenant Ludlow, already suffering from two dangerous wounds. He placed himself beside the younger officer and the two strove in every way to encourage the men. But Ludlow was felled with a gaping wound across the forehead. Budd, struck down, fell through the hatchway to the deck beneath. The men, thus deprived of all command, gave way in confusion, and the ship was in the hands of the British. A few marines, the last to submit, kept up a fire through the hatchway, but soon were silenced.

No American hauled down the flag. To that extent, at least, Captain Lawrence's dying command was obeyed. As an English officer, Lieutenant Watts, seized the halyards to strike the colors, it seemed as though fate was loath to see that starry banner disgraced, for he had scarce completed his task when a stray grapeshot from his own ship struck him and he fell dead.

The battle had been a sanguinary one. On the *Shannon* were 33 dead and 50 wounded. The *Chesapeake* lost her commander, Captain James Lawrence, and every commissioned officer, so that when the British came aboard none was left to throw the private signal book overboard. Forty-seven of her crew were killed and 99 wounded. The marines lost their commander, Lieutenant Broom, 11 killed and 20 wounded.

The year 1813 was marked by a number of actions between the smaller vessels of the United States navy and enemy ships. Typical of these was the sharp combat between the *Enterprise* and *Boxer,* in which five of the marines on the former ship were wounded. The marines fought on land as well, notably at the battle of Craney's Island, near Norfolk, where a party of 50 marines from the *Constitution,* under Lieutenant Breckinridge, formed part of the defending force. An enemy fleet of 14 sailors endeavored to take the batteries, but was successfully beaten off. At the battle of Fort George at the mouth of the Niagara River, a force of about 100 marines was engaged and received commendation for their services from the officer in general command.

CHAPTER IV

War of 1812, Continued.—Porter's Cruise in the Pacific.—
Services of the Boy Farragut.—Marines at Nukahivah.—
Defeat of the *Essex*.—Burning of Washington.—Battle
of New Orleans.

ONE of the most picturesque features of the War
of 1812, and one in which the United States marines
took a goodly part, was the cruise of the United
States ship *Essex*, which began in 1812 and ended
in 1814. The ship was a stout frigate of 32 guns,
only 26, however, being in fact mounted. She was
commanded by Captain David Porter, father of Admiral David D. Porter, of Civil War fame, and she
carried among her midshipmen a 12-year-old boy,
David Glasgow Farragut, whose name was destined
to be the brightest of all in American naval annals
for fully a century.

The ship carried 40 marines, under command of
Lieutenant James M. Gamble. In October she
sailed under a roving commission to cruise the seas,
destroy British commerce and give battle to such
vessels of the British navy as she might safely engage. After a brief cruise in the Atlantic, Porter
made his way around the Horn and into the Pacific.
Most of the South American countries were at that
time strongly under the influence of Great Britain,

so that Porter could not expect a friendly reception in their ports. For food and water, therefore, he must rely upon the prizes he might take, or upon visits to some of the uncivilized islands in which British influence was still unknown. This made the enterprise of entering that enormous, and little known ocean the more perilous.

The voyage around the Horn was peculiarly tempestuous, and though it was begun the last of January, it was March before the *Essex* was fairly in the Pacific. Fortune awaited her there. One after another British ships were overhauled, captured and put into service under the Stars and Stripes until Porter found himself commanding quite a fleet. Besides the *Essex*, he had the *Georgianna*, 16 guns; *Atlantic*, 6 guns; *Greenwich*, 10 guns; *Montezuma*, 10 guns; and *Seringapatam*, 10 guns. Naturally the necessity of equipping each of these vessels with American officers, and with at least enough American seamen to control the whole crew, put a heavy charge on Porter's limited supply of men. The marines were used but sparingly. He knew that before long he would have to make descents upon the Pacific Islands for food and water, and while he hoped that the visits might be peaceful, yet he recognized the necessity for conserving his supply of marines to lead landing parties.

How great was the strain upon Porter's force is indicated by the fact that he was obliged to put Midshipman Farragut, aged 12 years, in command of one of the prizes. The boy's description of his experience is worth repeating:

"I was sent as prize-master to the *Barclay*," he writes. "This was an important event in my life; and, when it was decided that I was to take the ship to Valparaiso, I felt no little pride at finding myself in command at 12 years of age. This vessel had been recaptured from a Spanish *guarda costa*. The captain and his mate were on board; and I was to control the men sent from our frigate, while the captain was to navigate the vessel. Captain Porter, having failed to dispose of the prizes as it was understood he intended, gave orders for the *Essex Junior* and all the prizes to start for Valparaiso. This arrangement caused great dissatisfaction on the part of the captain of the *Barclay*, a violent-tempered old fellow; and, when the day arrived for our separation from the squadron, he was furious, and very plainly intimated to me that I would 'find myself off New Zealand in the morning,' to which I most decidedly demurred. We were lying still, while the other ships were fast disappearing from view; the *Commodore* going north, and the *Essex Junior* with her convoy steering to the south for Valparaiso.

"I considered that my day of trial had arrived (for I was a little afraid of the old fellow, as everyone else was). But the time had come for me at least to play the man: so I mustered up courage, and informed the captain that I desired the topsail filled away. He replied that he would shoot any man who dared to touch a rope without his orders; he 'would go his own course, and had no idea of trusting himself with a d—d nutshell;' and then he went below for his pistols. I called my right-hand man of the crew and told him my situation; I also informed him that I wanted the main topsail filled. He answered with a clear 'Aye, aye, sir!' in a manner which was not to be misunderstood, and my confidence was perfectly restored. From that moment I became master of the vessel, and immediately gave all necessary orders for making sail, notifying the captain not to come on deck with his pistols unless he wished to go overboard; for I would really have had very little trouble in having such an order obeyed."

Porter had made of the Island of Nukahivah, one of the Marquesas group, a rendezvous, building there a fort, which he manned with marines under command of Lieutenant John M. Gamble, a young and spirited officer of that corps. Lieutenant Gamble was also vested with command of three prizes, the *Seringapatam,* the *Greenwich* and the *Sir Andrew Hammond,* which were moored under the guns of the fort. Having made these dispositions, Captain Porter, with the *Essex,* sailed away in search of more prizes.

But the frigate had scarcely disappeared when the natives began to show indications of turbulence. The sailors, who in many cases had formed tender attachments for native women, were inclined to be sympathetic with the islanders. With the aid of his trusty marines, however, Gamble put down the natives without bloodshed. Then he found himself with a mutiny on his hands. Captain Porter and the *Essex* had been gone two months when Lieutenant Gamble concluded he could by no means hope longer for their return and so made preparations for sailing away from the islands. To this action many of his men demurred strongly. Many of them were not American seamen, but sailors of various nationalities who had been captured with the prizes, and had cheerfully transferred their allegiance, as was quite commonly the practice with the roving seamen of that day. They were now not at all eager to leave the island home which they had occupied

for three months. In those days the islands of the
South Pacific, still untouched by the white man, were
justly entitled to the name of " tropical paradise "
so often conferred upon them by voyagers. Their
people were generous and hospitable. The women
beautiful and smiling, eager to win the approbation
and affection of visitors. The food, of tropical
fruits and vegetables, poultry, fresh pork and fish,
was lavish in quantity, and by its freshness a joyous
relief to the jack-tars long fed on moldy ship's
biscuit and " salt horse." Moreover, many of the
sailors had entered into relations with the native
girls which both were loath to break.

Accordingly, when news of Gamble's purpose of
sailing spread in the fleet, there was ominous mut-
tering among the men before the mast. They had
no desire to leave their comfortable quarters with
unlimited shore leave, and take to the arduous duties
of sea service again. Lieutenant Gamble, discerning
signs of a mutiny, had all the small arms carried on
board the *Greenwich,* on which ship he lived. His
force had consisted of 20 marines, but not all of
these proved faithful, and it was diminished by death
and desertion until only eight remained. Wounded
by a ball in the foot, received in an action with the
mutineers, Gamble retained his determination,
fought off the natives in a pitched battle, and, with
but four men fit for duty, sailed in the *Sir Andrew
Hammond* for the Sandwich Islands. He arrived
in safety, only to fall into the hands of the British.

Long after, when both he and Porter had escaped from British captivity, the latter wrote to the secretary of the navy:

" Captain Gamble at all times greatly distinguished himself by his activity in every enterprise engaged in by the force under my command, and in many critical encounters with the natives of Madison's Island rendered essential services, and at all times distinguished himself by his coolness and bravery. I therefore do, with pleasure, recommend him to the department as an officer deserving of its patronage. I now avail myself of the opportunity of assuring you that no marine officer in the service ever had such strong claims as Captain Gamble, and that none have been in such conspicuous and critical situations, and that none could have extricated themselves from them more to their honor."

The *Essex* had been prevented from returning to the rendezvous in the Marquesas by a piece of bad fortune which compelled Captain Porter, after a most one-sided action, to surrender to the British.

The *Essex,* with her consort, the *Essex, Jr.,* and a number of prizes, had put into the harbor of Valparaiso in February of 1814. There they remained some weeks. They had been in Valparaiso only a few days when the British men-of-war *Cherub* and *Phœbe* hove in sight. It was early dawn, after a night during which the hospitality of the *Essex* had been extended to the people of the city in the form of a ball, and the ship's cordage and decks were covered with lanterns and flowers, while the awnings that shielded the dancers were still in place. It was a neutral port, and the American captain had every right to believe himself secure against any attack.   Nevertheless he was watchful and as the two British ships came on into the harbor, propelled by wind and tide, apprehensive.   For the two vessels drifted in such a way that they bade fair to foul the *Essex*—whether by accident or with hostile intent only subsequent events would show.   Porter had his men at quarters and was ready for whatever might happen.

In his journal the boy Farragut thus described the course of the incident:

" We were all at quarters, and cleared for action, waiting with breathless anxiety for the command from Captain Porter to board, when the English captain appeared, standing on the after-gun, in a pea-jacket, and in plain hearing said,—

" ' Captain Hillyar's compliments to Captain Porter, and hopes he is well.'

" Porter replied, ' Very well, I thank you.   But I hope you will not come too near, for fear some accident might take place which would be disagreeable to you.'   And, with a wave of his trumpet, the kedge-anchors went up to our yardarms, ready to grapple the enemy.

" Captain Hillyar braced back his yards, and remarked to Porter that, if he did fall aboard him, he begged to assure the captain that it would be entirely accidental.

" ' Well,' said Porter, ' you have no business where you are.   If you touch a rope-yarn of this ship, I shall board instantly.' "

If it had not been for a watchful marine the affair might have wound up in a fight, notwithstanding

Captain Porter's forbearance. One of the crew of the *Essex*, who had acquired more than his share of grog, was standing by a gun with a lighted brand in his hand ready to fire the piece. His hazy faculties suggested that he saw an Englishman grinning at him through one of the *Phœbe's* ports.

"I'll soon stop your making faces, my fine fellow," he shouted in high dudgeon, and was about to fire when a marine on guard toppled him over with a blow of his musket. Had that gun been fired, a general combat would have followed and nothing could have saved the *Phœbe*.

Porter was very ill-requited for the self-restraint and fairness he manifested on this occasion. For the time came when the two British ships caught him at a disadvantage and showed no hesitation in attacking him. A heavy gale had caused the parting of one of the cables of the *Essex* and blew the ship out to sea. In beating back her foretopmast was carried away and with it several of her men. Crippled thus, the ship could not make her way back into the harbor against the gale, and Porter took refuge in a little cove, where unfortunately he had no room to maneuver the ship.

The *Essex* was but half-pistol shot from the shore, and the laws of civilized nations declare that a belligerent within three miles of a neutral shore is safe from attack. Captain Hillyar, of the British flotilla, had assured Porter of his intention of respecting the neutrality of the port under all circumstances. But the sight of the American ship thus delivered by fortune into his hand overcame his honorable intent, and he quickly brought up his ships *Phœbe* and *Cherub* to the attack.

The action that followed was hotly contested, but for the Americans hopeless from the start. The *Essex* was for a time aground and incapable of movement, so that the enemy had only to pick his position where the American broadsides could not be brought to bear, and pound away at his leisure. There was no chance to get at the British ships with the favorite American device of boarding. Nor was there much opportunity for the marines to practice their musketry. The most effective fire the Americans were able to deliver was from three long guns which Porter took from the gun deck and mounted in his cabin, firing through the stern windows. The enemy's fire was murderous. One shot entered a port and killed four men at a gun, taking off the heads of the last two. The decks were strewn with dead, the cockpit was full and the enemy's shot not infrequently penetrated it, killing the wounded under the surgeon's hands.

Midshipman Farragut, aged 12, fought throughout the battle, and in his journal has recorded some of its most picturesque incidents.

" I performed the duty of captain's aid, quarter-gunner, powder boy and, in fact, did everything that was required of me," he writes. " When my services were not required for other purposes I generally assisted in working a gun;

would run and bring powder from the boys and send them back for more, until the captain wanted me to carry a message; and this continued to occupy me during the action."

Once during the action a midshipman came running up to Porter with the report that a gunner had deserted his post. Porter's reply was to turn to Farragut with the command, " Do your duty, sir! " The youngster seized a pistol and ran to find the recreant seaman, whom it was his duty to shoot dead. But the man had slipped overboard and swum ashore.

The *Essex* was fought until it was evident that there was no longer a chance of saving her, or disabling her adversaries. Then she surrendered to fortuitous circumstances and a treacherous enemy. The battle had been unusually sanguinary. When the time came to call a council of war prior to surrendering, Porter found that he had but one commissioned officer living and fit for service. In all, out of her complement of 255 men, the *Essex* had 58 killed, 66 wounded and 36 missing—probably drowned in trying to swim ashore. On the enemy ships the *Phœbe* lost 4 killed and 7 wounded out of her crew of 300; the *Cherub* 1 killed and 3 wounded out of 121 in all.

The records of the time do not give in detail the mortality among the marines, but Captain Porter in his report especially praises the gallantry of Lieutenant Samuel B. Johnston of that corps.

We cannot dismiss the affair of the *Essex* without

telling of a second battle in which Midshipman Farragut, then a prisoner on the victorious *Phœbe*, was one of the belligerents and the victor. The great admiral told of it years after in his memoirs thus:

" I was so mortified at our capture that I could not refrain from tears," he writes. "While in this uncomfortable state, I was aroused by hearing a young reefer call out,—

" ' A prize! a prize! Ho, boys, a fine grunter, by Jove.'

" I saw at once that he had under his arm a pet pig belonging to our ship, called ' Murphy.' I claimed the animal as my own.

" ' Ah,' said he, ' but you are a prisoner, and your pig also! '

" ' We always respect private property,' I replied; and, as I had seized hold of ' Murphy,' I determined not to let go unless ' compelled by superior force.'

" This was fun for the oldsters, who immediately sung out,—

" ' Go it, my little Yankee. If you can thrash Shorty, you can have your pig.'

" ' Agreed,' cried I.

" A ring was formed in an open space, and at it we went. I soon found that my antagonist's pugilistic education did not come up to mine. In fact, he was no match for me, and was compelled to give up the pig. So I took Master Murphy under my arm, feeling that I had in some degree wiped out the disgrace of the defeat."

Perhaps the land service in which the men of the marine corps won their greatest credit was the abortive defense of Washington in August, 1814. As every American knows, the capital fell and was burned by the British. As every American ought to know, the futile defense of Washington was a scathing commentary upon the lack of preparation for war in the United States at that time—a lack which persisted even until the beginning of the war in which we are now (1918) engaged. In the effort to save Washington from the ignominy of foreign capture the marines fought bravely, but ineffectively. Perhaps their bravery was set off, as it certainly was rendered futile, by the poltroonery of the militia by whose sides they fought.

In the spring of 1814 the activities of the British forces in the lower Chesapeake aroused the fears of the American authorities for the safety of Washington. But their fears seem to have been all that was aroused. Though the danger was imminent, nothing could stir them to effective action. A proclamation calling for 15,000 troops was met with indifference by the surrounding country, and though the command of this paper army was given to General Winder, the most considerable force he was ever able to lead was a few hundred militiamen.

The naval defense of the capital was entrusted to Commodore Barney, a veteran who had served with distinction in the Revolution, and in the early years of the second war with England had commanded the Baltimore privateer *Rossie*. Barney exerted every effort to collect a fighting force, and by June he had gathered together 26 gunboats and barges and about 900 men. They were mostly sea-fighters, though it turned out most of their fighting in this peculiarly ill-fated campaign was on land, and

among them was a fair proportion of marines, later
to be added to. In a slight brush with the enemy,
June 1st, Barney was victorious, but as he was
pursuing the retreating foe down the bay his hopes
were dashed by the appearance of the British 74-
gun ship *Dragon*. It was then Barney's turn to flee,
and he led his forces up the Patuxent River, where
they were blockaded by the superior British force.
Here he was joined by Lieutenant Miller, with a
force of marines from the Washington barracks.

Desultory fighting went on between the Americans
and the British on the Patuxent for a month or two,
and it was during this period that the forces under
'Admiral Cockburn committed against the people
on the Chesapeake coasts those atrocities which long
made the name of England feared and hated in that
region.

It was not until August that the long-apprehended
attack upon the capital took definite form. News
came to Captain Barney that the enemy had landed
four or five thousand men at Benedict and was marching on Washington. Leaving his flotilla in command
of Lieutenant Frazer, with orders to burn the boats
if attacked in force, Barney, with about 500 men,
including all the marines in his command, marched
to Washington and took up quarters in the marine
barracks there. Additional troops were now coming
up to General Winder's aid, and he soon had a force
of about 3,000, including about 1,400 regulars, more
than half of whom were the sailors and marines

of Barney's command. Upon the latter, as we shall see, fell the brunt of the fighting.

Against this American force the foe advanced with an army of about 7,000 men. In it were included veteran forces like the Twenty-first Fusileers, and two battalions of Royal Marines. A detachment of marine artillery also accompanied the British advance.

It soon became apparent that the hostile forces would clash at Bladensburg, a spot a few miles from the center of Washington, where to-day, more than 100 years later, the outlines of the trenches thrown up by the Americans are still plainly discernible.

Barney here assumed command of the American artillery, while Captain Miller, of the marines, took command of the several hundred members of that corps and of the sailors from the flotilla. At the very first assault of the enemy the militia fled, but the marine detachment stood firm. The British charged gallantly with their light troops of the Eighty-fifth, the Fourth and the Forty-fourth regiments, and the First Battalion of Royal Marines. But they were sturdily met by Captain Miller's forces and driven back. The marines manifested the utmost steadiness throughout the action, and to them, and to the bluejackets who fought by their side, is due such honor as the Americans might find in a day which redounded but little to the credit of the national arms. Had they been properly supported by General Winder's militia they might have saved the day, and the young nation would have been spared the ignominy of having its capital burned by a foreign foe. But these troops were by this time streaming back to Washington a mere disorderly rabble; and influenced by the spectacle of their rout the President and the higher officers of the government were fleeing for safety in every sort of conveyance that could be pressed into service.

Meanwhile, the marines stood steadily to their guns and drove the invaders back upon their supporting column. Recognizing the sturdiness of this defense the British made no further effort to attack Captain Miller's front, but centered their attention upon the disordered militia. By driving those troops back they could turn Miller's flank and take him in the rear. The situation was fast becoming hopeless for the Americans. Captain Barney, Captain Miller and several other officers were wounded. In the face of irresistible forces the retreat was ordered, but it had been so long delayed that it was impossible to bring off either the guns, or the two wounded commanders, both of whom fell into the enemy's hands. They were treated with the utmost consideration by their captors, who were loud in their praises of the valor of the sailors—with whom in accordance with the custom of the time they included the marines.

"Of the sailors," wrote Mr. Gleig, a subaltern in the British army, " it would be injustice not to speak in the terms which their conduct merits. They were employed as gunners; and not only did they serve their guns with a quickness and precision which astonished their assailants, but they stood until some of them were actually bayonetted with fuses in their hands; nor was it until their leader was wounded and taken, and they saw themselves deserted on all sides by the soldiers, that they quitted the field."

In this action the marines lost their commander, Captain Miller, seriously wounded, and Captain Alexander Sevier, wounded. Fully one-third of the rank and file were put out of action. The precise figures are not available, for the official records make no distinction between marines and sailors, nor, for that matter, between the men of Barney's command and those of General Winder, who fled at the first fire.

After burning and pillaging Washington the British moved back down Chesapeake Bay, plundering and ravaging as they went. They had laid plans for the capture of Baltimore, and after one or two false starts finally got their forces under way. In the hotly contested action at Fort McHenry, which gave the inspiration to Francis Scott Key's national anthem, "The Star-Spangled Banner," the marines under Captain Anthony Gale and Lieutenant Breckinridge took an active and gallant part. Even after the fort itself was silenced, though not defeated, a small battery, thrown out in advance and manned almost entirely by men of the corps, continued an active response to the enemy's warships.

Not long after the repulse at Fort McHenry the British made their preparations for the capture of New Orleans. This was to have been the culminating achievement of the war, on their part. They gathered together a great expedition, part naval and part military, with the troops composed largely of veterans who had served with Wellington in the Spanish peninsula. For months before the actual assault British armed vessels lurked in the water-logged territory of the Mississippi delta, spying out new ways of reaching the Crescent City and striving to enlist the inhabitants, who were partly Indian, partly Spanish and partly French, on the British side. They sought even the aid of Lafitte, the famous pirate of Barataria, but that worthy, though the state of Louisiana was at the moment proceeding against him, spurned the British offers, and with a detachment of his men fought in Jackson's line on the plain of Chalmette.

Two days before Christmas the British—who had made their way in luggers, barges, schooners and all sorts of small craft through the bayous and lagoons, though not without some opposition from the navy—deployed on the broad level plain at Chalmette, about ten miles below New Orleans. General Andrew Jackson, who had been put in command of the defense of the city, marched against them with about 1,500 men, including a considerable detachment of marines. The armed schooner *Carolina*, commanded by Captain Patterson, at the same

ABOVE: A HEAVY BATTERY OF SEARCH LIGHTS
BELOW: FIELD TELEPHONE IN ACTION

time dropped down the river and took up a position on the British flank. Shortly after nightfall the two opened a vigorous fire on the enemy, who were taken by surprise. The fire from the *Carolina* was particularly effective, until the enemy hit upon the expedient of sheltering himself under the steep bank of the levee where the shots could not reach him. When dawn came they mounted a battery on the top of the levee and returned the *Carolina's* fire with spirit. The corvette *Louisiana* came down to the aid of the *Carolina* and for a time the artillery duel was vigorous; but the British, using red-hot shot, set the American schooner on fire and she was soon destroyed. The action, however, plunged the invaders into confusion, delayed their attack on New Orleans for more than two weeks and gave General Jackson time to prepare for the victory which made his name famous throughout the world. In this preliminary action the marines lost eight killed and eight wounded.

Meantime, New Orleans was getting adequately armed for her defense. There had been long and inexplicable delay in recognizing the threat of the British expedition. There is even some reason to believe that had it not been for a stop at Fayal of the British squadron bringing the Pakenham expedition the troops might have reached the mouth of the Mississippi in time to take the city before General Jackson could make preparation for its defense. But in the harbor of Fayal they encountered the American privateer, *General Armstrong,* commanded by Captain Samuel C. Reid. The British having something like ten times his guns and man power, set gayly about capturing him. But Reid put up so savage a defense before scuttling his vessel that the three men-of-war that attacked him were obliged to lay up for repairs. The New Orleans expedition was delayed for weeks, and Jackson was able to gather the motley line of fighters that on January 8, 1815, put the flower of King George's army to flight.

Before the British and the Americans clashed in this final battle of the War of 1812 peace commissioners in far-off medieval Ghent had met and signed a treaty of peace, which curiously enough ignored the main issue of the war, namely the impressment of American seamen. The battle of New Orleans was therefore fought between two armies nominally at peace. But there was then no ocean cable to bring news swiftly, and though the carnage was dreadful and deplorable, Americans may at least find compensation in the thought that they won the last battle of the War of 1812, though prior to that the land battles had been all to their discredit. Only on the sea had the young nation won any glory.

It was a strange and ill-assorted force that General Jackson arrayed on that January morning behind the straight line he had drawn from the Mississippi to the swamps. There were gaunt riflemen from Tennessee and Kentucky, men in coonskin caps skilled in picking off game in the forests, and not long unused to Indian warfare. There were pirates from Barataria—Dominique You with a crew of red-capped nondescripts serving a seven-pounder brass piece; gay creoles from the Crescent City; swarthy Spaniards and mulattoes, militia and regulars from all the adjacent states, and bluejackets and marines from the United States ships on the southern station.

The story of that battle is familiar to every American schoolboy. How the picked troops of Wellington's peninsula campaign in three attacks went down before Jackson's nondescripts; how Major General Pakenham and Major General Gibbs both fell in leading the assaults; how Jackson discovered that sugar in hogsheads was no substitute for sand in bags in building redoubts, and that cotton bales were too light and too inflammable to make good breast-works, and how a little four-foot ditch which the British engineers, though with ample time to recon-noiter, had failed to note, contributed to the British defeat—these are all parts of the story that must be left for the more extended histories. Enough here to note that the marines held a share of the defensive line, fought with great valor and lost early in their action their commander, Major Carmack, who was seriously wounded. In his report of the Battle of New Orleans, Commodore Patterson, who com-manded the naval forces, said:

" To Major Daniel Carmack, commanding the marines of this station, I am indebted for the prompt-ness with which my requisitions have been complied with, and the strong desire he has always maintained to further as far as in his power, my views."

Despite the treaty of peace, still unknown in the United States and to the vessels cruising the lonely reaches of the high seas, the war on the ocean continued. In a notable action between the famous *Constitution* and the two British ships, the *Cyane* and *Levant,* the marines played a gallant part under their commander, Captain Archibald Henderson, who was especially mentioned in the official report. In a later disastrous action, in which the *President* was forced by four British ships to surrender, the marines lost heavily, and of their commander, Commodore Stephen Decatur said in his report: "Lieutenant Twiggs displayed great zeal, his men were well supplied and their fire was incomparable." Last of all the sea actions of the war was that between the brigs *Hornet* and *Penguin.* It lasted only 22 minutes, when the British surrendered, but in that brief space of time the Englishman lost 14 killed and 28 wounded, while on the *Hornet* one was killed and 10 wounded. Major Collum relates this incident of the fight:

" Private Michael Smith, marine, who had served under the gallant Porter in the *Essex* when she was captured by the British, received a shot through the upper part of the thigh which fractured the bone, and nearly at the same moment had the same leg broken immediately above the knee by the spankerboom of the *Hornet,* which was carried away by the enemy's bowsprit while afoul of her. In this situation, while bleeding upon the deck and unable to rise, he was seen to make frequent exertions to discharge his musket at the enemy on the topgallant forecastle of the *Penguin*. This, however, the gallant fellow was unable to accomplish, and was compelled to submit to be carried below."

Plucky Michael Smith at least goes down into history by name. The student of the War of 1812, our most glorious naval war, will bitterly regret that the official chroniclers of the time were so impersonal in their reports, and so slovenly in their failure to discriminate between the marines and the other branches of the service. Nevertheless, there was glory enough for all and we may be sure the marines earned their share.

CHAPTER V

Dull Days for the Marines.—The Mutiny of the *Somers.*—
The Revolt of the Charlestown Convicts.—The Pirates
of Quallah Batoo.—Marine Campaigns Against the Indians.—The Wilkes Exploring Expedition.

WITH the end of the War of 1812 the young republic settled down to a period of peaceful growth
and development, not to be interrupted for some 30
years when, once more, war clouds began to gather
to the south of our boundaries. For a large part
of this epoch, the work which the marine corps was
called upon to do was chiefly of a routine character.
But, though the thrills and opportunities of war
times were missing, there was plenty of work to
be done, and the corps showed efficiency and patience
in its every-day service in the same degree to which
it had displayed preparedness and valor during the
late war with Great Britain.

Of course, in those early days of our national
existence, both the extent of our territory and the
size of our naval establishment were comparatively
small. Our navy was not the proud and powerful
fighting machine which it grew to be in the later days
of the 19th century. It was not even what it had
been during the War of 1812. There were not a

great many ships and those that we had were mostly
of modest tonnage. The number of our navy yards,
too, was much smaller than it is to-day. On the
other hand, the marine corps itself was an exceedingly modest establishment. Considering this fact
and the further fact that ways and means of communication were slow and difficult, the corps had its
hands full in its attempt to supply a guard to all
the United States ships in commission and to protect
properly the property of the government on land.

However, true to the spirit of preparedness and
efficiency which the marine corps displayed at all
times, from the day it had been founded, it did
whatever was to be done to the best of its ability,
frequently under trying conditions, in the face of
great difficulties, and with apparently little appreciation either on the part of the government or on that
of the country at large. The early annual reports
of the various secretaries of the navy to the presi-
dents do not have very much to say about the work
of the marine corps, and the reports of its commanding officers consist chiefly in pleas for increases in its
size, and for proper provisions for the housing of
the small detachments stationed at our few navy
yards. From the fact that these are frequently repeated year after year, it becomes clear that Congress was not any too liberal with supplying the
necessary moneys for the proper development and
maintenance of the corps. It is the more to the
latter's credit that it never failed the country when

called upon to do some special bit of work. This is especially creditable in view of the fact that there were great difficulties in the way of properly training the corps as a unit. For its limited membership was most of the time scattered in the form of small detachments among the vessels of the navy and at the yards. It was rare indeed, as one report of its commanding officer of those days says in a rather plaintive tone, that as much as a whole company of marines was ever assembled at any one point.

Discipline on warships in the early part of the 19th century was not what it is to-day. The crews were then not made up from the flower of the country's youth. Conditions of life aboard a warship, too, were far from ideal, and, everything considered, it is rather astounding that one did not hear more frequently of mutinous outbreaks. In the few instances of that type of which there is a record, the presence of the marines, not forming part of the crew, but a separate body of guardians of governmental property and used much in the manner of latter-day policemen, always tended to suppress outbreaks quickly and, indeed, most of the time to prevent them entirely. As an instance of this there may be cited the grateful commendations of the marines by the commanding officer of the United States ship *Potomac* to the effect that the presence of a marine detachment prevented mutiny by their promptness in quelling a serious outbreak of the crew at Port Mahon in 1836.

A few years later, in 1842, Commander A. S. MacKenzie, of the United States brig *Somers,* thought it necessary to execute, by hanging, an acting midshipman, a boatswain's mate and a seaman for attempted mutiny on the high sea. When tried somewhat later by court-martial for this action and for the causes leading up to it, the commander stated, with regret and as part of his defense, that " the *Somers* had no marines, a body of men distinct from the crew in organization and feeling, on whom, in ordinary ships of war, the police and discipline greatly depend, and who form a counterpoise and check to the turbulent spirits of the common seamen."

However, there was on that ship at that time one member of the marine corps, Sergeant M. H. Garty, traveling as a passenger and having been invalided home on account of serious illness. Of him the commander speaks in the following highly laudatory terms:

" Of the conduct of Sergeant Garty I will only say that it was worthy of the noble corps to which he has the honor to belong; confined to his hammock by a malady which threatened to be dangerous, at the moment when the conspiracy was discovered, he rose upon his feet a well man. Throughout the whole period his conduct was calm, steady and soldier-like. But when his duty was done and health no longer indispensable to its performance, his malady returned upon him, and he is still in his hammock. In view of this fine conduct, I respectfully recommend that Sergeant Garty be promoted to a second lieutenancy in the marine corps. Should I pass without dishonor through the ordeal that probably awaits me, and attain in due time to the command of a vessel entitled to a marine officer, I ask no better fortune than to have the services of Sergeant Garty in that capacity."

In this particular instance there has always been doubt, however, whether any actual mutiny was planned, and whether the unfortunate midshipman, Philip Spencer, was not sacrificed to the misconstruction put upon an innocent boyish prank by an hysterical commander. The boy—he was hardly more—was the founder of a well-known college secret fraternity, the Chi Psi. A lot of writing in Greek characters found in his neckcloth, which Commander MacKenzie thought to be memoranda of a plot, turned out to be part of the ritual of this order. Spencer was hanged, but the commander, though acquitted by court-martial, left the navy under a cloud.

Of a somewhat similar nature, though really outside of their proper line of duty, was the service which a detachment of marines, stationed at Charlestown, Mass., were called upon to render in 1824 in connection with a mutiny at the Massachusetts State Prison. In accordance with the harsh prison rules of these early days three convicts had been sentenced to be publicly whipped, in punishment for some offense committed by them. The culprits, confined to solitary cells, escaped from these on the day set for their punishment and made their way to the dining hall, a large dark room. There they were joined by the other inmates of the prison, who rushed from the workshops, arming themselves with clubs, knives, hammers and with whatever other weapons they could procure. The outbreak had been so sudden and unexpected that it found the wardens and keepers utterly unprepared and entirely incapable of meeting the serious revolt. A general jail delivery, and much bloodshed seemed unavoidable, especially as all the officers of the institution lost their heads, as well as their courage. The single exception was a subordinate member of the prison management who, as soon as he heard of the occurrence, sent a request to Major Wainwright, commanding officer of the marine guard at the navy yard, to come to the assistance of the prison authorities. While the prison official was trying to persuade the convicts to desist from their mutiny, the marines arrived. The convicts refused to submit, except upon the promise of remission of the punishment of their three comrades. This the prison officials refused to give. Further developments are best related by quoting in part from the description of the occurrence contained in the " New England Galaxy " of 1828:

" Major Wainwright was requested to order his men to fire down upon the convicts through the little windows, first with powder and then with ball, till they were willing to retreat. But he took a wiser as well as a bolder course. Relying upon the effect which firm determination would have upon men so critically situated, he ordered the door to be thrown open, and marched in at the head of 30 men, who filed through the passage and formed at the end of the hall, opposite the crowd of criminals, grouped together at the other end. He stated that he was empowered to quell the rebellion; that he should not quit that hall alive till every convict had returned to his duty. The latter replied that they would fight to the last unless the sentence of flogging was remitted.

" Major Wainwright now ordered his marines to load their pieces, and that they might not be suspected of trifling, each man was told to hold up to view the bullet which he afterwards put into his gun. This only caused a growl of determination, and no one blanched, or seemed disposed to shirk from the foremost exposure. They knew that their numbers would enable them to bear down and destroy the handful of marines, after the first discharge.

" The marines were ordered to take aim; their guns were presented; but not a prisoner stirred, except to grasp more firmly his weapon. Still desirous, if possible, to avoid such a slaughter as must follow the discharge of the guns, the major advanced a step or two and spoke even more firmly than before, urging them to depart. Again, and while looking directly into the muzzles of the guns, which they had seen loaded with ball, they declared their intention of fighting it out. The intrepid officer then took out his watch and told his men to hold their pieces aimed at the prisoners, but not to fire till they had orders. Then, turning to the convicts, he said: ' You must leave this hall. I give you three minutes to decide. If at the end of that time a man remains, he shall be shot dead. I speak no more.' No more tragic situation than this can be conceived; at one end of the hall a fearless multitude of desperate and powerful men waiting for the assault; at the other a little band of well-disciplined marines, waiting with leveled muskets and ready at the least motion or sign to begin the carnage, and their tall commander holding up his watch to count the lapse of the three allotted minutes. For two minutes not a person nor a muscle was moved; not a sound was heard in the unwonted stillness of the prison, except the labored breathings of the infuriated wretches as they began to pant between fear and revenge. At the expiration of two minutes, during which they had faced the ministers of death with unfaltering eyes, two or three of those in the rear, and nearest to the further entrance, went slowly out; a few more followed the example, dropping out quietly and deliberately; and before half of the last minute was gone, every man was struck by the panic and crowded for the exit, and the hall was cleared as if by magic. Thus the steady firmness of moral force, and the strong effect of deliberate determination, cowed the most daring men, and prevented a scene of carnage, which would have instantly followed the least precipitancy of exertion of physical force by officers or their subordinates."

The account is silent about the further fate of the wretched convicts, and though not indulging in an overly loud praise of the brave little band of marines, and their calm, heroic commander, it shows clearly enough that, once again, some marines had lived up to the spirit of their corps to face the enemy, against what seemed overwhelming odds, calmly and bravely and to accomplish completely that for which they had been called into action.

Still another instance of the availability of the marine corps for civic needs occurred in 1835, when New York City was devastated by a great fire. The municipal authorities found it impossible to cope unaided with the conditions created by the conflagration, dangerous alike to public peace and safety. Upon their request the national government ordered to their assistance a detachment of marines from the Brooklyn navy yard, under the command of First Lieutenant J. G. Reynolds. They were used to guard public and private property and, following their custom, they did this with so much efficiency that the municipal authorities later passed a vote of thanks to this little group of marines and their able commander.

During all these years the marine corps had done its full share of whatever other work fell to the lot of our navy. Foremost among the undertakings of the United States navy in the third and fourth decades of the 19th century—1820 to 1840—was the determined effort to wipe out the pirates who were seriously interfering with American commerce in the West Indies, and to give protection to our merchant marine in whatever part of the globe it needed protection. The former purpose was quickly accomplished, once the federal government had decided definitely to act against the ever-increasing insolence of pirates operating off the islands of Porto Rico, San Domingo and Cuba. This decision was made in 1821, and before long the various strongholds of the pirates had been wiped out and American merchantmen, as well as those sailing under the flags of other countries, could carry on their legitimate business in peace and without molestation. Detailed records regarding the participation of the marine corps in the navy's work of cleaning up the Caribbean islands are singularly lacking, however, though the actual fact of their active participation is well established.

The next event of note in the history of the marine corps is more typical of the work they like to do. Even in its early days its slogan, which since has become so famous, " First to fight," was true to its spirit. Nothing was dearer to their hearts than to form a landing party and to have the first shot at some enemy of their country, who, for the time being was out of reach of its ship's guns. Such an opportunity came to the marines serving on board the United States frigate *Potomac* in 1832.

Grilling under a tropical sun on the northwestern coast of Sumatra lies a Malay hamlet—or town, perhaps it would be called, as it had nearly 4,000 savage inhabitants—rejoicing in the picturesque name of Quallah Batoo. Few hotter places are ever visited by civilized man, and curiously enough the product which in that day took Yankee traders to that unfriendly coast was as hot as the climate— namely, a very superior order of Cayenne pepper. In February of 1831 one of those Salem brigs, which at that time carried Yankee sailors and the American flag to all strange quarters of the world, lay at anchor half a mile or more from the harbor's mouth. We might better say from the mouth of a roaring torrential river which enters the sea at that point with such force as to break a way through the bars by which the coast is guarded, leaving an open- ing for small boats. But there is no harbor proper, and a heavy surf beating at all times on the shore makes landing perilous. The few traders that called at the port were accustomed to receive their cargoes in native boats that made their way out through the surf and slowly and laboriously carried to the ships their full load.

This particular brig was called the *Friendship,* and on a scorching day her captain and his second mate with four seamen were ashore at the trading depot, weighing the pepper and disposing it in the boats for carriage to the ship. The remainder of the crew were on board attending to the stowage.

No fiercer nor more criminal race exists than the Malays, particularly those of the seafaring towns. Captain Endicott noticed that the boats leaving the trading posts stopped near the mouth of the river, and seemed to continue their voyage with larger crews, but he supposed that this was merely the precaution of taking on more oarsmen to fight the increasing surf. What really happened was that the more or less peaceful oarsmen left the boats and their places were taken by armed warriors. These, on reaching the ship, concealed their character until fairly aboard, when they killed the mate and three sailors and bound two others for subsequent torture. Three slipped overboard, and after a long swim reached a point on the shore where there were no hostile tribesmen. The pirates who had seized the ship rifled her of everything of value, sending it ashore in their boats, and even cutting the copper bolts out of her timbers. Then they ran her ashore.

Captain Endicott, after a vain effort to retake his ship, made his escape in a small boat from the scene of the murders, and at a harbor some 20 miles to the south found three American merchant vessels, to whose captains he told his tale. It is characteristic of the self-reliance and of the hearty good fellowship existing between the Yankee skippers of that day that these three vessels were promptly got under way and the next day appeared before Quallah Batoo, demanding Captain Endicott's ship and complete reparation for his loss. All were armed, as was the custom of those days of piracy, and when the Rajah of Quallah Batoo insolently refused to deliver the ship, they first subjected his town and forts to a spirited bombardment, and then sent off three boatloads of armed sailors, who after a lively fight recovered the *Friendship*. On boarding his ship Captain Endicott found everything of value gone, including a chest with $12,000 in cash in it. In all, the loss to his owners was more than $40,000 and his cruise had to be abandoned.

When this news reached the United States the navy department determined upon a punitive expedition. At that time the American merchant marine was rapidly attaining the height of its glory and it was necessary for its further development that respect for the flag should be enforced upon even the most savage and distant nations or tribes. Accordingly, the 44-gun frigate *Potomac* was ordered to sail for the scene of the crime. She was one of the smartest and best equipped vessels of the navy, under command of Commodore John Downes, and carrying a large detachment of marines under Lieutenants Alvin Edson and J. H. Terrett. Approaching Quallah Batoo her captain slewed up the yards, loosened the cordage and strove in every way to give to the formerly trim and shipshape man-of-war the slovenly appearance of a merchant ship. Disguised thus the vessel approached within a few miles of the shore without arousing special suspicion, although large numbers of the natives gathered on the beach to study the character of the newcomer.

It was known that four forts, really heavy palisades, defended the town. One was on each side and one in the center. At midnight, landing parties, including all the marines, silently left the ship and with muffled oars pulled across the three miles of tossing water that intervened between them and the shore. The night was dark, but one of the officers leading the expedition writes that for a time they feared their presence would be betrayed by a meteor of amazing brilliancy that shot across the heavens immediately above, making everything for a moment as bright as day. Their landing, however, was effected without opposition and the force prepared to advance at dawn. The marines were given the van of the attack and carried with them the only piece of artillery of the entire company, a six-pounder upon which they had conferred the name of " Betty Baker."

With daylight they began to advance along the beach, the marines under Lieutenant Edson leading the vanguard. Apparently the natives had become suspicious of the stranger in their harbor, for their scouts were seen almost as soon as the landing party had reached shore. Besides the marines there were three divisions of seamen. Each of these four groups was to attack one of the forts. The one beyond the town had been assigned to Lieutenant Edson and his command. They went at their assigned task with good will, and in spite of determined and brave resistance on the part of the Malays, their stronghold, after some few hours' severe fighting, succumbed to the superior discipline and equipment and to the usual dash of the marines. They finally stormed the fort.

In the meantime, matters had not been going equally well with the force attacking the principal fort, south of the town and near the beach. They discovered, anchored in a little creek, three armed schooners, crowded with Malays. " Betty Baker " was turned loose on these with murderous effect. The natives on shore were fighting with savage desperation. But at the critical moment the marines, as well as one of the other divisions which had also successfully achieved its objective, came up with vigor and encouraged by their recent successes, stationed themselves advantageously and poured a devastating cross-fire into the ranks of the Malays.

It was at this moment that the Rajah himself rushed from the fort and led his men in hand-to-hand attack on the invaders, sustaining cutlass and bullet wounds until cut down by a marine. When he fell a woman, richly garbed in the barbaric costume of the tribe, sprang into the fight, seized a cutlass and fought like a tigress over his body until slain. Not until most of the Malays had been killed or wounded did they yield their stronghold. The last fort was attacked then and was taken in quick order by an assault in which bluejackets and marines shared.

About two and a half hours had elapsed since the beginning of the fighting. All the forts were in the hands of the United States forces. The town itself had been fired during the progress of the fight and most of it was burned down. The Malays had lost heavily, among their dead being the very rajah who had been the chief instigator of the attack against the *Friendship*. The object of the expedition had been fulfilled, though in its accomplishment two of our men had given their lives, and two officers and nine men had been wounded. Of these losses the marines bore their full share. Private B. J. Brown had made the supreme sacrifice for his country's honor. Private D. H. Cole had been wounded so severely that he later succumbed. Lieutenant Edson himself, too, had been wounded and so had Private J. A. Huster. Humble submission on the part of

ANTI-AIRCRAFT GUN ABOARD SHIP MANNED BY
MARINES

the natives was exacted and thereafter piratical out-
rages were infrequent.

A few years later an opportunity came to the
marine corps to show again its fighting value as a
unit. In those days there were frequent difficulties
between settlers in outlying districts and the Indians.
One outbreak of this type, more severe than usual,
occurred in 1836 in Georgia, where Creek Indians
were attacking with special savageness the doughty
pioneers who were attempting to change the southern wilderness into farmlands. As was frequently
the case, our military forces were utterly inadequate
to meet the emergency. As soon as word reached
Washington of these difficulties the commanding officer of the marine corps, Colonel Archibald Henderson, proffered his services, suggesting that the
marine detachments stationed at the various navy
yards be temporarily relieved by civilian guards; and
be then combined into a battalion to put the Indians
in their proper places. His offer was immediately
accepted.

Early in June, 1836, the necessary concentration
had been effected at Washington. From there the
battalion, under the command of Colonel Henderson
himself, went by way of Norfolk to Augusta, Ga.,
from where they marched in two weeks to the seat
of the trouble near Columbus, Ga., a distance of
224 miles, no mean achievement in those days of
poor roads and sparsely settled country. They encamped on June 23rd about 15 miles below Colum-

bus on the western bank of the Chattahoochee at Camp Henderson. This had been fortified by them with great haste in accordance with orders from General Scott, and was to serve as a base for the eastern wing of the army. Though the marines undoubtedly would have preferred to do some actual campaigning in the open, they did the work assigned to them with their usual promptness and efficiency. They had occasional relief from their arduous camp duties by pursuing Indians who were noticed lurking around almost every night. From time to time, too, there would be an alarm to the effect that some Indians were concentrating in force near by. Then a company or two of marines, enforced, perhaps, by some Georgia volunteers, would attempt a pursuit, but invariably the wily savages had fled by the time the marines arrived at their last camping place, where frequently fires still burning and horses left behind would testify to the precipitancy of their flight and to the respect in which they held our sea-soldiers.

The second battalion of marines, 160 men strong, had reached Milledgeville, Ga., on June 24th, 1836, under command of Lieutenant Colonel W. H. Freeman, and from there proceeded to Fort Mitchell, Ala.

In the meantime, it had been determined to send the marines to Florida, where the Indians were giving a great deal of trouble at that time. The two battalions, therefore, were consolidated into one regiment of six companies, and immedately left for

Florida. Arriving at Apalachiola, Fla., on October 16, 1836, the regiment was attached to the army operating under General Jessup. Throughout the balance of that year the marines participated in the operations carried on by General Jessup. They distinguished themselves especially at the battle of Wahoo Swamp, where First Lieutenant A. Ross, cited for gallantry, was mortally wounded.

With even greater glory did the marines cover themselves at the battle of Hatchee-Lustee, January 27, 1837, and the military operations immediately preceding it and lasting from January 23rd to the day of the battle. On the 23rd a company of marines, under the command of Captain J. Harris, forming part of a strong force under Lieutenant Colonel Caulfield, U. S. A., participated in the attack on Osuchee, one of the more important Indian chiefs. He had been located with a large force of Indians in a swamp on the shores of Lake Apopka. So quickly did our troops move upon him that he found no opportunity to evade them. He himself lost his life, together with three of his men, nine of whom were captured, together with eight negroes, of whom a goodly number were fighting with the Indians.

On January 27, 1837, the main force of the Indians was located on the Hatchee-Lustee, near and in the Great Cypress Swamp. Without loss of time our forces attacked. A rapid charge secured the enemy's horses and baggage, together with 25 Indians

and negroes. Colonel Henderson, himself always
in the midst of the fighting, ordered one company of
his command to guard this booty. With the balance
of his troops he promptly followed the Indians into
the swamp to which they had fled. He drove them
across the Hatchee-Lustee and crossed the river
with his force in the face of heavy fire from the
enemy, who was then driven into an even more dense
swamp, where he soon was dispersed completely.
In his official report of the engagement the commander of the marine corps says: " The regular
troops, both artillery and marines, displayed great
bravery and the most untiring and determined per-
severance. The marines, however, I cannot refrain
from mentioning in a particular manner. The killed
and wounded show where they were, and render
any further comment from me unnecessary." Two
non-commissioned officers and four privates paid
with their lives for the glory of having vanquished
the cruel savages.

A few months later Colonel Henderson was recalled to Washington in connection with his duties
as commanding officer of the corps. General Jessup,
at that time, issued the following order from his
headquarters, dated Tampa Bay, May 22, 1837.

" The presence of Colonel Henderson being required at
the headquarters of his corps, he will proceed to Washington
City and report to the adjutant general of the army. The
major general commanding would be forgetful of what is
due to merit, and would do injustice to his own feelings

were he to omit on the present occasion the expression of the high sense he entertains of the distinguished and valuable services rendered by the colonel. He tenders him his warmest thanks for the able, zealous, and cheerful support he has on every occasion received from him, both in Florida and Alabama and begs him to accept his best wishes for his future fame and happiness. . . ."

Colonel Henderson arrived in Washington about a year after he had left it with the corps for Georgia. The marine corps remained with General Jessup's army under the command of Lieutenant Colonel S. Miller. How the country felt towards the marine corps is shown by an extract from a contemporaneous newspaper report of his arrival, printed in the " National Intelligencer."

" We are glad to learn that Colonel Henderson, and the officers accompanying him, have returned to their families in good health. They have suffered much in common with all with whom they have served, not less from the climate, and the peculiar nature of the country which has been the theater of the war, than from the necessary hardships of the service in so wild and destitute a region. The gallant corps, which it is the good fortune of Colonel Henderson to command, has always been distinguished wheresoever duty has called it. In the present case the corps' deserves peculiar commendation, from having volunteered in the war in Florida. . . . Its commander deserves the praise of having proven himself worthy of his post, both by his gallantry in the field, and by patience and good example under all difficulties; and he, his officers and men have most honorably maintained the pledge which they gave to the government and to their country when they first tendered their services. The corps remains in Florida under the veteran and gallant Colonel Miller, to make farther sacrifices and endure fresh hardships. . . ."

In close relation to the Florida war against the Indians stands the work done by the so-called " Mosquito Fleet " from June, 1838, to August, 1842. The fleet consisted of a varying number of United States boats, supplemented by a large number of canoes. It was under the command of Lieutenant J. I. McLaughlin, U. S. N., and had attached to it, from 1839 to 1842, a force of marines, varying from two companies to 130 men. From 1839 to 1840 they were under the command of First Lieutenant G. H. Terrett, with Lieutenants T. R. Wilson and R. D. Taylor serving under him, and from 1840 to 1842 under First Lieutenant T. T. Sloan, assisted by the same subordinate officers. The marines also garrisoned Indian Key on the eastern coast of Florida, which was the base of the fleet, as well as Fort Dallas. The chief object of the " Mosquito Fleet's " activities were to penetrate into the heart of the Everglades, a water-logged country about which there was practically nothing known then, and to prove to the Indians, by the showing of a strong force, the wisdom of submitting to the government of the United States.

This object was accomplished by means of a number of scouting trips in which the marines took a leading part. One of them, begun in November, 1841, lasted for 22 days and resulted in the gain of much information regarding the difficult country through which it led. The marines had charge of two other scouting expeditions, one under Lieutenant Sloan, made for the purpose of carefully exploring the entire territory between the Miami and New Rivers. A number of Indian settlements were discovered, but the inhabitants fleeing as soon as the approach of the white forces became known, there were no hostile developments. On another trip, led by Lieutenant Taylor, the water gave out and Private Kingsburg died on the return trip to camp from exhaustion.

On the 9th of June, 1842, the " Mosquito Fleet " was ordered back to Norfolk, Va. During the entire period of the marine corps' service in Florida its losses in dead amounted to one lieutenant, 10 non-commissioned officers and 38 privates. Of these, 19 lost their lives while on sea service, while 30 died as a result of military operations on land. Of the latter, seven died in action or as the result of wounds received in action, 23 more dying of disease and accidents.

In 1836 Congress had passed an act permitting the employment of portions of the marine corps for the purpose of exploring those seas in which the United States were interested either on account of its fisheries or its trade. On March 20, 1838, Lieutenant C. Wilkes, U. S. N., was appointed to the command of an expedition of that type, and on August 11, 1838, he received his instructions from the navy department ordering him " to explore and survey the Southern Ocean . . ." The expedition was primarily for the purpose of promoting commerce and navigation, but was also to do everything in its power " to extend the bounds of science, and to promote the acquisition of knowledge."

The squadron was to consist of two United States sloops, one brig, one store ship and two tenders. To these were attached eight noncommissioned officers and 22 privates of the marine corps. The squadron sailed from Hampton Roads August 19, 1838, and from then on, for three years and ten months cruised all over the world, with frequent crossings of the Pacific Ocean and extensive cruising among its islands. One of the tenders and one of the sloops was lost at sea, the others returning safely to New York in June, 1842. Of the many places at which the squadron touched may be mentioned: Madeira, Cape de Verde Islands, Rio, Callao, Sydney, New Zealand, Friendly Island, Fiji Islands, Honolulu and the mouth of the Columbia River. In a number of instances difficulties arose with natives which required the sending of armed landing parties. In all these affairs the members of the marine corps acquitted themselves with great credit, and added to the luster of their branch of the naval service, and the Wilkes expedition resulted in many valuable contributions to science.

It seems a curious fact to recall to-day that in 1843, while the United States permitted negro slavery within its borders, and had hundreds of thousands of slaves in its southern states, it was nevertheless pledged by the Hay-Warburton treaty to aid Great Britain in the suppression of the slave trade. This aid was to be given by the maintenance of a squadron of not less than 80 guns on the African coast. In February of that year Captain Matthew Galbraith Perry, later to become famous as the officer who opened Japan to civilization, was in command of this squadron, made up of four men-of-war. He had hardly arrived at his station when he learned that shortly before two American trading vessels had been seized by African natives. The captain, mate and cook of one were murdered and the captain of the other had been tied to a post, while for three hours the three women and children entertained themselves and tortured him by sticking thorns into his flesh.

Once again it was time to enforce respect for the American flag upon savages, and the brig of war *Porpoise,* under Lieutenant Steelwagen, was sent to the Berribee coast to demand the restoration of the cargoes and the surrender of the murderers.

A large stockade sheltered the offending negro tribe and in it they were presided over by a native king rejoicing in the title and name of King Crack O. This potentate with high dignity invited Captain Perry to a conference in his royal domain. The American officer, though warned that the savage was treacherous, landed with a small guard of marines and proceeded to the council hall. In the midst of the conference the king, who was a gigantic negro, carrying a spear which bore on its butt 12 notches, indicating the number of men he had slain with it, seized Perry with one hand and sought to impale him. Instantly the sergeant of marines, who had been warned to be on watch for just such a maneuver, shot the king and bayoneted him twice. But the giant, frothing at the mouth, fought fiercely until other men came to the sergeant's aid and put an end to him. In the end the Americans burned that town and three others and the affrighted and overawed Berribees soon were eager to conclude a treaty.

One fact of importance in the history of the marine corps, which occurred during this period, was a change in its uniform. Up to 1839 it had been a green coat with white or buff facings. In that year, to take effect on July 4, 1840, it was changed to blue with red facings, colors which have since been made famous by their wearers the world over.

It should be of considerable interest to know something about the organization of the corps previous to the Mexican War. Reports from its commanding officer tell us that in October, 1842, it consisted of one colonel, one lieutenant colonel, four majors, 13 captains, 20 first lieutenants, 20 second lieutenants, 228 noncommissioned officers, 19 musicians, 63 drummers and fifers and 949 privates.

Besides furnishing detachments to most United States ships then in commission, they also garrisoned their headquarters at Washington and the United

States navy yards at New York (Brooklyn); Charlestown, Mass.; Gosport, Va.; Philadelphia, Pa.; Portsmouth, N. H.; and Pensacola, Fla. Figures regarding the pay received by the various ranks are interesting, showing a slight increase since the days of 1812. The commanding officer drew the monthly salary of $75; the lieutenant colonel followed with $60; the majors with $50; captains, if commanding a post or if at sea, $50; if not so engaged, $40; first lieutenants, $25; sergeant majors and quartermaster sergeants, $17; sergeants, $13; corporals, $9; drummers and fifers, $8; and privates, $7. In the case of commissioned officers certain service allowances for rations, servants, etc., increased their remunerations so that the aggregate annual salaries received by the various grades were: colonel, $1,946.40; lieutenant colonel, $1,620; major, $1,353.60; captains (post commanders or on sea service), $1,269.60; captains (regular service), $856.80; first lieutenants, $736.80; second lieutenants, $676.80.

In spite of these low salaries, the general average of efficiency and valor, both among officers and men, seems to have been very high, though life, at times, must have presented some very serious financial problems, especially to a married officer with boys and girls to clothe and school.

CHAPTER VI

War in Mexico.—Marines Landed at Point Isabel.—Plan
of the Mexican Campaign.—The Capture of Vera Cruz.
—The Storming of Chapultepec.—Santa Anna at Puebla.

DURING 1845 and the early part of 1846 the war
clouds were gradually gathering over Mexico and
the United States. There had been for some time
considerable friction between the two nations. In
1845, nine years after the independence of Texas
from Mexico had been acknowledged by the United
States, the annexation of that territory to the United
States made war inevitable. With the annexation
of the " Lone Star " state Mexico and the United
States became neighbors, and the opportunities for
friction along the long boundary of the Rio Grande
became suddenly greatly multiplied. They have
scarcely been lessened for one moment since.

Though war was not declared officially between
Mexico and the United States until May, 1846—
on May 12th on the part of the United States and
on May 23rd on that of Mexico—hostilities between
the armed forces of the two countries began as early
as April. In the latter part of that month General
Zachary Taylor, in command of the United States
forces in Texas, was stationed at Fort Brown, now

Brownsville, opposite the Mexican town of Matamoras, near the mouth of the Rio Grande. His base was at Point Isabel, somewhat to the northeast on the Gulf of Mexico. Receiving information that the Mexicans were concentrating a large force, apparently for the purpose of cutting him off from his base, he decided to march back to Point Isabel before their plan could be carried out. He arrived there safely and at once proceeded to strengthen his position at that place. Four days later, May 6th, the Gulf squadron, under the command of Commodore Conner, U. S. N., arrived and landed 500 marines and bluejackets under the command of Captain Gregory of the U. S. S. *Raritan* to assist in the defense of the Point.

This was the first active participation of the marine corps in the Mexican War, and was followed, as we shall presently learn, by service as continuous as it was courageous and effective. Much of it, as far as it was rendered in the eastern theater of the war, was performed in coöperation with the army. It matters little, however, to the marine corps, though always considering itself an integral part of the navy, whether its fighting is to be done with either branch of the service—it is always done to the best of its power, and General Taylor, as well as later General Scott, frequently and in unmistakable terms expressed his appreciation of the corps' work.

The combined military and naval operations of

the United States forces against Mexico consisted of three distinct phases: General Taylor's military operations in the east and the naval operations of the Gulf squadron, first under Commodore Conner and later under Commodore Perry; the naval operations of the Pacific squadron, commanded in turn by Commodores Sloat, Stockton and Shubrick, and the military operations of General S. W. Kearny in California; finally the military operations of the army of occupation under General Winfield Scott in the interior of Mexico.

The marine corps did its share of the work in all these theaters of war and did it equally well in each one. Although these various operations were not consecutive, we will consider them separately for the sake of greater clearness.

We have already heard how General Taylor had returned to his base at Point Isabel and how, with the assistance of a landing party of marines from the Gulf squadron, he had increased its ability to resist a Mexican attack. On May 7, 1846, he decided to return to Fort Brown, and took with him part of the marines who, at first, had been designated to act as part of Point Isabel's garrison. These took part in the engagements at Palo Alto, May 8th, and at Resaca de la Palma the following day, acquitting themselves creditably and contributing their share to the success with which both of these engagements ended for the United States forces.

Encouraged by these successes, General Taylor immediately proceeded to make his preparations for the capture of Matamoras. A detachment of marines and seamen from the men-of-war *Cumberland* and *Potomac* of Commodore Conner's squadron, about 200 strong and under command of Captain Aulick, with First Lieutenants D. D. Baker and A. Garland in command of the marines, were ordered to sail up the Rio Grande and to effect a junction with part of General Taylor's forces at the Rancho de la Burrita, about half way between the Gulf and Matamoras. This was done promptly, and a post was established on the right side of the river without any opposition. As soon as General Taylor received word of the successful carrying out of this protective movement he crossed the river with his main force, and occupied Matamoras on May 18th, without a shot having been fired, the Mexicans having abandoned the town.

Then came a summer of excessive heat, and early fall with its fierce tropical storms. Throughout all this period the Gulf squadron maintained a strict blockade of Vera Cruz. There was little glory to be gained out of this work, except that which comes from a sense of duty well performed, and of that the marines deserved their full share.

At last, in October, 1846, came another chance for more active work. Commodore M. C. Perry, second in command of the squadron, with the steam frigate *Mississippi,* a small steamer, a steam revenue cutter and four schooners sailed on an expedition with the object of ascending the Tabasco River. As usual, a detachment of marines was on board. The expedition started on October 16th and reached the bar at the mouth of the river on the 23rd. The same day the town of Frontera, and in its harbor two small steamers and some other boats, were taken without any opposition having been encountered. On the following morning some of the United States ships sailed up the Tabasco and after a day's journey arrived before the town of San Juan Baptista, the capital of the department of Tabasco. After a short cannonade the town was taken. Not having a large enough force to garrison the town, Commodore Perry seized some merchant vessels lying at anchor and returned to the squadron off Vera Cruz.

On November 12, 1846, the *Mississippi, Princeton* and three sailing frigates left the squadron and sailed for Tampico, about half way between Vera Cruz and Matamoras, and second only to the former in importance as a port on the eastern coast of Mexico. At daylight on November 14th these boats arrived before the bar of Tampico and there were joined by the vessels blockading this port. A detachment of marines was on each of the two steam frigates, under the command of First Lieutenants D. D. Baker, A. Garland and W. Lang and Second Lieutenant J. D. Simms. They formed part of the force, consisting all told of 300 officers and men, which was sent across the bar, a little later that morning, in boats. They sailed up the river, encountering no opposition, both the fort at the entrance and the town itself having been abandoned by their Mexican garrisons some weeks before.

About this time it had been decided in Washington to send another general to the Gulf, not to supersede Taylor, but to engage in a separate campaign which was to have its basis in the landing of large additional forces at Vera Cruz, and as its chief objective the occupation of eastern Mexico and, if possible, the capture of the capital. For this command General Winfield Scott was chosen. He arrived about the middle of February, 1847, off Lobos Island, about seven miles off shore and about 60 miles south of Tampico, which was to serve as rendezvous for all the transports bringing Scott's force, estimated at some 13,000 men. On March 2nd he set sail with all his ships for Vera Cruz.

In the meantime, Commodore Conner had been acquainted with the plans of the new campaign and had worked out the difficult problem of landing such a large force with all its necessary equipment, supplies, etc. It must be remembered that steam navigation in those days was still in its infancy and that the problems involved in an undertaking of this type were much more difficult than they would be to-day. However, thanks to the efficiency of the Commodore, of his staff and, indeed, of every unit of his squadron, as well as to the carefully worked out and equally carefully executed plans of General Scott, coöperation between what most likely was then the largest naval force ever assembled by the United States and the army, resulted in the successful carrying out of all details of landing.

On March 9, 1847, between daylight and ten o'clock in the evening of the same day, about 12,000 men, with rations for two days, horses, field artillery, etc., had been landed safely. Not a shot was fired against them and not a man was lost. The next day General Scott himself landed, and for the next few days part of his forces and a large part of the naval forces, including the marines, were kept busy landing the heavy artillery, ammunition and supplies for the army.

Throughout this whole operation, so carefully planned and so successfully carried out, the marines of the entire Gulf squadron played an important part. They were under the command of the following officers, attached to the various ships of the squadron: Captain Alvin Edson; First Lieutenants A. Garland and R. C. Caldwell; Second Lieutenants W. B. Slack, J. D. Simms, G. Adams and F. G. Mayson.

In his report of the landing, Commodore Conner says: " On board the *Raritan,* off Sacrificios, March 10, 1847 . . . General Scott has now with him upward of 11,000 men. At his request, I permitted the marines of the squadron, under Captain Edson, to join him, as a part of the Third Regiment of artillery."

Attached in this manner they took part in the siege of Vera Cruz, which lasted from March 10th to March 29th, when the greatest of the Mexican ports surrendered to the forces of the United States. The work done by the marines in the trenches and beside the guns is described by the commanding general of the brigade to which they were attached, Brigadier General Worth, in the following words of praise, forming part of an order, issued the day before the surrender of Vera Cruz: " The general of brigade avails himself of the occasion on separating from Captain Edson, his officers and men, to express his high appreciation of the energy, zeal and thorough soldiership, which marked their effective coöperation during our association and also to tender his cordial thanks and respects."

General Scott now began his preparations for an advance into the interior. The marines, for the time being, returned to their several ships and, almost at once, were employed in the various expeditions undertaken by Commodore Perry, who, on March 21, 1847, had relieved Commodore Conner, whose health had given out under the strain of his arduous work and the long stay in these tropic waters, then still infested everywhere with yellow fever.

The first of these was directed against Alvarado, about 30 miles from Vera Cruz. The U. S. steamer *Scourge,* manned by bluejackets and marines, captured the forts and town without receiving any opposition. A few days later the new commander of the squadron determined to occupy Tuxpan, about halfway between Vera Cruz and Tampico and the only place of importance on the Gulf not yet occupied by United States forces. On April 12, 1847, Commodore Perry started with the steam vessels of the squadron. The sailing boats, having started some days before, were to meet him off Lobos Island. The concentration took place promptly on the 17th, and on the next day the entire fighting force of the squadron was detached to the smaller vessels, which were then towed up the river to attack the forts and town. There were, all told, almost 1,500 officers, seamen and marines, the latter being led by Captain A. Edson, ably supported by First Lieutenants Garland, Caldwell and Slack and by Second Lieutenants Kintzing, Adams and Mayson. As soon as the ships approached the forts, the landing parties were transferred to the boats, which were run ashore, and from which the marines and seamen jumped out and immediately began the assault which, in every instance, was successful. The resistance encountered was only feeble, so that the object of the expedition was achieved with the small loss of three killed and 11 wounded.

It will be recalled that Commodore Perry, in October, 1846, had made a successful expedition to the Tabasco River, without, however, occupying San Juan Baptista, the capital of the state of Tabasco,

BOAT DRILL ON THE HUDSON

and frequently called by the name of the state. He now decided that it would be desirable to put a garrison of United States troops into this important city. Early in June he started with some of his ships and with a considerable force—some 1,500 marines and bluejackets—for the mouth of the river. In due time this point was reached and the river was ascended to within a short distance of the town. The larger part of the marines and seamen were landed to attack the town by land, while the boats were to assist from the river. Without meeting much opposition the town was occupied and the United States flag was promptly raised over it.

On June 22, 1847, Commodore Perry decided to return with his main force to Vera Cruz. At the newly captured town he left a small garrison of marines under the command of First Lieutenant W. B. Slack, with Second Lieutenant G. Adams as second in command. They were supported by the United States brig *Ætna* and the two small steamers, *Spitfire* and *Scourge*. The other officers of the marine corps—Captain Alvin Edson, First Lieutenants F. G. Kintzing and R. C. Caldwell and Second Lieutenant F. G. Mayson—together with the largest part of the marines—returned with the squadron.

Immediately after the departure of the commodore, Lieutenant Slack made his preparations to hold his post against any possible attacks. Three field pieces were landed and brought to the plaza, commanding the approaches. The garrison guard was also quartered there, numbering 28 marines. The balance of the marines, 69 men, under Second Lieutenant Adams, were quartered so that, in case of an alarm, they could march immediately to the plaza. On that very night a small Mexican force of about 200 men attempted to drive the guard and artillery from the center of the city. The latter, one of the field-pieces being handled by seven marines, under a corporal, all of them having served formerly in the regular artillery, quickly dispersed the attackers. From then on, though no further massed attack was made, Mexican troops could be observed moving continuously from point to point on the outskirts of the city and regularly, every night, the sentinels thrown out by Lieutenant Slack would be fired on. This kept the entire garrison continuously under arms and, considering its smallness, its distance from the source of possible reënforcements, and the ability of the Mexicans to oppose to it a much larger force, conditions assumed a rather dangerous state.

Fortunately, on June 26th, Captain Bigelow, U. S. S. *Scorpion,* arrived from the squadron and, as soon as he had heard from Captain Van Brunt, U. S. N., and in command of the small boats in the river, how affairs stood on land, he dispatched a boat to Commodore Perry with a request for reënforcements. Three days later these arrived on the *Vixen,* consisting of 55 marines under First Lieutenant Kintzing and 50 seamen. Captain Bigelow decided that it would be best to attack the enemy, lurking in the vicinity, and thus end the continuous expectation of an attack on his part. With about 125 bluejackets, two of the field-pieces, and 115 marines under Lieutenant Slack, he left the town on June 30th. On the march to a nearby Indian village, where the Mexicans were supposed to have concentrated, he was attacked. The marines, ably assisted by the field artillery, quickly brought the Mexican fire to an end, not, however, until Captain Bigelow's force had suffered the loss of two men killed and three wounded, among the latter being Lieutenant Kintzing.

For a few days after this engagement the garrison was left in peace. Sniping, however, soon began again. In the meantime, sickness, too, had made heavy inroads on the small force, about one-half of the garrison being in the hospital. Commodore Perry, therefore, decided to abandon the place, and in accordance with his orders, Lieutenant Slack, on July 22, 1847, hauled down his colors under the proper ceremonies and to the tune of " Hail, Columbia " marched his men aboard the boats and sailed for Frontera at the mouth of the river. In advising the secretary of the navy of these developments, Commodore Perry says: " I feel myself called upon to invite the attention of the department to the zeal and gallantry with which all the officers, seamen and marines of the detachment left by me at Tabasco performed their arduous duties in defending the city against a most active enemy."

During July the marine corps suffered a severe loss through the death of Captain Alvin Edson, attached to the U. S. S. *Raritan* of the Gulf squadron, who died at sea on the 15th of the month. He was a gallant and able officer and had taken a prominent part in all the operations of the marine corps attached to Commodore Perry's ships.

After Commodore Perry had left Tabasco, he lay for some time off the mouth of the river. He then sailed for Vera Cruz with his squadron. Soon after his arrival there, he received an order from Washington to detach the marines of the squadron and to attach them to the forces of Brigadier General Franklin Pierce, who, at about the same time, had arrived at Vera Cruz from the north with reënforcements for General Scott.

In regard to this measure the commodore wrote to the secretary of the navy, in a report, dated U. S. Flagship *Mississippi*, Anton Lizardo, July 4, 1847:

"Since the receipt of your dispatch of the 21st of May, received on the 1st inst., I have had an interview with Brigadier General Pierce, whose brigade the marines ordered to be detached from the squadron are to join. General Pierce has fully agreed with me that the small force of marines in the squadron, about 190 effective men, will be of little advantage to him, and that the consequences of withdrawing them, and the necessity of the immediate evacuation of Tabasco, and of weakening other posts in our possession (measures that will be indispensable by the detachment of the marines in the squadron), will produce a most pernicious influence with the enemy, who always claims as a triumph any retrograde movement of ours. I beg to be understood that the order of the 21st of May will be obeyed in part immediately, however it may inconvenience the ships of the squadron; and the withdrawal of the marines from Tabasco, Laguna, Frontera and Alvarado will be postponed only till I can receive reply to this communication or hear sooner from the department on the subject. This arrangement can produce very little delay, as it will require considerable time to collect together the marines, dispersed as they are along the coast, at points the extremes of which embrace a distance of nearly six hundred miles in extent. I shall await with much interest your communications, and hope that you will not only soon be able to replace the marines withdrawn from the squadron, but add to their number."

In the meantime, the authorities at Washington apparently had reached a similar conclusion. For, even previous to the receipt of Commodore Perry's request, they had dispatched an additional battalion of marines. They were under command of Lieutenant Colonel S. E. Watson. Having sailed from Fort Hamilton, New York harbor, in June, 1847, they were debarked at Vera Cruz and, by August 6th, had joined General Scott's army at Puebla. There they were assigned to the fourth division, commanded by Brigadier General J. A. Quitman, forming, together with Pennsylvania volunteers, its second brigade, which was put under the command of Lieutenant Colonel Watson.

By this time General Scott's preparations for his march into the valley of Mexico had been completed. One of the divisions left Puebla on August 7, 1847, and the next day the marines, with the other parts of their division, followed. Puebla was left in charge of a small garrison of 393 men, including among their number a small detachment of marines; there were also some 1,800 men in the hospital. All of these were under the command of Colonel Thomas Childs, U. S. A.

Without meeting any notable opposition General Scott's army reached the valley of Mexico about August 12th. The Mexicans continued to withdraw, while the United States forces gradually pushed their way forward. On August 19th, General Scott ordered that part of General Quitman's division, including the marines, to remain in reserve at San Augustine de las Cuevas. In announcing this decision, he wrote to the secretary of war on August 27th:

"I regret having been obliged, on the 20th, to leave Major General Quitman, an able commander, with a part of his division—the fine second Pennsylvania volunteers and the veteran detachment of United States marines—at our important depot, San Augustine. It was there that I had placed our sick and wounded, the siege, supply and baggage trains. If these had been lost, the army would have been driven almost to despair; and, considering the enemy's very great excess of numbers, and the many approaches to the depot, it might well have become, emphatically, the post of honor."

These two days, August 19th and 20th, were, indeed, red-letter days in General Scott's campaign. They brought his signal success over the Mexican forces at Contreras and Churubusco and thus opened the way for the assault on Mexico City itself. Though the marines had been entrusted with the highly responsible duty of guarding the rear of the army and its supplies and thus deprived of the privilege of participating in the actual fighting, they were soon to get an opportunity to show their prowess in combat.

First, however, came the futile armistice arranged between General Scott and N. P. Trist, special representative of President Polk, and President Santa Anna of Mexico, lasting from August 21 to September 6, 1847. Hostilities were resumed on the latter day, and on September 8th the sanguinary battle of Molino del Rey was fought. The marines then were still in reserve at San Augustine. On September 9th, however, General Scott ordered them, together with the Pennsylvania volunteers, to advance to Coyoacan, just west of Churubusco.

By that time General Scott had decided to attempt the capture of Mexico City by an assault against Chapultepec. Under this name is known a hill topped by a citadel about two and a half miles west of the capital. It is a narrow, volcanic ridge of rock about 200 feet above the level country, by which it is surrounded. On three sides—to the north, east and south—it is extremely precipitous. Only in the west it is sufficiently sloping to permit military operations against it, though even there the ground offers many natural difficulties. Its crest is occupied by a palace begun in 1783. After 1833 it was used as a military college of the Republic of Mexico. It was in 1847 still used for that purpose, and not until much later did it become the famous presidential palace and pleasure ground which adds so much to the appearance of the city of Mexico. But even then it was surrounded by a park, enclosed by high walls. At the time of General Scott's campaign the palace could be reached only by one road, winding its way up along the southerly side of the hill. To the west there were a series of solid stone buildings—Molino del Rey.

This formidable position seemed to General Scott and many of his officers the first obstacle that had to be overcome before the capital itself could be attacked. He decided to attempt this undertaking at once, and to General Quitman's division was assigned the difficult task of making the assault. It was to be supported by another division commanded by General Pillow and still another under General Worth was to assist.

Quitman's entire division, including the marines, was ordered to join these other forces by daylight on September 11, 1847, at Piedad, about two miles southeast of Chapultepec. Batteries had been erected southwest of the hill and these were to be supported by the marines and their fellow fighters. During the following day Chapultepec was continuously bombarded by the United States artillery.

The assault itself had been set for September 13th. Two storming parties, each numbering 250 men, were organized and were well supplied with scaling-ladders, pickaxes and crowbars. Both were under the command of marine officers—Major Levi Twiggs and Captain J. G. Reynolds—a signal expression of confidence in the valor and efficiency of that corps on the part of the commanding general. They were supported by the entire marine battalion under Lieutenant Colonel Watson, so that the corps carried the burden of the most difficult and dangerous part of the assault on its shoulders. It acquitted itself with its customary dash, against which the Mexican opposition could not avail for long. The storming parties and their support, the marines, rushed forward in the very face of the Mexican batteries, and long before the day was over, their work, combined with that of the artillery and parts of the other divisions, wrested the entire hill from the Mexicans and cleared all the surrounding ground of Mexican troops. The way was clear now to the two western gates of the capital.

As soon as the hill had been taken General Quitman gathered his entire division and with it moved directly against the city of Mexico, along the Tacubaya Causeway. Carrying all obstacles and in the face of a tremendous fire of artillery and small arms from the batteries at the gate of Belen, through which the causeway entered the city, and from nearby roads still occupied by large bodies of

Mexicans, the marines and the other units of Quitman's division pressed onward.

About two o'clock in the afternoon the gate was in the hands of the United States forces. From then until dark the marines and their fellow victors were subjected to a steady fire of artillery from the Mexican batteries at the citadel and at other points. By that time the second gate had been taken, too. During the night the Mexicans withdrew and at dawn the city surrendered.

Cautiously Quitman now moved his forces along the city's streets towards the National Palace. There they found bands of natives bent on looting. They were quickly driven out. To 40 marines under Lieutenant A. S. Nicholson, fell the honor of taking charge of the palace and of hoisting on it the United States flag for which they had fought so valiantly. They quickly put it in readiness for the commanding general, who entered the palace with his staff at about eight o'clock on the morning of September 14, 1847.

It was this exploit of first raising the American flag over the ancient citadel of the Mexicans that gave the author of the " Marines' Hymn," printed at the end of this volume, the inspiration for his first line—" From the Halls of Montezuma——"

September 13 and 14, 1847, thus became red-letter days in the long calendar of honorable achievement standing to the credit of the marine corps. Their successes, however, were not gained without serious losses. Major Levi Twiggs was killed leading the first assault against Chapultepec. Corporal Graham and Privates Egbert, McLaughlin, Herbert, Banks and Kelly laid down their lives for their country before the Gate of Belen. At Chapultepec, and before the gates of Mexico City, too, the following officers received wounds: First Lieutenants D. D. Baker and J. S. Develin and Second Lieutenant C. A. Henderson. The same price for their valor was paid by Sergeants Montgomery, Orr, Roach, Tansill, Wilson and Curran; and Privates Seebeck, Milburn, Rooney, Fogg, McGihen, Phœnix, Williamson, Briggs, Connor, Quinn, Smith, Stevens, McDonald, Cooper and Linns.

Out of 27 brevets awarded to officers of the marine corps for gallant and meritorious service during the Mexican War, 13 were earned before Chapultepec and Mexico City on September 13, 1847. The proud possessors of this distinction and the respective ranks awarded were: Lieutenant colonel—Major W. Dulaney; major—Captains J. B. Reynolds and G. H. Terrett; captain—First Lieutenants D. D. Baker, J. D. Simms and W. L. Young; first lieutenant—Second Lieutenants C. A. McCawley, T. Field, C. A. Henderson, A. S. Nicholson, J. S. Nicholson, F. Norvell, E. McD. Reynolds. Lieutenant and Adjutant Baker was especially mentioned " as conspicuous for his bravery and efficiency."

That the rank and file of the corps was equal in its display of courage to that of its officers is frequently testified to by the reports of the commanding generals. General Scott, in reviewing his entire campaign, says that " he had placed the marines where the hardest work was to be accomplished and that he had never found his confidence misplaced." General Quitman states: " The storming parties, led by the gallant officers of the marine corps, who had volunteered for this desperate service, rushed forward like a resistless tide."

During the weeks that were gaining laurels for General Scott's army, fighting its way to Mexico City, affairs in its rear were not progressing so favorably for the forces of the United States. Hardly had General Scott's troops marched out of Puebla (August 7, 1847) when the small garrison left there under Colonel J. Childs was faced by the outbreak of open hostility on the part of the populace. Among Colonel Child's force, consisting of about 400 effectives and some 1,800 invalids, in varying stages of sickness, were, of course, some marines. Bravely they shared with the other troops the anxieties caused by continuous sniping, waylaying of straggling men and similar guerilla methods of warfare. By the middle of September affairs had reached such a state that the garrison was practically besieged at its station in the San José barracks on the outskirts of the city. However, fortunately for the United States forces, the Mexicans were poorly armed and lacking in proper leadership, so that they did not succeed in making much of an impression on the watchful garrison. Still there were many anxious and trying days and the little band of soldiers and marines had a hard time of it. Though some of the sick had recovered and had thus increased the garrison to about 500 men, this was not a sufficient number to keep up the necessary watchfulness without putting a great strain on officers and men. To make matters worse Santa Anna, after the evacuation of Mexico City, decided to attempt to recoup his defeats by attacking the rear of General Scott's army. He assembled whatever was left of his beaten army and brought it to Puebla, hoping by a siege and capture of this place to cut off General Scott's army from its base of supplies and reënforcements.

He arrived before Puebla on September 21, 1847. His equipment was little better than that of the Mexican troops already there and his success, therefore, not any greater. Still, he formally demanded from Colonel Childs a surrender of the town, a demand which was promptly refused.

Just then Santa Anna received word that a new United States force was approaching from the direction of Vera Cruz and he decided to make an attack on it. This relieved the Puebla garrison, even though some Mexican troops remained behind and carried on the siege in a rather desultory fashion. The approaching force was under command of General Lane, and consisted of various units—artillery, infantry, marines—forming reënforcements for Gen-

eral Scott and numbering about 2,500. He had left
Vera Cruz on September 19th, and at Jalapa had
overtaken another United States force under Major
Lally, which had left Vera Cruz on August 6, 1847,
with about 14 companies of various regiments and
some marines, and a train of 64 wagons. All the
way to Jalapa he had been constantly harassed by
guerilla forces, with which he had fought numerous
engagements, during all of which the marines acquitted themselves most creditably. On one of these
occasions, at National Bridge on August 12th, Lieutenant Adams of the marine corps had distinguished
himself especially by his gallantry, but unfortunately
had been severely wounded. For his bravery he was
brevetted first lieutenant.

General Lane and Major Lally now joined forces
and left Jalapa on October 1, 1847, for Puebla.
On the ninth they fought an engagement with Santa
Anna at Huamantla, to the north of the Puebla
road. Here, too, the marines lived up to their long-
established reputation and helped to gain the day for
the United States arms.

On October 12th General Lane's forces reached
Puebla and occupied it in spite of considerable
sniping, and relieved Colonel Childs and his men,
who from then on remained unmolested. The siege
of Puebla had caused a number of casualties in the
garrison, among which the share of the marine detachment was two men wounded.

CHAPTER VII

CONSPICUOUS as had been the part played by the
marine corps in connection with the military and
naval operations of the Mexican war along the east
coast and in Mexico itself, the detachments of the
corps attached to the Pacific squadron were not to be
outdone in their eagerness and readiness to serve their
country. In some ways the difficulties of the United
States forces in the Pacific were greater, perhaps,
than those of their brethren in the east. They were
much further away from their home bases and could
be reached by the Washington government only after
long delays and in the face of many difficulties.
There were, of course, no transcontinental railroads
or Panama Canal in those days. No telegraphs or
telephones made it possible to keep in touch with
affairs or to send or receive orders almost as soon
as they had been issued. Travel was slow, even
for the fastest mails and most important dispatches.
The only way to get reënforcements to the Pacific
was around Cape Horn, and almost the only way to

send instructions was to send them by special messenger along the same road. For the overland route was then so undeveloped that it took almost as long, and was so insecure that no reliance could be placed on it.

When our difficulties with Mexico assumed a threatening outlook in the latter part of 1845, it was decided at Washington to send special instructions to the representatives of the United States government in or near the Mexican possessions on the Pacific. The most important among these were Commodore Sloat, in command of the Pacific squadron, then at Mazatlan, at the entrance to the Gulf of California; Mr. Larkin, the United States consul at Monterey in California, and Captain John C. Fremont, U. S. A., then on his famous exploring expedition in the Rocky Mountains. As bearer of these special and highly confidential instructions the administration chose First Lieutenant A. H. Gillespie, U. S. Marine Corps. He was to travel through Mexico, using his own name, but disguising himself and his object in the character of a merchant in search of health and amusement. He left Washington about November 1, 1845, and by December had reached Mexico City. There he was delayed by the revolution then in progress. However, he finally got away and reached Mazatlan, where he found Commodore Sloat, who assisted him in reaching Mr. Larkin at Monterey, which latter place Lieutenant Gillespie reached on April 17, 1846, six months after he had made his start. After a short rest he set out again to find Captain Fremont, whom he met on May 9, 1846, in Oregon. So intelligently had Lieutenant Gillespie carried out his instructions that not a suspicion of the true purpose of his journey became known. He later served with distinction as a member of the marine corps attached to the Pacific squadron and on December 6, 1847, was brevetted major.

On June 7, 1846, Commodore Sloat, then off Mazatlan aboard the *Savannah,* and accompanied by some boats of his squadron, received word of the opening battles of the Mexican War—Resaca de la Palma and Palo-Alto. At once he sailed north, leaving one of his boats, the *Warren,* at Mazatlan. He reached Monterey on July 2nd, where he found two more of his vessels and heard that the *Portsmouth* was at Yerba Buena (San Francisco). As soon as he reached Monterey 250 marines and blue-jackets were landed, the former under the command of Captain W. Marston, and Second Lieutenants W. A. T. Maddox and H. W. Queen. The United States flag was hoisted by this force, part of which was detached to garrison the town, under the command of Lieutenants Maddox and Queen. Just after Commodore Sloat had taken possession of the place the British 80-gun ship-of-the-line *Collingwood* entered the bay. The times were turbulent, and her commander would have been justified in landing a force himself. He was, no doubt, bitterly disappointed to find the Americans already in occupation. "It was a day of excitement when we entered Monterey," writes Fremont in his Memoirs. "Four of our men-of-war were lying in the harbor, and also the *Collingwood*. Looking out over the bay the dark hulls of the war vessels and the slumbering cannon still looked ominous and threatening. There lay the pieces on the great chess-board before me with which the game for an empire had been played." Admiral Seymour, of the British navy, would perhaps have found added pleasure in seizing the port from the fact that in the harbor lay the *Cyane* and *Levant*, captured from the British in 1815, and which he could thus have easily retaken.

Yerba Buena was occupied on July 9th. The people of the district were called upon, in a proclamation, to form a militia company with its own officers. The custom house was taken over and a guard of marines was placed there, under the command of Second Lieutenant H. B. Watson, who was appointed military commander of the place, with authority over the marines of his command as well as over the newly formed local militia.

In the meantime, Commodore Stockton had arrived in the Pacific from Norfolk, Va., by way of Cape Horn, on the U. S. frigate *Congress*. Commodore Sloat's health having broken down, he turned the command of the squadron over to Stockton, who by July 15, 1846, had reached Monterey. On August 1st he sailed south. His first stop was

Santa Barbara, where the United States colors were unfurled to the breezes of the Pacific Ocean and a small force of marines was left. On the 6th he arrived off San Pedro and a week later made a junction with Major Fremont's forces, with which Lieutenant Gillespie had thrown in his lot. Enlarging this force by the landing of a brigade of marines and seamen, the commodore marched upon Los Angeles, which he occupied in the name of the United States government on August 13, 1846. This having been accomplished, it was decided that a sufficiently large part of California had come under the control of the United States to warrant the establishment of a more or less stable civil government for the entire state. Major Fremont was made its head and Lieutenant Gillespie military governor and commander of the troops on land. Commodore Stockton then left for Monterey on September 2, 1846.

By the end of that month difficulties began to develop in the way of the Los Angeles garrison. The Mexicans, knowing that it would take some time to get reënforcements from the squadron, decided to attempt to retake some of the ground lost, and invested Los Angeles. Lieutenant Gillespie managed to get word to the commodore, who immediately started with the main portion of the squadron for San Pedro, leaving Lieutenant Maddox with a small force of marines to hold Monterey. As soon as the squadron had disappeared from Monterey, the Mexicans began a siege of that town, too. Lieutenant Maddox immediately dispatched a boat, hoping to be able to intercept the squadron and to bring back part of it. Before being able to catch up with Commodore Stockton's ships, this messenger fell in with the *Congress* on her way from San Francisco convoying a transport with Major Fremont and additional reënforcements destined for Los Angeles. It was decided to use part of this force to relieve Lieutenant Maddox at Monterey, a purpose which was promptly accomplished. The balance of Major Fremont's command proceeded to Los Angeles.

There affairs had rapidly reached a critical stage. Though a determined effort was made by a combined force of marines and sailors under Captain Mervine, U. S. N., to reach Lieutenant Gillespie, the latter's resources quickly gave out and he was forced to surrender with his small garrison to which the Mexicans granted liberal terms enabling this brave officer to join the main force before long. In recognition of his many services he was raised to a captaincy in November of that year and he was put in command of a force which was about to attack the Mexicans in their camp at San Bernardo. Before this plan could be put into execution word was received that Brigadier General S. W. Kearny, with additional military forces, had reached California from New Mexico and was to assume command of all military forces in the new territory. It was decided to have Captain Gillespie effect a junction with

DRESS PARADE ABOARD SHIP

Kearny's troops and to coöperate with him. The Mexicans immediately afterwards succeeded in inflicting on General Kearny a serious defeat at San Pasqual, resulting in heavy losses to his command, both the General and Captain Gillespie being among the wounded. As soon as Commodore Stockton, then at San Diego, heard of Kearny's difficulties he sent a force of marines under Lieutenant Gray to his assistance and, with his forces augmented by these new troops, Kearny made San Diego on December 12, 1846.

A few days afterwards Stockton decided to make an attempt to reoccupy Los Angeles. On December 29th he left San Diego with about 500 men, about 400 of whom were marines and sailors, the former under Captain Gillespie. On January 8, 1847, a serious engagement took place between this force and a slightly larger force of Mexicans at San Gabriel from which the United States forces emerged victoriously, though they suffered some losses, among the wounded being Captain Gillespie. On the following day another engagement occurred, equally satisfactory for the United States forces. On the morning of January 1, 1847, the latter entered Los Angeles and the Stars and Stripes once more waved over the city. Besides Captain Gillespie, Lieutenants J. Zeilin, J. C. Cash, W. A. T. Maddox and J. Wiley of the marines participated in this expedition.

While these events transpired in the southern part

of the state, the neighborhood of San Francisco, too, had seen considerable military activity. During the latter part of December, 1846, a small group of United States sailors had been attacked and some of them taken prisoners by the Mexicans. It was decided to start an expedition against the enemy and on December 29, 1846, about 100 officers and men left San Francisco under the command of Captain Ward Marston, U. S. Marine Corps. The marines participating in this expedition were commanded by Lieutenant Tansill. On January 2, 1847, they encountered the enemy. A successful attack was made which drove back the Mexicans. All the marines, officers as well as men, exhibited their usual coolness and were important factors in the successful outcome of the engagement. The Mexicans sent in a request for an interview with the United States commander, the outcome of which was first an armistice and later their capitulation, which included the surrender of their prisoners, laying down of their arms and return to their homes for more peaceful pursuits.

Another officer of the marine corps who was coming to the fore in these days was Lieutenant Maddox. At that period he was acting captain of mounted Monterey volunteers—a true " horse " marine—and a general order of the commodore in command of the squadron, dated February 1, 1847, speaks of him as follows: " For disinterested conduct the company of mounted volunteers, under

Lieutenant Maddox of the marine corps, acting as captain, is tendered the thanks of the commander-in-chief, and will without doubt receive the applause and due recompense from the general government."

Another change had taken place by now in the chief command of the squadron, Commodore W. B. Shubrick having succeeded Commodore Stockton. Under his direction the Mexican harbors of San José, San Lucas and La Paz in Lower California were seized. In command of the first of these another marine officer was put, Lieutenant Charles Heywood, who had under him four passed midshipmen and 20 marines. A blockade of Mazatlan was begun by the sloop *Cyane* and the frigate *Independence,* on both of which marines were serving. Later in the year the *Congress,* too, made its appearance there bearing the commander of the squadron. On November 11, 1847, a force of 600 marines and seamen was landed and occupied the town, the Mexicans promptly retreating. The largest part of the landing force was soon again withdrawn, but a small garrison, partly of marines, was left, and held this port for the United States to the end of the war.

But it was not held without the most untiring vigilance, and many weeks of almost continuous savage fighting. About the middle of November a large force of Americans unexpectedly appeared before the mission house and called upon Lieutenant Heywood to surrender. Taking account of forces he saw that he had 20 marines, 20 volunteers and 4 marine officers. So far as he could judge from the reconnaissance made from the roof of his stronghold the assailants outnumbered him nearly 10 to 1. He prepared for a desperate defense, feeling in his heart that its success would depend largely upon whether the enemy was provided with artillery. Hardly had he returned to them his defiance when that question was settled by the rapid fire of a six-pounder gun. The piece, however, was badly handled, did but little execution and was soon silenced by the nine-pounder which Heywood had mounted in an upper window. Under cover of the fire of their gun, however, the Mexicans made an assault at 10 o'clock at night, attacking both front and rear, but were beaten off.

The next night this assault was repeated in greater numbers and with more careful preparation on the part of the assailants. They rushed the front gate to the mission house in hopes of breaking through and capturing the nine-pound gun which had so harassed them the day before. At the same time another party attacked the house from the rear, being provided with scaling ladders and having the obvious purpose of reaching the roof. But both attacks were repulsed and the Mexicans were thrown into some confusion by the loss of their leader, who was killed by a discharge from Heywood's redoubtable nine-pounder. Luck, however, in the end saved the day for Heywood; for a Yankee whaler anchored in the bay, and the Mexicans, mistaking her for a man-of-war, retired. They carried their wounded with them, but left eight men dead on the field of battle. Heywood had but three wounded.

A small reënforcement was received by Heywood early in the following year, but this was largely offset by the misfortune of losing midshipmen Warley and Duncan, who with six men were on the beach in front of the house, never dreaming of danger. A large body of Mexican cavalry made a sudden dash along the shore and captured their whole party. The appearance of this force of cavalry was the precursor of another determined attack upon the mission house and its feeble garrison, now amounting to 57, of whom 27 were marines. The situation was not made easier for the defenders by the presence within the fort of about 50 women and children, who had sought shelter there when the town was raided by the Mexicans, and were dependent upon the garrison's rations.

Gradually the enemy brought up his forces and so thoroughly invested the mission house that no avenue either of retreat or of assistance remained open. Heywood, restive at thus being confined like a rat in a trap, determined to press the fighting himself. Accordingly, early in February, at the head of a party of 25 men, he made a sortie against the enemy, driving them from a house they held which commanded the gate of the fort. But as he had no men to hold the captured edifice he had to return to his works and the enemy returned to their house. Another sortie on the following day was equally successful for the moment and equally futile in the end. Indeed, it was more than futile; for Heywood lost one man, and though the Mexicans lost 15 killed or wounded, their greater numbers enabled them to stand this loss better than the Americans could spare their single brother in arms. From this time on it was the policy of the besiegers to occupy all buildings commanding the mission house and pick off the Americans one by one. By this sniping method they slew Midshipman McLanahan, who was mortally wounded by a bullet that entered through a window. The enemy also seized the point where the Americans had been obtaining their supply of water, but this move was checkmated by digging a well within the mission.

February 16th, nearly three months after the beginning of the investment of Heywood, the United States ship *Cyane*, Captain Du Pont, appeared in the harbor. Never was a more welcome sight to any eyes than was this vessel to Heywood's. Signals conveyed to the ship intelligence of the dire state of the men in the mission, and, at dawn the next morning, Captain Du Pont landed an expedition of 94 sailors and marines and attacked the enemy in his strongholds. The Mexicans showed no white feather. From behind trees, houses and sand hills they poured in a galling fire so that the landing force was compelled to fight for every inch of ground. The *Cyane* in the bay could not use her guns for fear of injuring her own people.

Du Pont's tactics were to drive the Mexicans to such a point that the fire from the mission house would take them in the rear. This was accomplished, and the Mexicans were massed at the junction of two streets, when, simultaneously, Heywood's men and the men from the ship charged furiously. The enemy broke and fled. Soon the marines were policing the town, in which order was restored, and nothing but a dim cloud on the horizon told of the whereabouts of the retreating foe. In this affair, the Mexicans lost 13 killed and a great number of wounded; the Americans had three killed and eight wounded. This was the last serious effort of the Mexicans to regain their ground on the western coast.

In October, 1847, Guaymas was shelled by the *Portsmouth* and the *Congress* and surrendered to those ships. Not having sufficient men to spare for a garrison, the United States flag was kept flying on a little island under the guns of the *Portsmouth,* which was left there until November 8th, when she was relieved by the *Dale.* On the 17th, Commander Selfridge made a landing at the head of about 65 marines and seamen, the former being commanded by Second Lieutenant R. Tansill. The Mexicans attacked at once and Commander Selfridge was severely wounded. The accurate and sustained rifle fire of his small force of marines and seamen, however, promptly drove back the Mexicans, who evacuated the town.

Military and naval operations in the Pacific and the adjoining territory were discontinued as soon as word was received of the temporary suspension of hostilities in the east and were not again taken up.

How the last commander of the Pacific squadron, during the period of the Mexican War, valued the services of the marines may be seen from the following extract from the report of Commodore Shubrick, dated "On Board the *Independence,* Mazatlan, February 21, 1848":

"The marines have behaved with the fidelity and constancy which characterizes the valuable corps, and I embrace this opportunity respectfully to recommend that ships coming to this station be allowed as large a complement as possible. The service would be greatly benefited by doubling the number allowed to each ship, and reducing to the same extent, if necessary, the complement of landsmen and ordinary seamen. The want of marines is strongly felt in all operations on shore."

The following officers of the corps had been attached to one or another of the various ships of the Pacific squadron, 1846-1848: Captains W. Marston, J. Edelin, H. B. Tyler, A. H. Gillespie, J. L. Hardy; First Lieutenants J. Zeilin, W. A. T. Maddox; Second Lieutenants H. W. Queen, J. W. Curtis, H. B. Watson, W. W. Russell, R. Tansill, J. C. Cash, J. A. Buchanan and J. Wiley. Of these the following were brevetted for "gallant and meritorious services": Major—Captain Zeilin, Captain Marston;

captain—First Lieutenants Maddox, Russell, Tansill and Watson.

While peace negotiations were about to be begun in March, 1848, a second battalion of marines, under the command of Major John Harris, left New York. It was to coöperate with the Gulf squadron on the Isthmus of Tehuantepec. However, upon its arrival at Vera Cruz the armistice had been concluded and the battalion saw no active service. It acted for some time as garrison of Alvarado. It consisted of four companies of 90 men each and, besides its commander, was directed by the following officers: Captain N. S. Waldron; First Lieutenants A. S. Taylor, W. L. Shuttleworth, J. Watson; Second Lieutenants J. R. F. Tatnall, G. R. Graham, J. H. Jones, J. H. Broome, G. F. Lindsay, W. S. Boyd.

The services of the marine corps during the Mexican War was one of both quality and quantity. Members of the corps participated in practically every important undertaking, both on land and on sea, in the east and in the west. All told, there had been during the period of the war, with the Gulf squadron, 1,050 marines; with the Pacific squadron, 402; and with the army, 317. One remarkable feature of their record is the fact that there does not stand against them a single execution for military offenses, a record which cannot be claimed by any other unit that fought in our army against Mexico.

The officers of the corps made a record which at

least equalled that of the rank and file. Twenty-seven out of a comparatively small number were brevetted for gallant conduct and service before the enemy.

In spite of all these facts Congress, watchful even in these present days of lavish war expenditures and always rather strongly anti-militaristic, even while the war was still being fought, seemed to become afraid that if the claims of the corps for extension were to be based on the merits of its conduct, such an extension, always desired and recommended by the commanding officer of the marine corps, by the secretary of the navy, by most officers of the navy, and certainly by the corps itself, would have to be granted. It, therefore, decided the matter adversely before the end of the war and before such well based claims as courage and fidelity could be legitimately put forward by the well-wishers of the corps of whom there were legion, then as now.

On March 2, 1847, Congress passed an act directing that " at the termination of the Mexican War the marine corps was to be reduced, both in men and officers, to a number not exceeding the number in service at the date of the act." This was accomplished, as far as the men were concerned, by discharging the necessary number as they arrived in the United States. The duty of reducing the number of officers was more difficult. It was necessary to drop from the rolls four captains, four first lieutenants and four second lieutenants. The disagreeable problem was finally solved by organizing a board of officers of rank superior to that of captain, who were instructed to designate the officers who could best be spared from the service. The report of this board was carried out, without, of course, any blame being attached to the officers thus dropped.

Despite this action of Congress, the secretary of the navy of those days, J. Y. Mason, in his annual report to the President, James K. Polk, says: " The efficiency of our ships of war would be promoted if the marine guard allowed by the regulations could be enlarged; and an increase of the rank and file of the corps from 1,000 to 1,500 would, in my judgment, be highly beneficial. Such an increase of the noncommissioned officers and privates would justify an additional number of commissioned officers equal to the number dismissed."

At the end of the war, by a joint resolution of Congress, approved on the 10th of August, 1848, the officers, noncommissioned officers, privates and musicians of the marine corps, who had served with the army in the war with Mexico, were placed in all respects as to bounty land and other remuneration, in addition to ordinary pay, on a footing with the corresponding ranks of the army. The wording of the resolution was somewhat uncertain, unfortunately, and the secretary of the navy refused to interpret it as meaning all members of the corps who had seen active service during the war, whether on land or on sea. He restricted it, though with regret, to those who had been attached to the army, though there can be no doubt that those that had been attached to various boats of the Gulf and Pacific squadrons deserved this recognition equally well.

CHAPTER VIII

AFTER the Mexican War the national government, as usual, reduced largely the armed forces of the nation. The marines suffered with the rest. Although year after year secretaries of the navy recommended an increase in the size of the corps, an increase made the more necessary by the substitution of steam for sails in the navy, and the accompanying increase in the number of ships, Congress was deaf to their appeals. Yet at this time the development of the corps in efficiency was notable. It had for its commander General Archibald Henderson, who had entered the corps as a second lieutenant in 1806 and served until 1859. An enthusiast upon the subject of the marines and their services, a fighter himself, an earnest observer of the motto, " First to Fight," he exerted every quality for the advancement of the corps. But his was a long and uphill fight and not until just before his death did he see its fruits becoming apparent.

In 1851 the corps consisted of a brigadier general commanding, 66 commissioned officers and

1,154 noncommissioned officers and privates. At this figure it stuck for years. In his endeavors to secure congressional authority for the increase of the corps, General Henderson wrote to commanders of squadrons and other high officers in the American navy asking their opinion as to the desirability of such an increase. In his annual reports appear letters from the most eminent officers of the service, urging the further development of the corps and giving cogent reasons for it. But it was of little avail. Not until 1858 could any increase be secured and then it was only to 1,852 officers and men. Yet the service of the corps was not unappreciated, for in 1859 Secretary of the Navy Isaac Toucey, in his report, said: " The marine corps is an indispensable branch of the naval service. At home we have had occasion to appreciate its prompt and disciplined energy in maintaining law, order and government against outbreaks of illegal violence. It is a gallant little band upon which rest the most widely extended duties at home and in every sea and clime, without sufficient numbers to perform them."

In the second half of the 19th century Cuba began to be a source of trouble to the United States government—a part which she continued to play until the nation wisely and firmly intervened and took her away from the crushing domination of Spain.

For decades the sympathy of the people of the United States for the Cubans, seeking freedom from Spain, found its expression in filibustering expeditions which carried arms and other aid to the Cuban insurrectos. Observance of international law compelled the government to suppress these expeditions with a heavy hand, and in this task the marines more than once were landed in Cuba, partly for the purpose of apprehending the invaders, partly in order to suppress riotous outbreaks in the streets of Havana. Indeed, an article might be written about the benevolent part played in all parts of the world in saving foreign but friendly governments from riotous outbreaks of their own citizens. It was because of their constant employment in service of this kind that the principle grew up that landing marines was not to be considered an act of war, though landing troops would be.

In 1853 the United States undertook a task which came near to changing the history of the world, and will always exercise a marked influence upon it. Up to that time Japan had been a hermit nation. No foreigners were allowed to land in its ports. It neither sought trade with other nations nor even permitted it. Foreign ships, compelled by stress of weather or lack of supplies to seek shelter in its harbors, encountered savage hostility. Sailors shipwrecked on its shores were reduced to slavery and not infrequently murdered. This situation the United States determined to correct by opening Japan to civilization.

By so doing we created a new and vigorous competitor in the markets of the world, and a military and naval rival of no mean proportions. In a great section of the United States apprehension of Japan's power is such that the people rue the day when by action of our government she was induced to study modern and civilized methods of government, industry and military and naval efficiency.

Whether advantageous or not, however, the job was well done. It was entrusted to Commodore Matthew C. Perry who, with a fleet of 10 ships, one of the most powerful squadrons ever sent out up to that time, was dispatched to Japan to make a show of naval force and to negotiate peacefully, if possible, a treaty of commercial intercourse between the two nations.

It is impossible to give in detail here the methods by which Commodore Perry met and set at nought the mediæval conceptions of dignity and etiquette with which the court of the Mikado was hedged about. If the Japanese insisted upon deference and reverence being shown to their ruler, so Perry's subordinate officers insisted upon like deference being shown to him. The Mikado was invisible, and the commodore clung to his cabin and deputed subordinate officers to meet the envoys which the Japanese sent to treat with him. Japanese dignity insisted on prescribing the distance from the capital at which the fleet should anchor. Perry insisted that he would anchor where he desired. He bore a letter from the President of the United States to the Mikado. That is, he was the personal repre-

sentative, the *alter ego,* so to speak, of the President.
To no one save a special officer of like relationship
to the Mikado would this letter be delivered. The
story of the long-continued clash between the rival
pretensions to extreme and lofty dignity is amusing
reading in the light of present-day commonsense.
It lasted for weeks, but finally Perry landed amicably
with an escort, including all the marines on his
flotilla and some 400 officers and bluejackets besides, proceeded in stately procession to a house
specially built and endowed with the quality of a
palace of the Mikado. There the letter was duly
delivered and, promising to return in six months for
an answer, the commodore sailed away.

Upon his return after another protracted duel of
diplomacy, etiquette and ceremony, and a shore visit
—escorted this time by more than 500 officers and
men—the Japanese acquiesced in all of the sugges-
tions made in the President's letter and a most
liberal treaty was negotiated. Commodore Perry
in his report mentioned with especial commendation
the part played by the marines in these ceremonies.

China, like Japan, engaged much of the diplo-
matic attention in those days of the American navy.
While Perry was at Jeddo, marines from the United
States sloop of war *Plymouth* were landed at Shang-
hai to coöperate with English marines in protecting
English and American residents of that port against
Chinese insurrection. There was heavy fighting, in

which the Americans lost two men, killed. The year following, 1855, English and American marines again landed on Chinese territory—this time at Khulan—where they practically annihilated a piratical force. Eight Americans were killed, two of whom were marines, and in the cemetery of Happy Valley at Hongkong there stands to-day a monument to the memory of the bluejackets and marines of the United States ship *Powhatan* and the British ship *Rattler* who fell in this action.

Always the Asiatic coast has been the scene of activity of the United States naval forces, both bluejackets and marines. Present-day Americans, of course, recall the part taken by our forces at the time of the Boxer Rebellion. The earlier services were much of the same sort. In 1856 Commodore Armstrong landed a heavy force from the *Portsmouth* and *Levant* at Canton. The English were then engaged in an attack upon the governor's palace, and in spite of their neutral character, some of the younger American officers, carried away by their enthusiasm, permitted their forces to join in this attack. Commodore Armstrong repudiated this action and strove to check the fighting, but by this time the Chinese in turn had their passions aroused and fired from several ports upon the American flag. The result was a general battle, in the course of which a heavy landing force, composed mainly of marines, was thrown against the forts and occupied them. Later they repelled a counter-attack from a force of over 5,000 Chinese. In the end four forts, all planned by European officers, built of granite, and defended by more than 170 guns, were carried by the Yankee sailors and marines. It was a fight without true diplomatic reason. To some extent it was the spontaneous outburst of the spirit expressed by Commodore Tatnall years later when he went to the aid of British forces in another Chinese port with the cry, " Blood is thicker than water." But however indefensible from the standpoint of international law the action might have been, it was not without its advantages to the general cause of civilization, for it led to a new and much more liberal treaty between the United States and the empire of China.

Central and South America have always been active in giving military employment to the ever-ready men of the marine corps. In those Latin-American countries insurrections and actual revolutions were for half a century of more than annual occurrence. In these later days the great republics of Brazil, Argentina and Chile are established on as firm a basis as any governments of the world and would spurn the idea that foreign intervention was necessary to maintain order in their cities. Only the Central American nations now invite the occasional attention of the marines, but during the latter half of the last century turbulence in South America frequently called them to those coasts. It was in 1855 that the ship *Germantown* was at anchor in

the harbor of the town of Montevideo. On shore,
one of the customary revolutions was running its
usual course with much noise and turbulence, much
looting and menace to the lives and property of foreign residents but without much serious fighting. Beside the American ship there were English, French
and Spanish men-of-war in the harbor, and Captain
Lynch, of the *Germantown,* suggested joint action
for the protection of foreign residents. He himself
landed about 100 of his marines, under command of
First Lieutenant Nicholson, who occupied the
United States consulate and the custom house. This
officer, moved by motives of humanity, went somewhat beyond the scope of his orders, but for so
doing afterwards received the approval of his superior authorities. The insurgents, finding themselves outfought and outnumbered, had surrendered
to the government forces. The latter, after a practice too common in these South American brawls,
were about to massacre them all, when Lieutenant
Nicholson mustered his marines and marched them
to a point between the two forces. Here he protected the weaker faction and harangued the victors
until they agreed to abandon their murderous pro-
gram and to submit to the regular courts the question of the punishment of the insurrectos. Montevideo was more than once the scene of marine activity, and in 1858 a joint force from several men-of-
war of various nationalities was landed, all under
the command of Flag Officer Forrest of the United

MACHINE GUNNERS OF THE U. S. MARINE CORPS READY
FOR ACTION AND ON THE MARCH

States navy. Marines from the United States ships *St. Lawrence* and *Falmouth* formed part of the landing force, which remained in command of the town for 10 days.

Central America, even more turbulent than South America, had witnessed on many occasions the occupation of sundry of its ports by American marine forces. This occurred in 1853, when the *Cyane* and the *Albany* sent some 50 marines ashore at San Juan to rescue American residents. A year later the same town was bombarded by the American forces. Curiously enough, the marines were afterward called upon to rescue Nicaragua from the notorious filibuster, Walker, who once was able to conquer the country and become its president. Afterwards, however, defeated by an uprising of the natives, he was forced to flee and surrender himself and his expedition to marines from a United States ship in the harbor.

Certain of the activities of the marines on the soil of their native country read queerly to-day in the light of the development of our territory and subsequent history. The people of the thriving and progressive city of Seattle, Wash., if unversed in American history, would hardly believe that 60 years ago marines were landed from the sloop of war *Decatur* to drive off a force of several hundred Indians who had gathered with the obvious intention of raiding the town. A pitched battle was fought for more than six hours, when the Indians were driven off by the superior marksmanship of the marines.

New York even had occasion to call upon the soldiers of the sea for assistance in 1857, when a force of what were then called " Plug Uglies " from Baltimore was imported to influence a local election by their peculiar methods. History records that it was the " Know Nothing " party which employed these strong-armed mercenaries. At any rate, they outfought the local police and so terrorized the city that an appeal was sent to the President of the United States for military aid. He promptly referred the request to the commander of the marine barracks, and speedily, after the fashion of the force, two companies of the marines were on the way to New York. Here they were received by an excited and desperate mob. The rioters were armed with guns, pistols, sledge hammers, crowbars, knives and every imaginable weapon that would wound or kill. In some way they had possessed themselves of a small brass cannon, which they loaded to the muzzle and trained upon the marines, telling Captain Tyler, in command, that unless he withdrew his force they would surely fire. Just at that moment there stepped from the crowd of bystanders an elderly man in civilian's clothes, who walked up to the cannon and with folded arms stood directly before its muzzle.

Then he said to the rioters, " You had better think twice before you fire this gun. The rifles of

those marines are loaded with ball cartridges; many
of you are sure to be killed and wounded. I call
upon you in the name of the law to leave this place
in peace and order."

It was General Henderson, the commander-in-
chief of the marines, who, though not on duty at
the moment, had come in civilian garb to see how
his men acquitted themselves. But his bravery did
not cow the mob. Several pistol shots were fired
at him, all flying wide of the mark, and he passed
over to the side of Captain Tyler, to whom he said
curtly, "Take that gun." This was instantly accomplished, and the cannon was held despite two
charges on the part of the rioters. In one of them
a member of the mob was barely stopped from killing General Henderson, for he held a loaded pistol
within a few feet of the general's body and was
about to fire it when a blow from a musket wielded
by a marine laid him low.

Thus far the marines had withheld their fire,
having been instructed to subdue the mob, if possible,
without bloodshed. But at last a shot from a
rioter's pistol struck one of them in the face. His
comrades, losing their self-control at the spectacle,
emptied their rifles into the mob, with the result
that that body rapidly scattered. After a brief encampment in City Hall Park the marines returned
to Washington, leaving the city restored to order.

The first serious overt act to herald the coming
storm of civil war called the marines to active

service on the 16th of October, 1859. It was then
that the long-contested struggle of words and laws,
for and against the evil of slavery, first blazed forth
in active hostilities with swords and guns. It was
then that John Brown, fanatic and inspired prophet,
murderer and yet a friend to humanity, strove to
incite the insurrection of slaves in the south that
had long been his plan for the abolition of slavery.

On the night of the 16th a party of insurgents,
led by " Old John Brown, of Ossawattomie, Kan-
sas," had seized the armory, arsenal, rifle factory
and bridge at Harper's Ferry, a little town in West
Virginia just across the Virginia border on the Potomac, and had then imprisoned there as hostages
10 of the most notable residents of the vicinity,
using for that purpose the fire-engine house. The
news spread rapidly and early the next morning
volunteer companies from Virginia arrived. As soon
as the federal government had been advised of the
affair, Colonel Robert E. Lee, then still an officer
of the United States army, was dispatched from
Washington to assume command of the forces arrayed against the insurgent leader. He arrived at
about the same time, the evening of October 17th,
with some Maryland volunteers, and a special detail
of marines from Washington. The latter had been
sent by Colonel-Commandant Harris from marine
headquarters by special train, and consisted of 11
sergeants, 13 corporals, one bugler and 81 privates,
with a battery of howitzers, all under the command
of First Lieutenant Israel Green. With them was

also Major W. W. Russell, paymaster of the marine corps. Within an hour after they had received
their orders they were ready for entraining at the
Washington railway station. It was a considerable
army to send against one half-crazed, fanatical old
man.

Immediately upon his arrival on the scene of
action, Colonel Lee ordered the marines to proceed
to the armory grounds, to which the insurgents had
retreated, and to prevent their escape during the
night. Fearing that the lives of the hostages might
be endangered by an immediate assault, it was decided to wait until the next morning, when an unsuccessful attempt was made to persuade the insurgents
to surrender. While Lieutenant J. E. B. Stewart,
U. S. A., was carrying Colonel Lee's summons to
the insurgents under a flag of truce, all the forces
available were paraded within their sight in the
hope that their overwhelming numbers might be the
best argument for a surrender. However, even this
failed to shake Brown's determination to make a
stand.

Colonel Lee, fearing just such an outcome, had
prepared a storming party of 12 marines, under
Lieutenant Green, who were to assault the engine
house with the least possible delay after Lieutenant
Stewart had signalled that his mission had failed.
The marines had been placed close to the objective
of their assault, but secure from its fire. Three of
them had been furnished with heavy sledge hammers
with which to break in the doors.

As expected, the insurgents refused to surrender. Lieutenant Stewart gave the signal as he left the building and the marines at once advanced to the door and began to attack. The fire engines had been placed against the doors, and the latter were further fastened by ropes against which the blows of the hammers were powerless. They were dropped, therefore, and a heavy ladder was called into use as a battering-ram, with which the door was quickly broken down sufficiently to permit the storming party of marines to enter. Just then a shot from one of the insurgents mortally wounded Private Quinn. The rest, led by Lieutenant Green and Major Russell, quickly ended the contest. The insurgents who resisted were bayoneted. Their leader, John Brown, was cut down by the sword of Lieutenant Green, and the citizens who had been made prisoners were promptly protected. The whole was over in a few minutes, not, however, until another marine, Private Rupert, had been wounded.

When the captured insurgents were brought out to be conveyed to prison, the attitude of the citizens became so threatening that Colonel Lee ordered the marines to protect their prisoners against any harm. This order was carried out with the same fidelity with which, only a short time before, they had risked their own lives fighting these very same men.

A party of marines was then detached under Lieutenant Stewart to proceed to a farm in Maryland, about four and a half miles from Harper's Ferry, which had been used as a depot by the insurgents. There they found a large number of pikes and other material, which was brought to the armory at Harper's Ferry.

The next day the insurgents were turned over to the proper civil authorities and, under escort of a detachment of marines, were safely taken to Charlestown. Later that day a false alarm of another armed attack at a place about four and a half miles distant was given. Though doubting its correctness, Colonel Lee, with Lieutenant Green and his marines, immediately started for the reported seat of the trouble, but upon their arrival found that there was nothing to the report. He returned to Harper's Ferry and, together with the marines, entrained for Washington early on October 20th. In making his report to the Adjutant General, he said: " I must also ask to express my thanks to Lieutenant Stewart, Major Russell and Lieutenant Green for the aid afforded me, and my entire commendation of the conduct of the detachment of marines, who were at all times ready and prompt in the execution of any duty."

The year 1860, as far as the marine corps was concerned, was much like the proverbial calm before the storm. The dark clouds were gathering, to break a year later into civil war, but the nation was still blind, and its fighting forces were not increased.

CHAPTER IX

*The Civil War.—Destruction of Gosport Navy Yard.—
Marines and the Coastwise Forts.—The Monitor and
Merrimac.—The Taking of New Orleans.*

IN the cruel and bitterly contested war between the
people of our northern and southern states, beginning in 1861 and lasting four years, the navy—and
with it the marines—played a part which historians
have been slow to recognize adequately. Around
the Confederate coasts the navy threw a belt of
iron, past which the blockade runners could but
infrequently slip. Up and down the inland waterways with which the territory of the Confederacy
abounded, the river gunboats, and not a few ships
from salt water, fought their way, helping the armies
of Grant and Sherman in the work of cutting the
Confederacy in two.

In this service the marine corps took its full part.
It entered upon the war somewhat crippled, for the
question of loyalty to their states rather than to
the nation perplexed its officers as it did those of
other services. Six resignations and 14 dismissals
were caused by this divided allegiance. The north
was bitter then at those who put local loyalty above
national allegiance, but that bitterness has long since

died away, and right-thinking people recognize the fact that there was logic, and even patriotism in either point of view.

The marines were called early to active service. When Major Anderson, suspecting the temper of the South Carolinians, secretly transferred his army command from the mainland to Fort Sumter, in Charleston harbor, he had neither troops to garrison so large a work, nor provisions to sustain the troops he did have against a protracted siege. A relief expedition was speedily dispatched from the north. It was bungled, of course, for our knowledge of war was then limited and our equipment for it still more so. Instead of a warship, of which indeed we had too few, a merchantman, the *Star of the West*, was loaded with provisions, took aboard 250 marines and set forth to Anderson's relief. But at the first shot from the watchful Confederate batteries the *Star*—which was no shooting star—put her helm hard down and fled. A more fortunate relief expedition, in which the marines, under Lieutenant Cash, took part was that for the reënforcement of Fort Pickens, at the mouth of Pensacola harbor. Their success saved this fort for the Federal arms throughout the war.

It early appeared that the policy of President Lincoln was to hold, or recover, for the Union all national forts, navy yards and army posts in the Confederate territory, or, failing that, to destroy them. What was then—and is still—one of the largest navy yards in the country was in Virginian territory, at Gosport, right across the river from Norfolk. Though on the border, close to Fortress Monroe, which remained throughout the war in northern hands, and within sight of Hampton Roads, where for years the United States fleets rode safely at anchor, this post was just far enough within Confederate territory to be in daily danger of seizure. Accordingly, on the 19th of April, 1861, the ship *Pawnee,* with a force of marines under Lieutenant A. S. Nicholson, was ordered to the yard, where were already the *Pennsylvania,* the *Cumberland,* the *Merrimac*—destined to become famous in new form—the *Germantown, Plymouth* and *Dolphin.* The first three of these ships were then modern men-of-war, and the Confederate by sinking stone boats in the channel thought that they had secured them for the state of Virginia.

The marines from all the ships, together with the bluejackets, were ordered ashore and the work of destruction was speedily begun. About the gates of the yard the townspeople gathered, enraged to see the preparations for destroying so much war material that they had expected to save for the Confederacy. It proved possible to get the frigate *Cumberland* out, past the obstacles in the channel, and this was done by the sailors, while the marines laid the train of combustibles and disposed of the explosives where they would do the most damage. At midnight a rocket from the *Pawnee* gave the signal for setting the torch. All the men from the other ships and from the yard were crowded upon the *Pawnee* and the *Cumberland,* and as the flames broke out the two ships pulled away, the *Pawnee* under steam and towing the other. The other ships at the docks, with their tarred cordage and their decks filled with combustibles, made a magnificent spectacle as the flames roared high in air. Much, however, of the property in the yard was saved by the townspeople who, when the marines were withdrawn, rushed in and extinguished the flames wherever possible. The frigate *Merrimac,* though burned to the water's edge, was afterwards raised and, as an iron-clad ram, helped to revolutionize naval warfare.

In pursuance of the President's war policy joint military and naval expeditions were launched against the forts which guarded the harbors south of the capes of the Chesapeake. The actions that followed, though seemingly trifling to us to-day in the face of the colossal combats of the war in Europe, achieved results that were influential upon the whole later course of the war. Along the Potomac, the south shore of which was held by the Confederates, at Hatteras Inlet, at Port Royal and in Albemarle and Cumberland sounds the marines served with credit and success. They took an active and an efficient part in forging that part of the remorseless blockade which in the end did much to starve the South into subjection.

The marines fought, too, at that disastrous battle

of Manassas, or Bull Run, which first gave to the North some comprehension of the temper and the valor of the South. There was little glory for any federal command in that day of panic and defeat. The utmost that can be said for the marines—a battalion of whom, under Major John G. Reynolds, fought in the very thick of the battle—is that though sharing in the general defeat they yielded neither to panic nor rout but retired from the field in good order, an unbroken command. The marines who fought on this occasion were furthermore wholly untrained in the practice of war. " Not one," said Major Reynolds, in his report, " had been in the service more than three weeks, and many had hardly learned their facings, the officers likewise being but a short time in the service." Three hundred and fifty officers and men were in action. One officer, Lieutenant Hitchcock, was killed and eight privates. Major Reynolds and Lieutenants Zeilin, Hale and Hitchcock were especially singled out for commendatory mention in Colonel Porter's report.

A general reorganization of the armed forces of the United States was, of course, undertaken in this first year of the war, and the marines came in for some slight encouragement. Under the new law they were given 2,500 privates, 320 noncommissioned officers, 30 musicians, 60 drummers, 60 fifers—the corps seems always to have been great on music— and about 90 commissioned officers. The same year, however, saw the United States navy multiplied tenfold, with the result that the total force of marines was wholly inadequate to put detachments on each ship. To some degree this inadequacy was the less important because the Confederacy had literally no navy and there were no naval duels like those of the War of 1812, in which the marines played so gallant a part. On the other hand, there was more landing service and storming parties to be led. In work of this sort the marines were naturally preëminent.

Late in October, 1861, a joint military and naval expedition was sent from Hampton Roads to reduce the forts at the entrance to Port Royal. The magnificent harbor at that South Carolina port was a strong incentive to blockade runners, and was defended by two formidable earthworks on opposite sides of the entrance, Fort Walker and Fort Beauregard. The armada sent against it consisted of 48 vessels, the most formidable fleet ever gathered under the United States flag, so far as numbers were concerned. But it was a rather heterogeneous body of vessels. Almost anything that would float had been gathered from the northern harbors, and, as the sequel showed, one or two things that would not float. The naval operations were under command of Flag Officer Samuel F. Du Pont, while the 12,000 troops that accompanied the expedition were commanded by General William T. Sherman.

The action that ensued was entirely successful and almost bloodless. The forts were both taken without assault and merely as the result of the fire from the men-of-war. It was still early in the war and the Confederates had not learned to manifest that desperate valor and tenacity of resistance which came later to characterize them. They seemed to have surrendered when they saw that the battle was getting hot, rather than after any very serious loss, for in all they had but 11 killed and 48 wounded, while the national loss was but 8 killed and 23 wounded.

The forces of nature, indeed, offered a more savage resistance to the progress of this expedition than the human enemy himself. For the ships had hardly left Hampton Roads when one of the furious storms for which the neighborhood of Hatteras is famous came up and scattered the armada over the face of the waters. Two ships went down, the army transport, *Peerless,* and the *Governor,* which had on board 650 marines under command of Major John G. Reynolds. They were saved, with the loss of but seven men, by the most devoted exertions of the officers and crew of the *Sabine* and the *Isaac Smith.* In his report of this disaster, Major Reynolds said, after describing the dangerous situation of his ship on the morning of the 1st of November:

" At daybreak preparations were made for sending boats to our relief, although the sea was running high; and it being exceedingly dangerous for a boat to approach the guard of the steamer, in consequence the boats laid off and the men were obliged to jump into the sea, and thence hauled into the boats. All hands were thus providentially rescued from the wreck, with the exception, I am pained to say, of one corporal and six privates, who were drowned or killed by the crush or contact of the vessels. Those drowned were lost through their disobedience of orders in leaving the ranks or abandoning their posts. After the troops were safely reëmbarked every exertion was directed to securing the arms, accouterments, ammunition and other property which might have been saved after lightening the wreck. I am gratified at being able to say nearly all the arms were saved, and about half of the accouterments. Too much praise cannot be bestowed upon the officers and men under my command; all did nobly. The firmness with which they performed their duty is beyond all praise."

Another considerable expedition on the Atlantic coast was fitted out early in January, 1862, to proceed against Confederate fortifications in the waters of North Carolina. Seventeen light-draught vessels, under the command of Flag Officer Goldsborough, constituted the naval portion of this expedition, which was accompanied by 12,000 troops under General A. E. Burnside. The expedition was organized with the greatest secrecy. In the earlier instance of the attack on the forts at Port Royal some leakage at the capital had caused precise information as to its numbers and destination to be telegraphed to the Confederate government. This time the Federal authorities were determined that there should be no such betrayal. There was a suspicious pressure about the capital for information on the subject, and the story is told that one very prominent public man was most importunate in his demands upon the President that he at least should be informed. At last Mr. Lincoln said:

"Now I will tell you in great confidence where they are going, if you will promise not to speak of it to anyone."

The promise was solemnly given, whereupon the President continued:

"Well, now, my friend, that expedition is going to sea."

It became apparent early that going to sea was about as dangerous a thing as the expedition could undertake, for it was made up of a very sorry collection of unseaworthy craft. Indeed, nautical men were very dismal in their predictions of disaster. To some extent their prophecies of evil were fulfilled, for the *Pickett* was crushed between two large vessels, the old steamer *Pocahontas* was so battered by the waves that her officers were forced to run her ashore and 90 of 113 horses forming her cargo were drowned; the transport *City of New York* went ashore in a storm, was totally wrecked, and her officers and men were with difficulty rescued after clinging to the rigging all night, and the *Zouave* sank while crossing the bar, losing two of her officers.

Once within the sound, the expedition attacked and reduced one after another a series of small forts established by the enemy. There was more fighting than at Port Royal, and at Fort Bartow and the forts at New Berne marines were landed. In the course of the operations, which lasted, in all, until April, these waters were pretty thoroughly cleared of hostile works. After this was accomplished Major Reynolds and his marines were sent further south, taking and occupying Fort Clinch at Fernandina. To the marines the expedition was largely fighting without loss. In all, only a few wounded were reported.

An incident in which the marine corps took a part threatened for a time to embroil the United States with Great Britain and roused the liveliest hopes of the Confederacy that the latter country would intervene in its behalf.

Two commissioners from the Confederate states to Great Britain embarked from Havana on a British ship, the *Trent*. In the Bahama Channel this vessel was intercepted by the United States man-of-war *San Jacinto*, under command of Captain Wilkes. This officer's patriotism and zeal were far in excess of his respect for international law, and he fired a round shot across the bow of the British vessel, forced her to heave to, sent a file of marines on board and incontinently seized the Confederate envoys, removing them to his own vessel. It was, of course, all in flat defiance of international law and a grave affront to the British flag. Naturally, the British officers and citizens aboard the vessel thus rudely raided were highly indignant. Lieutenant Greer, who commanded the marines that boarded the *Trent*, says in his report:

"When I first went on board with the marines, and at intervals during my stay, the officers of the steamer made a great many irritating remarks to each other and to the passengers, which were evidently intended for our benefit. Among other things said were: 'Did you ever hear of such an outrage?' 'Marines on board! Why, this looks devilish like mutiny!' 'These Yankees will have to pay well for this.' 'This is the best thing in the world for the South; England will open the blockade.' 'We will have a good chance at them now. Did you ever hear of such a piratical act?' 'Why, this is a perfect Bull Run!' 'They would not have dared to have done it if an English man-of-war had been in sight!' The mail agent (a man in the uniform of a commander in the Royal Navy, I think) was very indignant and talkative, and tried several times to get me into a discussion of the matter. I told him I was not there for the purpose. He was very bitter; he told me that the English squadron would raise the blockade in 20 days after his report of this outrage got home; that the Northerners might as well give up now, etc."

For a time the international situation was menacing. Charles Francis Adams, then United States Minister to Great Britain, said afterwards that had the submarine cable been in existence nothing could have averted war. But the long time required for the exchange of diplomatic notes gave time for the public blood to cool, and the prompt action of the United States government in surrendering the Confederates and repudiating the action of Captain Wilkes smoothed out the difficulty and nothing came of it.

Early in March, 1862, occurred the naval action off Fortress Monroe, in which the chief antagonists were the *Monitor* and the *Merrimac,* the result of which revolutionized naval architecture and consigned wooden ships of war to the scrap heap. I have already referred to the fact that when the Portsmouth Navy Yard was destroyed the fine new United States frigate *Merrimac* lying there was burned to the water's edge. The hull was raised, put in drydock by the Confederates, repaired and fitted with a penthouse rising from almost the level of the water with sloping sides and covered with railroad iron. The sides were pierced for guns and from the house amidships rose a short and stubby smokestack. The deck fore and aft of this structure was practically level with the water and, indeed, when running with any rapidity, was submerged.

The fact that this vessel was in the course of construction was known in the north, but outside of naval circles aroused little comment. By one of those strange coincidences which influence the destinies of men as well as nations, there was building at the same time in a yard at Greenpoint, New York, another iron-clad vessel—from plans prepared by John Ericsson—named the *Monitor*. This vessel carried two guns in a circular turret mounted amidships. The *Merrimac* carried 10 guns in all. The peculiar appearance of the *Monitor* caused the sailors to call her " A cheese box on a raft." The *Merrimac's* appearance led the Yankee tars to refer to her as " a Yankee meeting house afloat."

On the 8th of March, in the magnificent harbor at Hampton Roads, there were anchored the United States ships *Cumberland, Congress, Minnesota,*

Roanoke and *St. Lawrence.* These were all wooden vessels of the old type but carrying heavy armament. Early that morning the *Merrimac* got up steam and coming down the Elizabeth River turned into the Roads. Her greatest weakness lay in a very insufficient engine so that she was able to make barely five knots an hour. Accordingly, the ships she was about to engage had every opportunity to prepare for her reception. When her smoke first rose over the tree tops they were in a state of complete unpreparedness, according to eye witnesses, with decks littered and the sailors' washing hanging in the rigging. But before she came up within range they were shipshape and cleared for action. The *Merrimac* made her way directly toward the *Cumberland,* reserving her fire until at short range. All of the United States ships within range opened upon her early, but the shot dropped impotently from her armored sides. When she was within easy range of the *Cumberland* she received its full broadside, but one of the officers on the Confederate ship stated afterwards that the shock was barely discernible. She, in return, opened fire on the *Cumberland* with her heavy guns; and that vessel, after an hour's gallant fighting, during which she had been rammed by the enemy, sunk at her moorings with her flag still defiantly flying. The *Congress* soon after was forced to surrender. The *Minnesota,* third of the large northern ships, had run aground, and after some hesitation the commander of the

ABCVE: WATCHING FOR A U-BOAT
BELOW: SKIRMISH DRILL ON THE QUARTERDECK OF A
BATTLESHIP

Merrimac determined to leave her where she was for the night, feeling that she would be easy prey in the morning. When his ship rammed the *Cumberland* it left the iron ram in the wound as it withdrew, and as a result the *Merrimac* was leaking badly. Accordingly, she withdrew up the river for repairs, expecting another field day on the morrow. Her losses had been trifling, being one killed and 21 wounded. These casualties were due to shots finding their way through the portholes, as the armor plating was not broken at any point. How fierce the fire was to which the *Merrimac* had been subjected was shown by the fact that nothing outside the plating escaped. The smokestack was riddled, the flagstaff repeatedly shot away and the protruding muzzles of guns chipped and in two instances broken off.

The *Merrimac* carried a small detachment of marines. On the northern ships the marine corps was well represented, and it is worth noting that the last shot fired at the *Merrimac* came in the shape of a volley from the rifles of the men of that corps. The first shot fired by the *Merrimac* killed nine marines serving a gun on the *Cumberland*. Of the service of the men of that corps on that ship under Lieutenant Heywood, Lieutenant Morris in command, spoke in the highest terms of eulogy in his report.

When the *Merrimac* came out the following day it was to no such holiday adventure as was the first action. During the night the little *Monitor* had arrived in Hampton Roads and was lying not far from the *Minnesota,* which it was her evident purpose to defend. The *Merrimac* came down as though to attack the latter vessel, but before her first broadside was discharged the *Monitor* placed herself in her path and the duel which was to change the entire course of future naval construction was fairly on. It is not pertinent to the purpose of this book to describe this action in detail. The *Monitor* carried no marines, the *Merrimac* but a few of the Confederate service. The whole world knows the outcome of this engagement. Baffled and beaten, the *Merrimac* returned to her anchorage near Norfolk, whence she never again came out to fight. In the end she was blown up by the Confederates as the advance of the Union armies up the peninsula menaced her safety. The *Monitor* was lost at sea on the last day of December, 1862.

Shortly after the destruction of the *Merrimac* the United States forces again took possession of the Norfolk Navy Yard, and it is worthy of note that the force which first entered that naval base was the one that had last left it when it was abandoned to the Confederates, namely, the United States marines.

Two or three days prior to this, by orders of the President, who desired to find out whether there was not a back door to Richmond that might be forced, three gunboats, the *Galena, Aroostook* and

Port Royal, under Commodore John Rodgers, were sent on a reconnoitering expedition up the James River. They were later joined by the *Monitor* and the *Naugatuck.* Little serious opposition was incurred until they had arrived at Drury's Bluff, eight miles from Richmond. This was in 1862, and looking back upon it it seems amazing that a Federal force should have then reached a point so close to the Confederate capital which beat off until 1864 the best efforts of the northern armies for its capture. On their way up the river the gunboats were continually harassed by sharpshooters and snipers on the banks. To meet this sort of opposition the marines were especially serviceable, and Commander Rodgers says of them: " The marines were efficient with their muskets, and they, when ordered to fill vacancies at the guns, did it well."

At Drury's Bluff a heavy battery was encountered and the channel was blocked with piles and sunken vessels. The gunboats engaged the batteries, but at a serious disadvantage; for the Confederate works were placed upon a bank so high upon the water that it was only with difficulty that the naval guns could be sufficiently elevated to tell effectively. In the end, the expedition was checked here. One marine was killed and several wounded.

During the remainder of the year 1862 the marines were engaged only in spluttering hostilities, widely spread, and of little bearing upon the war. Down on the Gulf of Mexico, at Pass Christian, a detachment of the corps on the United States blockading gunboat, *New London,* engaged in a sharp fight with two Confederate steamers. At St. Augustine, Florida, marines who had been put in occupation of the ancient Spanish fort, which was a decoration rather than a defense to that town, so commended themselves to the good opinion of the people of the little city, though the latter must have been of Confederate sympathies, that upon their departure the mayor and common council united in applauding their " polite and urbane course . . . and the conduct and discipline of the troops," and asked that they might, when compatible with the plans of the United States, be returned to that station. In Charleston harbor, where the Confederates were of course still holding Fort Sumter and the city itself, Commander Foxhall Parker landed a hundred marines on Morris Island and established there a heavy battery bearing on Sumter, against which it was used later with telling effect. And finally a sharp little action was fought on the banks of Santee River, in South Carolina, between Confederate cavalry and an expedition of marines which had been sent up the river to destroy a bridge which formed the sole connection between the city of Charleston and the interior of the state. The expedition failed of its purpose, not for any lack of gallantry or determination on the part of the marines, but because, being midsummer, the water in the river had fallen so low that the vessels could not proceed to their destination. At two points the marines landed and gave battle, once to some irregular Confederate cavalry, and the second time to a Confederate battery which had been shelling the vessels and which they effectively drove away.

Early in the following year the United States government made preparations for the capture of New Orleans. This great and cosmopolitan city was a very hotbed of Confederate sympathies. Situated some 90 miles up the swift-rolling Mississippi, it was protected by two forts on opposite sides of that river near its mouth—Fort St. Philip and Fort Jackson. Both were powerful works, as military architecture of that day stood. One weakness common to both was that they lay on the low mainland, and the river confined behind its mighty dikes or levees rolled along some 15 or 20 feet above their level, so that during the spring floods a steamer floating upon it towered high above the bastions of either fort. This would give to a fleet seeking to pass the forts a marked advantage, and would, indeed, have made it comparatively easy to reduce them had it been possible for an attacking fleet to remain in one position opposite them. But the depth of the river and the swiftness of its current made this impossible. The forts were made fairly impregnable to storming parties by the marshy character of the ground around them and the deep moat by which they were surrounded. In addition to the land defenses, New Orleans was further protected by a very considerable naval fleet, kept in the river, including a much-dreaded vessel, the Confederate ram *Manassas*, which, while building, was heralded far and wide as likely to prove a more formidable vessel than even the dreaded *Merrimac*.

From the beginning of the war the several mouths of the Mississippi were guarded by United States blockaders very successfully, for the business of blockade running was stopped and the grass grew on the once crowded levees of New Orleans. Occasional forays by Confederate naval forces harassed these blockaders, and in February the national government detailed Captain David Glasgow Farragut to the command of the western Gulf blockading squadron with instructions to take New Orleans. We have last seen Farragut a boy in his early teens serving as midshipman on the old *Essex*, commanding a prize, manned by men thrice his age, and acting as aid to Admiral Porter in the desperate battle between the *Essex* and two British men-of-war off Valparaiso. Since that time he had been engaged in the routine work of the navy and was recognized in the department as an officer of high ability, although perhaps few suspected that he would rise to the highest eminence in his country's naval service. On assignment to this service he was promoted to Admiral.

With a fleet of 25 men-of-war and 20 schooners Farragut passed the bar at the mouth of the Mississippi and either anchored or tied to the banks to complete his preparation for the attack. Some French and English naval officers, whose vessels were near by, visited him and warned him that to attack the forts with only wooden vessels such as composed his fleet would be madness and end in inevitable disaster.

"You may be right," said the old-time sailor, who, by the way, detested ironclads, "but I was sent here to make the attempt. I came to reduce or pass the forts and to take New Orleans and I shall try it on."

The fleet was quickly put in shape for action. The mortar schooners under the command of Captain Porter, who was a son of that Captain Porter whose aid Farragut had been at the Battle of Valparaiso, were moored close to the banks, their sails, spars and loose rigging sent down and their masts covered with willow boughs so that from a little distance they could not be distinguished from the long lines of willows that lined the river's banks. It was an early instance of camouflage, although our sailors had not then learned to call it by that name. Each schooner carried amidships one heavy mortar, and all were trained so that the great spherical bombs fell well within the walls of one or the other hostile forts. Their attack began on the 16th of April, and the roar of the mighty cannon could be heard in faraway New Orleans. The forts could respond but ineffectively with their heavy guns, as both the position and the disguise of the schooners

made it difficult to concentrate fire upon them.
Picked companies of riflemen, sent out from the
forts, made their way cautiously along the levees,
and tried to pick off the gunners at their work; but
they were met in turn by a fire from the decks of
the ships anchored amid stream and from marines
stationed in the upper rigging, whence they could
obtain a full view of all that was going on on the
river's banks. The forts suffered to some degree
from this fire. The wooden structures that stood
in the parade ground in Fort Jackson were set afire,
and the shells cut the levee in front of that fort,
letting in the great river and flooding all the country round about. Bnt as defensive works the two
fortifications seemed to be as strong and as uncon-
querable as ever. It had been Farragut's idea that
by this heavy cannonade the forts would be silenced
and his ships could ascend the river with but little
peril. In this anticipation he was disappointed, but
he went on industriously preparing his ships for the
assault, nevertheless. Twice they had to meet the
danger of great fire rafts, large floating structures
on which the Confederates had piled cords of pine
wood and other combustibles, set the torch to them
and sent them floating down the stream. Against
these the mortar boats, being tied firmly to the bank,
were helpless, so it was necessary to send out boats'
crews from the bigger ships prepared to grapple
with the rafts and tow them to spots where they
would be harmless. One hundred and fifty such

boats were manned, ready to put out into the river as soon as a bright ruddy glare up stream foretold the coming of another raft. By these tactics this form of Confederate attack was rendered entirely fruitless.

The bombardment by the mortar boats was kept up for six days. Then Farragut determined to begin the ascent of the river in defiance of the forts. He had first to destroy a chain of rafts and old hulks stretched across the river's channel, by which the Confederates had sought to further obstruct the upward passage of the fleet. This was done without delay. The fleet was prepared for a desperate struggle. With mud and paint the forms of the vessels were disguised, and chain cables were coiled over vulnerable parts or draped over the sides to protect the boilers. The decks were whitewashed so that during the night the men might see what they were about, even though the battle lanterns were extinguished while passing the forts. Hammocks and nettings were stretched overhead to catch flying splinters. Late at night Farragut, in his long boat, was pulled from ship to ship to examine each before the word to get under way was given.

At two o'clock on the morning of the 24th the fleet started up the river, headed by the *Cayuga*. The ships were at once detected by the forts, which opened upon them a vigorous fire, while from up the river came a fleet of Confederate vessels, some of them pushing fire rafts for the purpose of disputing the passage. Farragut's flagship, the *Hartford*, was the first to encounter serious trouble. In endeavoring to avoid a fire raft he ran ashore, upon which the Confederate ram *Manassas*, seeing her plight, caught up the fire raft and pushed it directly against the side of the stranded vessel. Bear in mind that these were wooden ships with which Farragut was operating. Almost instantly the tarred cordage of his flagship ignited, and the flames ran up the mast. The admiral paced the deck as cool as the fire was hot.

"Don't flinch from that fire, boys," he cried; "there's a hotter fire than that for those who don't do their duty."

The men on the *Hartford* fought the flames with hose and bucket and in time disengaged the flaming raft and pushed it off into the flaming river. Scarcely had they accomplished this when they saw a river steamer, unarmored but crowded with men, bearing down upon the *Hartford* with the evident intent of boarding her. Captain Broome, of the marines, with a crew selected from that corps, was working a bow gun on the *Hartford*. Carefully he trained the huge piece upon the approaching steamer. He stepped back, stooped for a last glance along the sights, then with a quick pull of the lanyard the great gun went off with a roar, followed instantly by a louder explosion from the oncoming steamer. When the smoke cleared away all looked eagerly for the enemy, but she had vanished as if by magic.

That single shot, striking her magazine, had blown her up with all on board.

Meantime, the *Manassas* had dashed fiercely at the *Brooklyn*, and that gallant old frigate, though built of wood and outclassed in her combat with her iron-skinned antagonist, met the issue of battle bravely. The ram failed to strike the *Brooklyn* fairly amidships, so that the wound inflicted was but slight. But the broadside from the *Brooklyn* was more effective. Many shots broke through the iron plating of the enemy. Backing off to gather headway, the ram again rushed at the frigate. This time she struck her prey full amidships. The shock was terrible, men on the gun deck of the *Brooklyn* were hurled from their feet with blood streaming from their nostrils, while the vessel itself heeled over farther and farther until it seemed as if she would be pressed down below the water by the weight of the ram. Yet, after all, little damage was done. The prow of the assailing vessel had struck one of the coils of chain cable which had been hung over the side of the *Brooklyn*, and had inflicted no wound upon the hull of the ship. The two vessels then drifted apart in the darkness. Presently the captain of the *Manassas* saw out of the darkness the great hull of the *Mississippi* bearing down upon him as if to ram. Hastily putting up his helm to avoid this new enemy, he ran his vessel ashore. There she lay helpless, while the *Mississippi*, taking up a position on which no gun of the Confederate could be brought to bear, pounded away at her with heavy shot until her crew fled to the shore, the vessel took fire and presently blew up.

This ended the battle in the river. Pushing on past the forts, which were for the time silenced, but not captured, the fleet made its way up to the city and anchored off the levee not far from the point at which Canal Street reaches the river. It was a scene of riot, turmoil and wholesale destruction. From the slums of the city all the worst elements of its population had flocked to the waterside. "To the levee!" was the cry; and, as the ships came slowly up against the current, the people who had had no word of the issue of the combat down the stream looked eagerly for the masts to appear above the tree tops. When they were seen to be crossed with yards, a cry of rage went up, for that fact told that they were seagoing vessels, not river boats, and of the former the Confederacy had none. The mob by the waterside was mad with rage, but throughout the city the better class of residents were almost equally out of their minds with fear. George W. Cable, the novelist, whose name is indissolubly linked with that of New Orleans, thus describes the scene at the river's brink:

"What a gathering!—the riff-raff of the wharves, the town, the gutters. Such women! such wrecks of women! and all the juvenile rag-tag. The lower steamboat landing, well covered with sugar, rice and molasses, was being rifled. The men smashed; the women scooped up the smashings. The river was overflowing the top of the levee. A rainstorm began to threaten. 'Are the Yankee ships in sight?' I asked of an idler. He pointed out the tops of their naked masts as they showed up across the huge bend of the river. They were engaging the batteries at Camp Chalmette, the old field of Jackson's renown. Presently that was over. Ah, me! I see them now as they come slowly round Slaughter-house Point, into full view: silent, so grim and terrible, black with men, heavy with deadly portent, the long-banished Stars and Stripes flying against the frowning sky. Oh, for the *Mississippi,* the *Mississippi!* Just then she came down upon them. But how? Drifting helplessly, a mass of flames.

"The crowds on the levee howled and screamed with rage. The swarming decks answered never a word; but one old tar on the *Hartford,* standing with lanyard in hand, beside a great pivot-gun, so plain to view that you could see him smile, silently patted its big black breech and blandly grinned."

Lieutenant Theodorus Bailey, with one companion, no more, was sent ashore to demand the surrender of the city. Shoulder to shoulder the two sailors marched, never faltering, through a mob which brandished weapons and threatened their lives at every step. At the city hall the mayor refused to surrender, saying that the city was in charge of the military. The officers went back to their ship with the flag still floating over the city hall. Two days later Farragut landed a detachment of marines from the *Pensacola* of 30 men, who marched through the riotous and turbulent crowd to the United States Mint, there hauled down the Confederate flag and hoisted the Stars and Stripes in its place. Later the whole battalion of marines, drawn from the different ships of the fleet, and commanded by Colonel Broome, was landed to take possession of the city until General Butler with the military force should arrive. A small detachment of them marched to the city hall, where the Confederate flag was still flying, dragging with them two small howitzers. These guns were trained on the mob in the street while two of the marines went to the roof to tear down the enemy banner. The crowd muttered darkly; the air was electric with the menace of a murderous outbreak. At the first shot from that mob the howitzers would be discharged, spreading death and wounds among the people. At that juncture the mayor, a slender young Creole, came down from his office, placed himself directly before one of the guns and with folded arms and calm eyes looked upon the gunners. He was determined that if there was to be a sacrifice he would be the first to go. It was a curious parallel to the action of General Henderson in New York, detailed in an earlier chapter. It had its effect upon the riotous crowd, for the flag fell slowly from the staff without any sign of the outbreak that was feared. A few sharp commands and the marines tramped away down the street with the howitzers clanking behind them. The crowd cheered for Mayor Monroe and dispersed.

CHAPTER X

THE fleet remained but briefly in New Orleans. Three days after the marines were put in control General Butler arrived with his army and assumed command. Thereupon, Farragut took his ships up the Mississippi River with the purpose of reducing the batteries along its banks by which the Confederates blocked it to all navigation. At the same time river steamers, remodeled and made into armor-plated gunboats, were fighting their way down from the north, the idea being to effect a juncture between the two fleets, open the river to unrestricted traffic and cut the Confederacy in two.

The first hard nut for the Federals to crack was at Port Hudson, about one-third of the way between New Orleans and Vicksburg, where the Confederates had erected ponderous batteries on the high bluffs that bordered the river, while the shifting sands and tortuous channels of the mighty stream made the course of the ships working their way against the current a most perilous one. But the tactics which had been applied at the forts below

New Orleans were adopted here once more. Porter, with his mortar schooners tied up below the works, opened upon them a vigorous fire, while the heavier ships, under command of Farragut himself, ran past. The forts endured a heavy and an effective fire, but were not reduced thereby. Only the northern fleet had accomplished its purpose by running by the batteries, and was prepared to continue its ascent of the river and attack the Confederate stronghold at Vicksburg. Reaching that point, it was determined to repeat these tactics, to pass the Vicksburg batteries, form a juncture with the river gunboats above and make the real attack upon the defenses of the town, fighting downstream.

While in this position, it was learned that the Confederates were building another iron-clad ram, the *Arkansas,* on the Yazoo River, which enters the Mississippi somewhat above Vicksburg. Three of the Federal ships were ordered to go up this river and destroy her. To their astonishment, they had hardly entered the Yazoo when they met the *Arkansas* coming down. This was more than they had bargained for. They had expected to destroy an unarmed hulk lying at its dock half finished. Instead, they encountered a heavily armored ship, carrying guns superior to theirs, and built for ramming. Incontinently they turned and fled, keeping up a fire with their after guns. Their practice was excellent, for an early shot struck the pilot house of the *Arkansas,* wounding the commander and the two pilots who were directing the course of the ship. Though crippled by this, the *Arkansas* kept on her course until, turning into the Mississippi, she encountered the full national fleet, and prepared to run through it and take shelter under the batteries of Vicksburg. Her one grave fault was in her engines, which were too weak for the size of the vessel. Indeed, her commander said afterwards that except for the current of the river she could hardly have made more than one mile an hour. Thus plodding along, she passed through the entire Federal fleet, receiving the heavy fire of its batteries on the way. Two 11-inch shells penetrated her armor, killed or wounded 16 of her people and set fire to her. In the end, however, she won clear and found a mooring place under the Vicksburg guns. Two later attempts by the Federals to attack and destroy her in this refuge failed, although pressed with the utmost gallantry. Both in the affairs with the *Arkansas* and in the task of engaging and passing the Vicksburg batteries, the marines gave a good account of themselves. Of their attitude during the latter engagement Commodore Wainwright, commanding the flagship *Hartford*, said, "The marine guard under command of Captain John L. Broome had charge of two broadside guns and fought them well, thus sustaining the reputation of that distinguished corps." Captain Broome was wounded seriously in the fight with the *Arkansas*.

It soon became apparent that Vicksburg could not

be taken by naval forces alone, and Farragut, with his seagoing vessels, returned down the river. Commodore Porter was left in the upper water in command of the river gunboats. He began a campaign in the Yazoo and in tributary bayous (in which mud was more present than water) that, because of its amphibious character, caused Lincoln to call his craft "web-footed gunboats." They plowed their way along through these narrow streams in which two boats could seldom pass, engaged from time to time by batteries or snipers on the banks. Porter had but few marines, for most of the members of that corps had been assigned to the seagoing ships. Such as he had, however, were peculiarly fitted for this class of warfare, keeping down the snipers on shore and picking off the gunners of the batteries. The commander of the flotilla had a theory that there was a back watergate to Vicksburg and he might find it, and so he tested one after another, the sluggish streams, often being forced to saw away the boughs of the trees that arched above them in order to pass. When a bridge impeded progress it was simply rammed. A final end to the expedition, however, came when it encountered a fort in the middle of the stream with a channel on either side blocked by sunken ships. It was clear that the commander at Vicksburg had heard of the expedition and was guarded against it. Thereupon Porter withdrew to the safer waters of the Mississippi. He made one other such expedition through another chain of bayous, when the Confederates rallied forces about him and bade fair to capture his fleet, thus giving to the history of the war the unusual incident of an army capturing a sea-going force. Happily, he was able to get word to Sherman, who with his army was in the vicinity, and who came promptly to the rescue. Thereafter, Porter avoided the backwaters of the Father of Waters.

A man of a lively sense of humor, Porter played one joke on the enemy which had curiously practical results. Being above Vicksburg, he took a large, flat boat, built it up with logs and lumber until it looked like a powerful ram, and provided it with two smokestacks, made of empty pork barrels, through which fires of tar and oakum sent forth clouds of black smoke. This vessel, of course destitute of a crew, he set afloat one night, and she drifted down the river, much to the alarm of the Confederates. Their batteries produced no effect upon her. Below Vicksburg they were building from the hull of a gunboat captured from the Federals a powerful ram. She was not completed, and in no condition for defense. Their first thought was that Porter had sent this mysterious ship down to capture her. In this conviction they set the torch to their nearly finished ram, and she was soon reduced to ashes.

Vicksburg fell to Grant's army on the 4th of July, 1863; and thereupon Porter, with his gun-

boats, sped down the river past the now silent batteries. Incorrigible in his zeal for exploring
secondary waterways, he thereupon took his fleet
up the Red River, where he narrowly escaped disaster from low water, and from the appearance of
a very considerable Confederate army, which bade
fair to cut him off from return to the Mississippi.
From the low water he was rescued by a dam built
across the rapids by the troops of a Maine regiment
under command of Colonel Bailey. From the Confederate forces he was delivered by the fortunate
appearance of a superior force under Sherman.
There are few more picturesque features of the
Civil War than the maneuvers of the web-footed
gunboats in the Mississippi and tributary streams.
But the subject is one largely foreign to this book.
Few members of the marine corps were assigned
to duty with these expeditions. Indeed, the commander-in-chief of that organization, in his official
report for 1863, deplored the fact that the size of
his command was so limited that he was unable even
to furnish detachments of marines to seagoing ships.

However, when it was determined to send Admiral Farragut back into the Gulf with instructions
to destroy the Confederate defenses of Mobile Bay,
he was furnished with a fleet made up mainly of
ocean vessels. They were mainly wooden, and besides having to encounter the land defenses of the
day they would have to meet a number of iron-cased
ships which the Confederates had there for purposes

THE FLYING MARINES: AEROPLANES OF THE U. S.
MARINE CORPS ABOVE; A HYDROPLANE BELOW

of defense. But, curiously enough, the most powerful ironclad, which was belatedly assigned to Farragut's force, the *Tecumseh,* was the very first vessel
to succumb to the Confederate attack, being sunk by
a torpedo with practically all on board early in the
action.

The Confederates had held Mobile from the beginning of the war. The entrance to the harbor was
guarded by the two forts, Gaines and Morgan.
Within the bay was a small Confederate fleet, of
which the ironclad ram *Tennessee* was the most
formidable. There had been occasional hostilities
in the neighborhood since the beginning of the war,
and on one occasion United States marines had
shown great gallantry in cutting out and destroying
a vessel, the *Wilder,* smuggling a valuable cargo.
Admiral Buchanan, in command of the Confederate
flotilla, had, at a later time, undertaken to attack
the United States blockading squadron, but was
balked by the fact that his chief vessel, the *Tennessee,* ran aground. Thereafter, the Confederates
planned no more offensive actions, but prepared to
strengthen the defenses of their harbors with mines
and torpedoes. It is interesting to note in passing,
particularly in view of the record of the great European war, that Farragut only reluctantly resorted
to the use of torpedoes. He wrote, " I have always
considered it (torpedo warfare) unworthy of a
chivalrous nation, but it does not do to give your
enemy such a decided superiority over you."

Early in August Farragut had under his command 21 wooden vessels and four ironclads. On the 4th of that month he made his plans to enter the harbor the next day. The ships were to advance in pairs, lashed together, one large and one small one in a pair. The *Brooklyn* led the file of wooden ships, while ahead of her went the *Monitor,* headed by the *Tecumseh.* Farragut, in his flagship, the *Hartford,* was in the center of the fleet. The advance began at two o'clock of the morning of a bright, breezy day. It was a perilous adventure. The channel was tortuous, and the vessels could only proceed with leadsmen in the chains rapidly taking soundings. Necessarily their progress was slow and they had to overcome obstructions, brave torpedoes and withstand the fire from the forts.

The gunners in the forts were slow in getting the range. When they did, however, secure it they gave no attention to the ironclad *Tecumseh* but concentrated their fire upon the *Hartford,* which was soon suffering seriously. One heavy shell struck squarely in the foremast, and had it exploded would have carried away that spar, together with a number of men who were in the foretop. But, curiously enough, the shell, instead of coming directly from the cannon, came tumbling end over end, and it was the blunt end and not the end with the percussion cap that struck the mast. Even as it was, the men aloft would have been thrown out by the shock, except that they could see the shell coming and prepared for it by seizing the rigging. It was about this time that Farragut, anxious to see the effect of his fire over the smoke that enveloped the ship, clambered first onto the gunwale and thence gradually up the shrouds, going a ratline at a time. Captain Drayton, noticing him, sent a quartermaster with a piece of line and instructions to tie the admiral to the rigging. This was done, despite Farragut's protest. Meantime, at the head of the line, the *Tecumseh* was making the best of her way toward the *Tennessee,* to which her commander, Craven, intended to give battle. In his eagerness he overlooked certain directions given to him for the avoidance of torpedoes, with which it was well known the harbor was strewn. Admiral Buchanan, for his part, in the conning tower of the *Tennessee* was preparing to meet the *Tecumseh* in deadly combat. He called his crew about him and addressed them, saying:

"Now, men, the enemy is coming, and I want you to do your duty; and you shall not have it to say when you leave this vessel that you were not near enough to the enemy, for I will meet them and then you can fight them along the sides of their own ships; and if I fall, lay me on one side and go on with the fight and never mind me, but whip and sink the Yankees, or fight until you sink yourselves, but do not surrender."

But Buchanan never met the *Tecumseh.* While he was peering through the bars of his pilot house at the ship which he was about to engage in battle, he heard a muffled explosion and saw a great column of water spring up by her side. In another moment, with a lurch to port, she had sunk, carrying down most of her crew. She had struck one of the torpedoes, of which but the day before Craven had said, " I don't care a pinch for them." Craven went down with his ship and the circumstances of his death make a classic tale in naval annals. One man at a time only could pass out of the pilot house. The commander and the pilot instinctively made for the doorway. Precedence meant life. Craven stepped back, courteously saying, " After you, pilot." " There was nothing after me," said the pilot, later, " for when I reached the last round of the ladder the vessel seemed to drop from under me."

The sudden loss of the *Tecumseh* had the effect of causing some disorder in the Federal line. It was then that the *Brooklyn* hesitated, in the face of what seemed to her commander a number of floating mines, but which, as a matter of fact, were a number of empty shell boxes thrown over from the Confederate gunboats. Her hesitation at once attracted the attention of Farragut, who inquired by signal what was the matter. The answer was, " torpedoes! " Thereupon the admiral shouted the message which has become one of the catch words of the service, " Damn the torpedoes! Go ahead! "

The good fortune which usually attends audacity was on the side of the *Hartford* that day. She passed directly through the line of torpedoes without disaster and took her place at the head of the Federal column. Instead of the lost ironclad, she now faced the *Tennessee,* and received from that vessel a heavy shot which, had it struck her beneath the water line, would infallibly have sunk her. As it was, it only added to the appalling execution which had been done on board the *Hartford,* the ship being fairly covered with dead and wounded men. Swinging to one side, she evaded a blow from the ram of the *Tennessee* and continued up the channel.

The other ships slowly followed, the smaller ones suffering severely from the heavy fire of the fort. But all observed to the fullest extent Farragut's favorite adage that " the safest way to prevent injury from an enemy is to strike hard yourself." They struck hard, running in close to the fort, and pouring grape and shrapnel in, until the Confederate gunners were fairly driven from their pieces. But they did not escape unscathed. A seven-inch shell passed through the *Oneida's* chain armor, pierced her boiler and put her out of the combat. The *Galena,* to which she was tied, towed her out of further danger. Meantime, the *Tennessee* was again bearing down upon the fleet, after having failed to ram the *Hartford,* and gave to both the *Brooklyn* and the *Richmond* the benefit of her broadside. Thereupon, the *Monongahela,* which had been provided with an iron prow, found opportunity to ram the Confederate. The vessel rammed did not suffer, but the assailant was seriously crip-

pled by twisting off its ram and had to run out of
the combat, leaking badly. One after another the
long line of Federal ships received iron messages
from the *Tennessee,* which by now was fighting almost alone. None, however, was destroyed, and
none had surrendered when the *Tennessee* ran under
the guns of Fort Morgan for a brief breathing spell.

There she lay quietly for an hour or two, while
the American fleet gathered out of range of the
forts in the upper bay. Farragut was discontented.
He had, it is true, passed the forts, and by so doing
had assured their ultimate loss to the Confederacy.
He had the city of Mobile at his command. He
had destroyed several of the enemy gunboats and
had himself lost only the monitor *Tecumseh.* But
the great Confederate ram still lay in safety under
the guns of the fort and Farragut announced to the
captain of his ship that later in the morning, as soon
as his people had had breakfast, he intended to go
for her.

Admiral Buchanan, however—the same Buchanan
that commanded the *Merrimac* in her fight with the
Monitor—had no intention of waiting until he was
attacked. At halfpast eight the Confederate ship
was seen to move slowly away from the guns of the
fort and to advance upon the Federal squadron. It
was a gallant defiance. At first Farragut could not
believe that his antagonist intended to give battle
to his whole fleet. After observing her a moment,
he exclaimed, " Buck's coming this way. Get under

way at once. We must be ready for him." The
admiral was quite right. Buchanan, a fighting sailor
if ever there was one, had had his ship examined by
his officers, who found its damages trifling. Thereupon he said to his captain, "Follow them up,
Johnston; we can't let them off that way."

Looking back upon the action, this seems a piece
of magnificent audacity. Buchanan must have known
the odds which he dared, because in the *Merrimac*
he had been beaten by the *Monitor;* but he now prepared to give battle to three monitors and nearly a
score of heavy warships. It is impossible here to
give the details of that Homeric contest. The Confederate ram fought one after another the ships
arrayed against it, doing deadly damage to them
and inflicting terrible execution upon their people.
It was repeatedly rammed by six of the fleet, and
by some of them more than once. Its plating long
withstood the pounding from the heavy guns of the
enemy, but in time the shock of repeated ramming
loosened her timbers and the *Tennessee* began to
leak. One shot, striking a shutter near which
Buchanan was standing, broke his leg, and he was
carried below to the surgeon's table. Captain
Johnston, succeeding to the command, fought the
vessel for some time, but found that the iron case-
mate was gradually being pounded to pieces, the
steering gear was jammed so that the vessel could
no longer be properly directed and it was impossible
for him longer to bring a gun to bear on the enemy.

In this virtually helpless state the *Tennessee* surrendered, after one of the most gallant naval actions known to history.

A curious feature about the battle of Mobile Bay was the extent to which personal friendship united the officers, Union and Confederate, who while on duty were officially enemies. When the *Tennessee* surrendered Captain Johnston went out on the deck, waving a white flag. Just then Commander Leroy of the *Ossipee* came along and shouted joyously, "Hello, Johnston, how are you? I'll send a boat alongside for you." The two had been close friends in the old United States navy. Captain Jouett, of the *Metacomet,* and Captain Murphy, of the Confederate ship *Selma,* also had been long-time friends. Jouett had long expected, as he expressed it, to catch Murphy and was prepared to entertain him. Accordingly, when the *Selma* struck her flag and Murphy came aboard to deliver his sword, Jouett put back the sword and said cheerily, " I'm glad to see you, Murphy. Come on, your breakfast is waiting for you." In the cabin Murphy saw a table laden with a meal which, including oysters, crabs beefsteak and wines, could hardly be called breakfast. Turning to Jouett in astonishment, he said, " Why didn't you let me know you had all this, I would have surrendered earlier."

The battle had been a sanguinary one. Of the part played in it by the marines we can only judge from the fact that in the reports not only of the admiral himself, but of the various captains, the marines were especially mentioned, and several of their officers received commendation and medals of honor. The losses of the corps were not heavy, being but three killed and 11 wounded. When the forts surrendered marines were sent ashore to occupy them until such time as the troops could come up.

We may pass over hastily certain other slight engagements on the shore of the Gulf and on inland waters to take up the attack made upon the formidable defensive works at Cape Fear, which protected the harbor of Wilmington, a port then in high favor with the blockade runners. Like other such expeditions, this was to be joint military and naval, with the military forces under the command of General Butler. Two forts guarded the entrance to the harbor, Fort Caswell and Fort Fisher. The latter was a formidable defensive work, with parapets 25 feet high and 10 or 12 feet thick, and mounted 44 guns. General Butler conceived an original, but a futile plan for reducing this fort without the loss of life that would attend a direct assault. A ship crammed to the decks with high explosives was to be anchored directly under its walls and touched off with fuses. This, it was thought, would level the walls with the ground and the storming parties might readily rush in. The expedient was tried with the utmost care in every detail. The vessel exploded with an enormous roar and a shock which set the waiting fleet rocking at its anchorage. But no sign of trepidation arose from the fort. Later, a captured Confederate said, " Say, that explosion was terrible. It woke us all up."

The day before Christmas the fort was engaged by the fleet in a vigorous cannonade lasting several hours. It was at that time perhaps the most stupendous and terrifying exhibition of the power of artillery which had ever been known, though of course, in comparison with the artillery fire of the European war, it would be trifling. Yet the fire of the fleet did but little damage to the fort. Some few frame buildings on the parade were set afire, but the fort itself, being practically a great mass of sand, was uninjured. It furnished an object lesson in the science of fortification which was not sufficiently understood at that moment. Not until the opening of the European war and the destruction of Liège did military men thoroughly comprehend that the best defense against the fire of heavy guns is a bank of earth. Masses of concrete, ponderous masonry, even wrought steel turrets, give way to the pounding of high explosives. But a bank of sand like that of Fort Fisher back in 1864 flies up into the air and then falls back to its prior position.

Pretty well convinced of the futility of its effort, the fleet drew off. But the next morning the attack was resumed, General Butler having landed a force of 3,000 men on the beach with the intention of charging when the fort should have been silenced. But that moment never came. Again, after a long bombardment, the fleet concluded that its efforts were fruitless and pulled out of action. Under those conditions Butler thought it inexpedient to charge, and the attack was abandoned. In the end, however, the navy was destined to win a great triumph at Fort Fisher, for on the 14th of January a landing force of 1,600 sailors and 400 marines gallantly assaulted the fort under cover of a heavy cannonade from the fleet. The losses of the naval column were exceedingly heavy. The whole attention of the defenders of the fort was centered upon them. The result was twofold. The naval column was beaten back with heavy loss, but meantime the army column, under the command of General Terry, attacking at a point from which the defenders' attention had been diverted, made their way into the fort successfully. The day after the victory, while the exultant Federal soldiers, sailors and marines were crowding into the fort, its principal magazine exploded, killing 200 of the victors and wounding 100 men. The losses of the marines in the two battles were heavy, but are not accurately reported in the official documents. All of the commanding officers in their reports spoke with especial commendation of the dash and gallantry of the members of the corps.

Charleston harbor, which had witnessed the first outbreak of the Civil War, became in 1863 once more the scene of naval activities, in which the marines took a prominent part. It was always a favorite resort for blockade runners, as Fort Sumter, perched in the very center of the entrance to the harbor, kept the blockaders at a distance. Moreover, the Confederates made several efforts with their somewhat rudimentary naval force to drive these blockaders away. The efforts were, however, without success, although they inflicted more or less loss upon the Federal forces, notably in the case of the man-of-war *Housatonic,* which was sunk by a submarine torpedo boat—the first instance of a successful attack of that character in history.

Most notable, however, of the actions in Charleston harbor was the futile effort to take Fort Sumter by a joint assault of sailors and marines. The fort had successfully defied bombardment from the sea for months. And although at this time the Federal forces had succeeded, after repeated attacks, in driving the Confederates from the works on Morris Island, they had not yet prepared that position for a further bombardment of Sumter.

That fort stands directly in the middle of the entrance to the harbor and about three-quarters of a mile from the shore on either side. It was at this time an old-fashioned edifice of brick, octagonal in shape, and surrounding a large parade. Since then it has been cut down and made into a modern harbor defense fortification by the United States government. In its original shape it would not withstand the fire of one of our modern warships for an hour. The walls of the fort then rose practically flush from the water's edge, making any effort to storm it most difficult. But on one side the heavy fire to which the fort had been subjected had brought down portions of the walls so that a sloping pile of débris seemed to make it possible for a storming party to land. It was shown by the final event, however, that this gave an insufficient foothold.

On the 8th of September, in the darkness of the night, an expedition of 34 officers and 413 men, nearly all marines, set out from the mainland with the purpose of assaulting the fort. It was to be attacked on two sides. One party was to attempt to scale the débris and gain the lofty parapet of the fort. The second was to try to gain entrance from their boats through the lower tier of embrasures which were little above the level of the water. A third party was to act as a reserve and follow up whichever of the others seemed to gain any success. It was shortly after midnight when the boats put out and they found nothing lacking in the vigilance of the Confederates. They had hardly approached within pistol shot of the fort before the sharp challenge rang out from the parapet, followed by the cry, " Turn out the guards! " A sharp fire of musketry followed and signal lights blazed from every point. The Confederate shore batteries opened fire on the fort, knowing that their shots would tell more on the attacking party than upon the defenders. About 150 of the marines got ashore at the foot of the débris, but instead of finding a rugged inclined plane leading to the parapet of the fort, they discovered that the forehanded Confederates had built a perpendicular range of masonry in anticipation of precisely such an assault. They were blocked absolutely, confined on a narrow strip of solid ground with the water behind them, a stone wall before them and on either hand the portholes of the fort blazing with a musketry fire directed down upon them. Hand grenades and even bricks hurled from the top of the parapet did deadly work among them. The boats which had brought them to this point were quickly cut to pieces by the fire of the fort, and, just at this juncture, a Confederate ram came out from the shore with a large locomotive headlight on her bow, which illuminated the scene and enabled the crew to pour destructive volleys upon the entrapped marines. Success was impossible. Delay meant annihilation. The men sought their boats for the purpose of retreat, but found that of the seven which had brought them three were wholly destroyed. Of this party 80 were killed and 10 officers and 104 men were missing.

The second party was no more successful. It had been expected to hold the boats close to the face of the fort while the men clambered in through the lower embrasures. But they found the water shallow and the bottom covered with sharp rocks, on which the boats bumped dangerously as the waves rose and fell. When the Confederate steamer bore down upon them they abandoned the effort to enter and made their way back to the mainland. Probably had any men been able to get in through the embrasures they would merely have been captured. In brief, the expedition, though gallantly conducted, was a complete failure, because the assailing force had not been sufficiently informed of the physical difficulties to be encountered. After this attack Sumter remained in the hands of the Confederates until Charleston was taken by the army from the mainland.

This was the last action of any considerable size or importance in which the marines participated in the Civil War. They were always in active service, but their small numbers and their wide distribution among scattered ships and posts made any considerable action on their part impossible. Yet they participated in sundry picturesque incidents which it would be impossible to enumerate here. Marines, for example, fought the rifle guns on the *Kearsage* in its successful battle with the Confederate cruiser *Alabama*, and it is a curious fact that after the assassination of President Lincoln, when the government at Washington, in a species of panic, was arresting every Confederate of importance, it was an officer of marines who was sent down to the outskirts of Mobile to arrest Commander Raphael Semmes of the *Alabama*, then living there in retirement.

In examining the record of the United States Marine Corps during the Civil War, and for that matter during all conflicts in which this government was engaged prior to the war with Spain, one is impressed

at once by the modesty of the officers of that corps
and by the very scant recognition which higher officials gave to their service. It is almost impossible
to disentangle the work of that corps from that of
the other branches of the armed service. In the
operations under Goldsborough and Porter on the
inland waterways it is absolutely impossible so to
do. Here and there a word of commendation in a
commander's report, and almost everywhere a line
or two in the reports of the dead and wounded, are
about all the records of the services of the marine
corps that we can disinter from the enormous mass
of material dealing with the history of the Civil War
in America.

CHAPTER XI

In Time of Peace.—The Marine Force Reduced.—Service
Against Mobs.—In China and Korea.—The Battle of the
Salee Forts.—Peace Duties Once More.—Intervention at
Panama.—The Disaster at Samoa.

WITH the close of the Civil War the people of the
United States turned joyously to peace. They were
weary of war and everything connected with it, and
this sentiment was reflected in the actions of Congress. Quickly the great armies were demobilized
and reabsorbed in the industrial life of the country.
The marine corps with its 2,500 men was but a small
factor in this situation, yet it did not escape the
pruning proclivities of a peaceful government.
While the law fixing its numbers was not changed,
it was impossible to bring it up to its statutory
strength because Congress refused to make the necessary appropriations for its support. As always, however, the marine corps strove to do its best and to
meet all calls made upon it.

In 1864 Colonel Jacob Zeilin had become commander-in-chief of the corps, and by act of Congress
was created a brigadier general, but in 1874 a spirit
of extreme economy overwhelmed Congress and it
reduced the size of the corps to 1,500 men and gave
the commandant the rank only of colonel. While

this could not affect General Zeilin, it did establish
the rank of his successor when he retired, and, accordingly, Colonel Charles G. McCawley, who succeeded him, although one of the most distinguished
officers the corps ever enjoyed, was limited to a
colonel's rank. In 1899 the rank of brigadier general was once more bestowed upon the commander
of the corps, who at that time was Colonel Charles
Heywood. The renewal of this rank was undoubtedly due to the fact that the nation was then in the
midst of the war with Spain, in which the marine
corps took a most creditable part.

Between 1866 and 1871 the activities of the marines were mainly in connection with domestic affairs. The war had left upon the national character a certain impress of lawlessness and turbulence
that manifested itself in riotous outbreaks in various
parts of the country, which grew out of very mis-
cellaneous causes. One of these causes was whiskey
—not wholly its use, though that no doubt contributed to the fire of the mobs, but springing mainly
from the efforts of the government to enforce the
internal revenue tax and to suppress illicit distil-
leries. Philadelphia and Brooklyn, though both
have the reputation of being peculiarly quiet and
peaceful cities, were the scenes of the most savage
of these outbreaks. In Brooklyn the section then
known as " Irish Town " was a veritable site of
civil war, and required the intervention of the marines no less than seven times. In service of this

character there is little glory and certainly no pleasure, for the forces of riot and outlawry against which the marines were arrayed were made up of their own countrymen and in some instances of their own neighbors. The records of the times show that they exercised the utmost restraint, usually dispersing the mobs without bloodshed. But there were instances of pitched battles, and in many cases they were attacked by sharpshooters firing from the roofs of adjoining buildings. In such cases it is hardly necessary now to say that the marines did their duty, and dispersed the rioters by force of arms.

During this period, other detachments were called upon to do work which was more to the liking of a marine. Our far-eastern squadron was then in Chinese waters, under the command of Admiral Bell. In those days, the island of Formosa, now part of Japan, still belonged to China and apparently did not suffer from any excess of government regulation. For when, in March, 1866, the officers and crew of the American bark, *Rover*, had been shipwrecked on the southeast end of the island a band of savages had fallen upon the unfortunate sailors and had murdered them in cold blood. It took some time before news of this dastardly deed reached the United States. As soon, however, as the facts had been established, the secretary of the navy instructed Admiral Bell to seek out the murderers and punish them, so that they, or their kind, would not again attempt to take

the lives of peaceful Americans. In June, 1867, he
therefore left Shanghai with the *Hartford* and the
Wyoming. Formosa was reached by June 13th, and
a landing party of 181 officers and men, including
43 marines, was sent ashore. Twenty of these,
under Captain James Forney, were immediately deployed forward as skirmishers. The terrain was
very difficult, a dense and almost impenetrable
thicket of bushes preventing rapid advance. For
about half a mile the little band of marines penetrated the unknown territory. The heat was terrible, and some of the men were temporarily in-
capacitated by it. At last contact was made with
the savages. A well-directed fire quickly routed
them. The marines and sailors pursued them as far
as prudence permitted, killing and wounding a large
number and destroying some native huts. When it
was thought that the savages had been sufficiently
punished and impressed with the danger of prac-
ticing their murderous habits upon American
citizens, the landing force was withdrawn and the
two ships returned to their station.

The other incident, in which marines played a
part, was nearer home. Off the east end of Long
Island is a smaller island, called Gardiner's Island.
News had come in July, 1869, to the ears of the
Federal government that a party of filibusters, planning an invasion of Cuba, had assembled there and
had built themselves a camp where they were busily
drilling and collecting supplies. Fifty marines

MARINES GETTING READY TO EMBARK FOR FRANCE

under Lieutenant Breese were dispatched from the Brooklyn Navy Yard on a revenue cutter. Taking the filibusters by surprise, the camp was surrounded, and 125 of them were captured and brought back to New York, where they were promptly tried for attempted breach of the neutrality laws.

Filibustering in those days was apparently quite a popular sport. For in the following year, 1870, another party of adventurers of many nationalities invaded Mexican territory on the Pacific coast. On the steamer *Forward*, flying the colors of San Salvador, they entered the Mexican port of Guaymas and, sending some 150 men ashore, had seized and robbed the custom house, forced contributions from the foreign merchants and even compelled the United States Consul to supply them with coal. The *Mohican* was lying then at Mazatlan. As soon as news reached her of the outrage she got under way. A few days later the *Forward* was caught at Boca Teacapan. Fifty marines and sailors put off from the *Mohican* in six boats and, under the protection of her guns, boarded the *Forward*, captured her crew and set her afire.

The year 1871 brought more troubles in Chinese waters. Another dependency of the Chinese empire, since then passed under Japanese control, Korea, had been a frequent offender in regard to the treatment accorded to shipwrecked sailors and passengers of American ships. The United States minister at the Chinese court was, therefore, instructed to arrange a treaty with the Korean authorities which would remedy existing conditions. In May, 1871, he sailed on the flagship of the Asiatic squadron, the *Colorado,* for the Boisee anchorage on the Korean river, Salee. After the fleet's arrival negotiations were begun immediately and seemed to be progressing favorably. In spite of this, however, some boats, engaged with the consent of local authorities, in making soundings and surveys, were suddenly and treacherously attacked by the Korean forts. Thanks to the prompt action of some small vessels of the fleet, the boats and their crews were saved, only two of our men being wounded.

Of course, the incident demanded that some definite action should be taken at once. It was decided to attempt first a peaceable adjustment. A demand was made upon the Korean authorities for an explanation. But when none was forthcoming, after 10 days had passed, it was concluded that more forcible means would have to be employed to secure the respect for the flag and dignity of the United States, to which they were entitled. The offending forts were to be attacked. Five hundred and seventy-five sailors with seven field pieces and 105 marines were detached from the various ships for this purpose. The marines formed in two companies and were under the command of Captain McLane Tilton.

On June 10th they left their ships, the *Colorado, Alaska* and *Benicia,* and embarked in boats, which

were towed up the river by the U. S. S. *Palos*. The
first line of fortifications was quickly reached. The
Palos anchored, the boats cast off and, under the
protection of her guns, pulled for the shore. A wide,
sloping beach, 200 yards from high-water mark,
was the first obstacle. Soft mud, reaching well over
the knees of the tallest man, made the landing difficult. Despite this, the marines advanced quickly
toward a square redoubt, fortifying a tongue of land
jutting out into the river, with grain fields and a
village in its rear.

In the meantime, the guns of one of the vessels
had been trained on the fortification, the fire from
which had quickly been silenced. Its garrison even
then was fleeing through the fields, firing a few shots
without effect. Without meeting any opposition, the
marines swept on, through the fields of grain and
the village. Soon the main body of the landing
force came up and took over the position. Again
the marines advanced toward a wooded knoll, apparently a burying ground, as it was covered with
hemispherical mounds. There they were ordered to
halt for the night. The main body was about three-
quarters of a mile further back. Beautiful wooded
hills and inundated rice fields were on all sides.
Still further away was the next fort, a square work
solidly built of granite and of formidable aspect.
Pickets were posted on the flanks and a 12-pounder
having been sent up from the main force, was placed
so as to command the junction of the only two ap-

proaches to the position which, in front, was protected by an inundated rice field. The marines were then divided into three reliefs, one being always on the alert, and there they bivouacked for the night, the first western force to spend a night in the hills of Korea.

The next morning the main body came up. Again the marines were ordered to advance. The second line of fortifications was their objective and it was entered without opposition, the garrison having fled. Quick work was made of making it harmless. The ramparts were torn down and some 60 old-fashioned breech-loading brass cannon were rolled without much trouble over the cliff into the river. To add to the up-to-dateness of the proceedings, a photographer was sent ashore from the *Monocacy*, who took a picture.

There was still the most formidable of the fortifications left, a circular stone edifice on the crest of the hill called by the Americans the Citadel. This proved to be the most difficult of the Korean positions. Yet at first it appeared to be undefended, the few natives who lurked about it being unarmed and rapidly disappearing as the American forces came into view. The road lay at the base of steep hills, or ran through the bottom of deep ravines. Soon from points of vantage isolated Koreans began firing upon the advancing column and before very long the fire was sustained as though a considerable force was engaged in it. The enemy hid in the tall grass. As they fired their heads would bob up for a moment and then disappear again. It was almost impossible to retaliate, but the marines suffered but little because the foe was armed only with antiquated matchlocks, which did little execution. Finally a piece of artillery, dragged to the battle line by prodigious efforts on the part of some sailors, sent a few charges of shrapnel into the grass and the Koreans were not heard from in that section thereafter.

The column had, by this time, come within about a third of a mile of the Citadel. The lay of the land was such that the advancing troops could approach close to the right face of the fort without being detected by the enemy. Accordingly, this line of attack was adopted, and the marine force had attained a position about 150 yards from the Citadel when they were perplexed by an unusual spectacle: a line of about 25 banners, placed in single file, a few feet apart, and at right angles to the advancing troops, extended across their path. What was the significance? In that country and at that time methods of war were primitive. It had been but a few years since the Chinese had relied upon terrifying masks, and even facial contortions, to strike terror into the hearts of their enemy. Just what the Koreans meant by their line of banners was yet to be determined. But Captain Tilton thought they portended some kind of an ambush and, accordingly, sent but four men forward to investigate. They had gathered in about 15 of the banners, when suddenly a tremendous fire was opened upon them from the redoubts and from the rank vegetation on the hill. The Koreans thereafter spurned concealment, dashing into the open, discharging their pieces and then dropping behind the parapet to reload. All the time they maintained a high, slow, melancholy chant, their historic battle song. Gradually the marines in small parties advanced closer and closer, they rushed down the steep bank of the ravine, and toiled painfully up the other side. But by this time the Koreans themselves were in a sorry plight. Their shots came at longer intervals and stones began to take the place of bullets. It was quite evident that their ammunition was exhausted, and with a cheer the front rank of the marines went over the crest of the fort. Their leader fell dead just as they were about to enter the works, being pierced by a bullet during the hand-to-hand struggle on the parapet. Admiral Rogers says of him, " The heroic McKee was first to mount the parapet and the first to leap into a hand-to-hand conflict. There he fell, as his father fell in Mexico, at the head of his men, first inside of the enemy's stormed works."

The remainder of the fight was brief but bloody. The Koreans neither sought quarter nor gave any, and, as they struggled with the band of invaders amongst them, they continued their melancholy song of battle. Their flag of yellow cotton with a Chinese character in black upon it, which floated over the Citadel, was torn down by one of the marines. All the defenders of the fort were slain or wounded. None escaped. Even the prisoners, of whom there were not more than 20, were wounded, and 243 dead Koreans were counted in the works. Fifty flags were taken and 481 pieces of ordnance. The latter were of no particular value to the victors, owing to their antiquated pattern. They were not retained, but destroyed by spiking or explosion. Despite the heavy loss on the side of the Koreans, there was, beside Lieutenant McKee, only one marine killed and two wounded. The heavy execution done among the Koreans is to be explained presumably by the fact that the expedition was a punitive one sent out to strike terror into the hearts of the natives. In his report of the affair, Commander Kimberly said:

" To Captain Tilton and his marines belongs the honor of first landing and last leaving the shore, in leading the advance on the march, in entering the forts and as acting as skirmishers. Chosen as the advance guard, on account of their steadiness and discipline, and looked to with confidence in case of difficulty, their whole behavior on the march and in the assault proved that it was not misplaced."

Followed now five years of comparatively commonplace service. Police duty in Boston on the occasion of two great fires, a very brief landing expedition in Panama when that province was in one of its recurrent revolutions against the government of Colombia and prompt and efficient aid furnished in the harbor of Callao, Peru, when an Italian vessel heavily loaded with explosives and on fire was towed out of the crowded harbor, constitute the main record of service. In 1874, a picturesque mobilization of the Atlantic fleet at Key West, intended to impress Spain with our power at the moment when it seemed as if war might grow out of the Virginius affair, gave the marines of that time an opportunity to display their discipline on shore. Nothing came of this, however; but it and the landing at Panama were curiously premonitory of the later action, by which both the Isthmian province and the island of Cuba were rescued from harassing control and erected into independent republics, owing an undying debt of gratitude to the United States.

Panama gave the marines a little more occupation in 1885, when its people fomented a revolution against Colombia which really for a time threatened to be successful. The United States had then a treaty with New Granada, one of the Colombian states, in which it guaranteed the protection of traffic across the Isthmus of Panama. At that moment, while we were thinking of the Panama Canal, we had not, as a nation, yet so determined upon its construction as to be willing to connive at a revolution as the means of securing the right of way across the Isthmus. That came years later.

But at this time the United States made good its treaty obligations by hurrying a naval force and a full battalion of marines down to Colon, which was threatened by the revolution. Panama City was in revolutionary hands, but in 12 hours the marines had proceeded thither and taken matters into their own control. Traffic was resumed on the Panama Railroad, each train carrying a detachment of marines. Before the revolutionists were thoroughly convinced that the United States was determined to maintain the authority of Colombia, three battalions of marines, numbering in all over 600 men, were distributed about the Isthmus. The city of Panama, in which the revolutionists had erected barricades, was very speedily taken by the marines, under Colonel Heywood, by the mere force of their appearance and discipline—for not a shot was necessary. Not long after troops were landed from Colombia, who took charge of the situation and the marines returned to their ship.

To-day Panama is one of the largest stations for the marines, over whose camp in the Canal Zone the United States flag flies, and the shouts of revolution are no longer heard.

In 1876-1877 the United States was the scene of labor disturbances, connected particularly with its railway systems, that for a time bade fair to attain the proportions of a true civil war. The marines were hastily summoned from their various posts and sent out to protect not only public property, but railway property as well, which they did with discretion and efficiency.

Not until 1882 do we find further record of marine service abroad. In that year the Egyptians rose in revolt against growing British domination, and for a time the property and even the lives of foreign inhabitants of Alexandria were in serious jeopardy. The United States ship *Lancaster*, lying at anchor in the harbor, became the place of refuge for imperiled Europeans, and later the American marines, together with those from sundry other men-of-war, were landed and maintained order in the city.

In March of 1885, nature with her irresistible forces broke up a game of international chess that was being played in the harbor of Apia at the island of Samoa in the Pacific Ocean. In so doing, it spoiled an early opportunity for that inevitable conflict between the United States and Germany, which finally broke in 1917.

At this time the two nations were diplomatically striving for the control of these Pacific islands, each giving a certain support to an aspirant for the position of king. While the diplomatists played with words and phrases three German men-of-war, one British and three of the United States, the *Trenton*, *Vandalia* and *Nipsic*, lay in the harbor and their ship's companies made faces at each other when they met. There was dynamite in the situation, but fate settled the proposition by sending down upon that group of islands one of the fiercest of the tropical hurricanes known to history. The harbor, though adequate for protection against the ordinary tempest, proved but a sorry place of refuge in the face of this gale. The vessels at once began to drag anchor. The captain of the British man-of-war *Caliope*, seeing that the situation was hopeless if he attempted to stick to his anchorage, got up steam and made for the open sea. It was a desperate venture. Whether the engines of the ship were strong enough to make headway against the gale could only be told by the trial. If they failed the ship would unquestionably be thrown upon the beach, and the lives of her 300 men be sacrificed. Nor could she steam out with a straight course, for the *Trenton* lay in her path and a jagged reef was but a few yards away. The *Trenton's* fires were out and she was helpless, but as the British ship nosed her way past, fighting for every foot against the roaring tempest, the men of the *Trenton*, facing death as they were, sprang into the rigging and gave three cheers for the *Caliope* as she passed out of the harbor in the teeth of the storm. Captain Kane, the British commander, said later, " Those ringing cheers of the American flagship pierced deep into my heart, and I will ever remember that mighty outburst of fellow feeling which I felt came from the bottom of the hearts of the gallant admiral and his men. Every man on board the *Caliope* felt as I did. It made us work to win. I can only say, ' God bless America and her noble sailors.' "

The *Trenton* played a great part that day.

Drifting about before the gale, helpless and apparently destined to go on the rocks to the complete sacrifice of her men, she strove to cheer on her fellows in misfortune. The flag was nailed to the mast, her men were ordered up into the rigging that their bodies might act as a sail to help direct the ship, her bands played patriotic and stirring airs and in the end she escaped disaster.

Of the three German ships two were driven on the beach with a heavy loss of men. Of the American squadron the *Nipsic* suffered in the same way. The others, though clinging to their anchorages, were desperately battered and torn and large numbers of their people washed away and drowned. A picturesque feature of the disaster was the effort of the Samoans to save the sailors thrown into the sea. A race of Herculean proportions and so used to the water as to be almost amphibious, they worked steadily in the roaring surf, singing a native tribal song, the sound of which rose even above the roar of the angry water. During the course of this disaster the marines on the American ship did their duty nobly. On the *Trenton* their first lieutenant and four men were lost. On the *Vandalia* one-half of the entire detachment were drowned, including their promising young commander, Lieutenant Sutton. Scarcely had the hurricane subsided, and made it possible for the ships' crews to seek the shore, when the marines were landed in force and assumed control of the situation. Despite the fragments of the German expedition, it was the United States marine corps that then ruled Samoa.

In 1891 the School of Application of the Marine Corps was established and for a long time exercised a great influence upon the personnel of the corps. Although many of the officers of this organization had been students at Annapolis or West Point, few were graduates, while the greater number had either risen from the ranks or been selected from civilian life. This school was, accordingly, established for the purpose of supplying such instruction to officers and men seeking promotion as would "keep pace with the progress made in the methods of warfare and thereby insure for the navy greater utility and continued efficiency on the part of its military arm." The school was maintained at Washington continuously up to the time of the Spanish-American War, which interrupted its work. After that contest, the work of instruction was conducted at the various posts of the marine corps. This educational work, beyond doubt, exercised a most beneficent influence upon the character and methods of the marine corps. No student of its progress can fail to be impressed with the fact that it was immediately upon the establishment of this school that the corps took its upward march in dignity and in standing, until it attained its present high reputation with the people and among the efficient military organizations of the world.

CHAPTER XII

In 1898 burst the storm with Spain which grew out of conditions in Cuba. This beautiful and fertile island, lying, so to speak, in the front yard of the United States, had long been a source of extreme embarrassment to this country. Spain, which at one time had the greatest colonial empire of any nation of the world, had proved a complete failure as an administrator of colonies. As a result, one by one her distant dependencies had broken away from her. South America, from being all Spanish, had become all republican. In the West Indies, which at one time had been wholly her territory, Cuba and Porto Rico were the only considerable islands remaining to her. Her administration of Cuban affairs had been such that for a half a century or more the island had been in a state of constant revolt, sometimes smoldering, sometimes active and aggressive. As we have seen before, the United States marines had been frequently landed to restore order, while the obligation of the United States to suppress filibustering had led to constant domestic difficulties with American citizens eager to aid the aspirations of the Cubans for liberty and self-government.

There was never a war more inevitable than that with Spain. The people of Cuba were too close neighbors of the United States to be willing to submit themselves to the antiquated and repressive colonial methods of Spain. And the people of the United States, in their turn, were so close to Cuba that they could not be ignorant of the barbaric and inhuman methods adopted by the Spaniards to suppress the Cuban uprisings—methods which were in the highest degree repugnant to all American ideas. Moreover, it was impossible that a populous and productive island like Cuba could lie within a few score miles of so great a market as that offered by the United States and submit to the commercial restrictions by which Spain sought to turn its trade away from the neighboring United States and divert it to distant Spanish ports.

Any careful student of history will recognize that war with Spain was inevitable. But the immediate cause for the outbreak was the mysterious destruction by explosion of the United States battleship *Maine*, which was lying in the harbor of Havana on the night of February 15, 1898, on a peaceful visit. There had already been a wide and vigorous agitation throughout the United States for intervention in Cuba. The barbarities of the so-called reconcentration policy by which Spain sought to suppress the revolution had made a great impression upon our people and, while American charity had done much to alleviate Cuban suffering, the conviction was rapidly growing that the situation could only be cured by cutting out the Spanish ulcer with the sword.

The *Maine* had been sent to Havana with no hostile purpose, merely that there might be a force of law and order in the harbor ready to protect peaceful citizens if the revolutionary agitation should suddenly blaze out in riot. The night was quiet, with the cool evening breeze of the tropics blowing gently across the harbor. A Spanish man-of-war, the *Alphonzo XIII*, lay at her moorings close by. And these two ships, with a Ward passenger liner all brightly illuminated, added picturesqueness to the evening scene. The bluejackets on the man-of-war, save those on watch, were peacefully swinging in their hammocks, while Captain Sigsbee and his officers were engaged in evening tasks or recreation. There was no thought of any serious danger impending. True, the town was hostile. The Spaniards in Havana regarded the presence of the *Maine* as offensive, and on the streets and in the cafés American officers and bluejackets were not infrequently jostled or insulted. But officially the two countries were at peace, and beyond the usual vigilance maintained on a man-of-war nothing was done by the officers of the *Maine* to suggest anything other than peaceful sentiments. No torpedo nettings were down, nor was a boat patrol maintained. Either of these acts would, under the circumstances, have been construed as offensive to Spanish dignity.

Suddenly without warning, at about nine-thirty, those on the *Maine* who lived to tell the tale heard a dull explosion with a slight shock, then a prolonged fierce, deep, furious roar which shook the ship to its very vitals. Startled observers on the other ships in the harbor saw the whole forward part of the American battleship suddenly becoming a flaming volcano, belching forth fire, shattered men, huge pieces of steel and bursting shells. The decks of the neighboring ships became places of danger, for portions of the steel hull of the battleship rained down upon them. In a few moments it was discovered that such parts of the shattered ship as seemed intact were blazing fiercely, and rapidly sinking.

There is ample evidence that on the stricken ship, despite the overwhelming nature of the calamity, the power of discipline still exerted itself, and that those men who were able to perform their duty went directly to their stations and did exactly what years of drill and teaching had accustomed them to do. In flooding the magazines and calling away the boats' crews, the men fairly anticipated the orders of their superior officers. A picturesque yarn, not wholly without some foundation in fact, depicted Captain Sigsbee rushing from his cabin door into the darkness, to be met by his orderly, Sergeant William Anthony, of the marines.

" I have to report, sir," said the orderly with a salute, " that the ship is blown up and sinking."

To some extent this story was demolished by Captain Sigsbee, who said that if there had been a salute it could not have been seen in the denseness of the darkness of the compartment between decks. But he went on to say that no salute or melodrama was needed to add to the heroism of this sergeant of marines, who kept his head and did his duty with calmness and efficiency.

Nothing could be done to save the ship, but its boats and those from the neighboring vessels plied busily about the harbor, picking up survivors and taking the wounded ashore to the hospitals. On the quarter deck which, as the after part of the ship settled in the ooze at the bottom of the harbor, remained a few feet above water, Captain Sigsbee stood, receiving reports and issuing orders. The flag, which had been hauled down at sunset, as is customary in the navy, was raised and floated defiantly over the wreck when the sun came up the following morning. There it stayed until the declaration of war. It hardly needed the daylight to show that the *Maine* was wrecked beyond repair, and as the morning wore on the reports from the hospitals and the life-saving boats brought the melancholy intelligence that 254 men had been killed outright. Thirteen others died in the hospital after a long illness. It is interesting to note that this loss was more than 17 times as great as the total losses of the United States navy during the war that followed.

In his first dispatch to the United States conveying news of the disaster, Captain Sigsbee said, " Public opinion should be suspended until further report." Public opinion was not so easy to control. Though it took nearly two months for an official investigation to report that the explosion was undoubtedly caused by a torpedo or mine set off under the ship, the people were convinced themselves that that was the fact long before. While the administration—as seems the custom of administrations in the United States—fought off a declaration of war as long as possible, the nation clamored for it. Public sentiment is well indicated by a story told of Captain Robley D. Evans, of the United States navy.

" If I had been in command of the fleet at Key West, in place of Admiral Sicard," said he, talking to the secretary of the navy, " I would have taken my entire squadron into Havana harbor the next morning and I then would have said to them, ' Now we'll investigate this matter and let you know what we think about it at once.' "

" If you had done that you would have been severely reprimanded," responded Secretary Long.

" Perhaps so," responded " Fighting Bob," " but the people would have made me president at the next election."

With more deliberation the United States set

about its official investigation. But the end was inevitable. The verdict was that the ship had been destroyed by an explosion from without, and this verdict was sustained by the fact that bottom plates of the ship were bent inward. The Spaniards, for their part, made their own investigation, reaching a diametrically opposite conclusion. The *impasse* was complete. Public sentiment was aroused to a fighting point, and on the 19th of April war was declared.

While this war was waged alike on sea and land, and great bodies of our citizens were called to the armies, it was, nevertheless, the fact that the decisive battles were sea battles. There were really but two,—the battle of Manila Bay and the battle off Santiago harbor. When these sea fights were ended, although Spain had considerable armies yet unconquered on the shore, the issue was practically determined. For those armies were cut off from their home base by thousands of miles of ocean, and Spain had no way of sending either reënforcements or supplies to them, for she had left no navy to protect the cargo ships.

Comparatively few people in the United States at the beginning of the war knew that Spain possessed in the Philippine Islands, off the coast of China, enormously valuable Asiatic colonies. Fewer yet knew that at the first rumblings of war the navy department had sent to its Asiatic station a fleet sufficient to cope with anything that Spain might

YANKEE BOYS OF THE MARINES AND POILUS TAKE A LESSON IN SIGNALLING

have in those waters and with a fighting admiral of the Farragut breed. But the uninformed and indifferent citizens of this Union awoke with a start when on the morning of the 1st of May, 1898, they read in their newspapers that Admiral Dewey, with an American fleet of six fighting ships, had entered the harbor of Manila and utterly demolished the Spanish fleet stationed there.

The exploit which had thus astonished the country was not accomplished without long and careful preparation. Dewey himself, a veteran sea fighter who had served with Farragut at New Orleans and Mobile, had been ordered to the Asiatic squadron with precisely this contingency in mind. He had been kept in constant touch with the developments that might lead to war, and he had kept his ships coaled and provisioned so that there might be no difficulty about leaving Hongkong harbor within 24 hours after the declaration of war, as international law prescribed. Measured by present-day standards, his fleet was but a puny one. A single modern dreadnought could easily have demolished it all without incurring serious damage. The most powerful vessel in the fleet was the *Olympia*, a mere protected cruiser. Nevertheless, the Spanish fleet with which he had to cope was vastly inferior. It had but two modern cruisers, the rest of the fleet being made up of gunboats and mosquito gunboats. They all mounted 44 guns as against Dewey's 53. But while the Spanish fleet was thus outclassed, it was not the chief danger which Dewey encountered in the battle of Manila Bay.

Swiftly upon the declaration of war came Dewey's orders by cable:

" Proceed at once against the Philippines. Commence at once operations, particularly against the Spanish fleet. You must capture vessels or destroy."

Incidentally this was the last order by cable that Dewey received for some months. The day following his fleet sailed, and his first act on reaching Manila Bay was to cut the cable and thus protect himself from interference from Washington.

Dewey knew, well enough, the inferiority of the Spanish fleet which he had to meet. What he did not know was the skill of the gunners in the shore batteries that commanded the entrance to Manila Bay, or the number of mines and torpedoes with which the channel giving entrance to the bay was probably strewn. His courage and dash was shown by his immediately leading his fleet through the darkness of night into the harbor without showing dread of either batteries or mines. His audacity was rewarded, for not a single torpedo or mine exploded, and although a flare of burning soot from the stack of one of his ships betrayed the presence of the fleet and the Spanish gunners opened fire, they failed to inflict any damage. Curiously enough, the first shot fired by the Americans, which was discharged without orders and entirely at random by a gunner on the *Boston,* dismantled a gun in the Spanish works and killed 30 men.

It is needless here to give the details of the battle of Manila Bay. In it the comparatively few marines on the little fleet participated only to the extent of manning the secondary batteries on the ships to which they were attached. Even after the Spanish fleet was wholly demolished and the forts silent there was little use for the marines, because with his slender force Dewey could not hold Manila or any considerable part of the mainland and, therefore, did not attempt to take possession until after the United States troops arrived, under the command of General Otis, some months later. A body of marines was ordered to land at Cavite to receive the surrender of the fort, navy yard and remaining Spanish vessels of war there. This they did on May 3rd, and the corps has always boasted, with truth, that they were first to raise the American flag over Spanish territory in the Spanish-American War.

We may take up later the services of the marines in the Philippine rebellion, but for the present we will shift our story, as the scene of active war shifted, to Cuba, where everybody had supposed the war would begin. The earlier days of the war on this coast saw only occasional bombardments of ports like Cardenas, San Juan or Santiago. The naval authorities thought that in view of the limited strength of our navy it would be unwise to risk the effort to send ships into Havana harbor. At that time, the loss of a single battleship would have been a national calamity. Active hostilities, therefore, were held up until the American army could be organized and equipped and made ready for transport to Cuba. While awaiting the completion of this work the navy was employed only in the blockade.

Some zest was added to this service by the fact that it was known that a considerable Spanish fleet, under command of Admiral Cervera, was on the high seas on its way toward the coast of the United States. There was some panic in our coastwise cities lest the coming armada should descend upon one of them, but the navy department resolutely kept the ships in the West Indies, and while the fleet sailed to intercept Cervera, it learned promptly when he had slipped into Santiago harbor and at once took up the task of blockading him there.

The strategic plan for the occupation of Cuba was both naval and military. To the navy was assigned the duty of blockading the Spanish fleet in Santiago, or of destroying it should it emerge from that port. The army was to land on the south side of Cuba and attack Santiago from its landward side.

Pursuant to this plan, there was gathered at Tampa, Florida, an army of about 17,000 men, under the command of General Shafter. As an army base, Tampa had the advantage of being the nearest to the Cuban coast of any good harbor in the United States. But this advantage was decidedly offset by the fact that it was reached by but one line of rail-road with small yardage facilities at the terminus, that its water supply was exceedingly limited and its climate scorching. A magnificent great winter hotel, promptly seized by the United States, made life tolerable for the officers who, as they sat on its broad piazzas sipping the cooling drinks that were common in those days when the idea of restricting the beverages of men in uniform had not gained currency, were inclined to question Sherman's maxim as to the hellishness of war. But for the men in the little shelter tents, eating the rations furnished by a government which had not yet learned the art of properly feeding an army, there was nothing cheering in the situation.

Indeed, the mobilization of the army at Tampa and its subsequent transfer to the south shore of Cuba afforded the most striking illustration of the lack of preparedness of the republic for war of any sort. The secretary of war, Hon. Russell A. Alger, said, himself, in June, " I do not believe that there was ever a nation on earth that attempted to embark on a war of such magnitude while so unprovided with everything necessary for a campaign."

As soon as it was learned that Cervera's fleet was securely bottled up in Santiago harbor, Shafter's army put out to sea. It could not very well move earlier, for there was a sore lack of warships to convoy the 32 transports that carried the troops, and it would have been madness to risk them afloat, with an enemy fleet roaming the ocean. As it was, the expedition went plowing gayly along, fully lighted and with no effort made to suppress unnecessary noises, so that a single torpedo boat, had the Spaniards possessed one, could have wrought havoc in its ranks. It was like an ocean circus parade, wrote one of the correspondents. It had been determined to land at a little port called Siboney, on the south shore of Cuba. Two or three weeks prior to the time of the sailing of the Shafter expedition, a force of about 600 marines had been landed by the navy at Guantanamo, about 20 miles from Siboney. They landed in the face of a very considerable force of Spanish soldiery and guerrillas lurking in the dense thickets which bordered the beach. The marines suspected their presence, and were surprised when their first boatload was permitted to land without opposition. It was learned later that the enemy conjectured that as soon as the first party had landed the boats would be sent off to bring stores. Accordingly, they thought they would lie in ambush, withholding their fire until the stores which they needed had been landed, when by an attack in force they could overwhelm the marines. But the latter beat them at that game, for, while the boats went back for additional men and stores, those who were first landed went to work systematically digging trenches and were fairly dug in before the enemy began his attack. It was savage while it lasted. A head lifted over the earthworks was sure to be struck by a flying bullet. So far as a response from the rifles of the marines was concerned, it could be only ineffective because the guerrillas were concealed in the jungle and the firing could be only at random. The ships lying off the harbor had the remedy to hand, but their crews were not informed as to the plight of the marines. It was necessary to signal, but no man could stand on the beach waving signal flags and escape that heavy fire.

It was a pitch dark night and the signalling could only be done with lanterns, which would, of course, make the signal man the most conspicuous target on the whole beach. Nevertheless, a volunteer was speedily found in the ranks of the marines, and, taking his stand, began the appeal for aid. The fire of the Mausers from the woods redoubled, and then there was done one of those things which have helped to give to the marine corps the indomitable *esprit de corps* which it has always manifested. Colonel Huntington, in command of the detachment, unwilling that any of his men should risk a danger which he did not share, clambered out of the trench and stood beside the signal man. Lieutenant Draper, from the comparative safety of the breast-work, pleaded with his chief to come back and not expose himself thus, but finding his entreaties fruitless, himself left his refuge and stood by the side of the waving lantern. There for five minutes or more, while the attention of the *Marblehead* was being sought, and the request that the woods be shelled was slowly spelled out, the three stood amidst the whistling hail of bullets. Then, suddenly, lightning flashed from the cruiser's side and the sharp detonations of exploding shells were heard in the neighboring jungle. The three men made their way back to the trenches and the rifle fire from the dark thicket slowly died away.

Stephen Crane, the author of " The Red Badge of Courage," and one of the most vivid of the correspondents in the Spanish War, tells of being with a detachment of marines operating against guerrillas on a densely wooded hillside. One of the gunboats, thinking to aid, opened fire on the hill, but its shells came nearer to the marines than they did to the enemy. It was necessary to signal to her to stop, else her fire would have destroyed our own men. The post of signal man would necessarily be one of grave danger and volunteers were called for. Sergeant Quick arose, and, announcing himself versed in the art of signalling, tied a fancy handkerchief on a stick, and proceeding to the top of the ridge began sending the message to the *Dolphin*.

" I watched his face," said Crane, " and it was serene as that of a man sitting in his own library, the embodiment of tranquillity and absorption in the work at hand. We gave him sole possession of that part of the ridge, for this marine with his back turned to the woods was wigwagging his message to the *Dolphin* while all Spain was shooting at him. But with bullets singing all around he showed not a single trace of nervousness or haste. I saw him betray only one sign of emotion. That was when an overhead branch of a tree, cut by a Mauser bullet, had sagged downward. His flag had been caught by the swaying limb and he looked over his shoulder to see what held it. Then he gave the flag an impatient jerk. He looked annoyed."

The greatest triumph of the marines in the Cuban campaign was not, however, in battle, for there were but few of them and the fighting was largely left to the soldiers. But they were victorious over the insidious and deadly enemy which inflicted upon the army its heaviest losses. The greatest reflection that was made upon the war department's conduct of the war sprung from the disease and death which stalked through our camps, and from the lack of preparation to encounter the climate of Cuba.

Indeed, looking back upon the campaign, one wonders that so far as the first expedition to Cuba was concerned, we were not overwhelmingly beaten and did not have inflicted upon us the most far-reaching of calamities by the enemy. Only the sluggishness of the Spaniards averted a tremendous disaster.

The army landed at Daiquiri. This was not a harbor, but merely a spot where there happened to be a pier reaching out into the open sea. Had a storm come up the landing vessels would have been forced to seek safety in the offing, and such portions of the troops as were ashore, separated from support and supplies, could have been cut off by a

Spanish attack. Even though the weather was favorable, General Shafter admitted that " It was not until nearly two weeks after the army landed that it was possible to place on shore three days' supplies in excess of those needed for daily consumption."

What would have been the outcome had one of the tropical hurricanes common in that latitude come up and driven the ships away for a week or more? Between starvation and the Spaniards the expedition must inevitably have been destroyed. There was prolonged delay, even with the good weather and the lack of any Spanish opposition, in getting the necessary material unpacked and landed. No provision had been made for large boats or lighters for landing purposes except one big scow that had been towed all the way from Tampa. For the rest a few lighters found abandoned on the beach had to serve. The expedition was in the hands of soldiers, landsmen not used to operating small boats, and this added to the delay. The transports were merely hired ships and their commanders not enlisted men, but men who owed their first allegiance to the owners of the vessels. The coast being treacherous and the danger of a hurricane always present, they thought it the part of caution to lie off from three to ten miles, often out of the reach of any form of signal. Moreover, the ships had been unscientifically packed. No one knew where anything was and officers in small boats sometimes had to make the round of the fleet to find the particular type of ammunition wanted at once. Articles belonging to the same branch of the service were not all packed together, so that many vessels of the fleet had to be visited in order to get a complete assortment of, for example, medical stores. It was reported that large quantities of stores of this character were carried back to the United States because they could not be found in season for use when wanted, although the surgeons on shore were almost frantic for the lack of surgical instruments, medicines and disinfectants. It was a state of chaos, bred of the inexperience of the quartermaster's department in outfitting a large expedition. Americans who recall the scandal attaching to this branch of the Shafter expedition found a certain grim satisfaction later in the fact that in 1916, in another and greater war, a British expedition to the Dardanelles had to turn around and return to Alexandria because the ships had been so unscientifically loaded that not even the men could be efficiently landed.

Neither the United States nor Great Britain was trained to war.

None of these errors in management attached to the operation of the marines. The motto of the navy is " Ever ready," and the marines are a naval arm. In time of peace every ship that is in commission is ready, as Admiral Evans said on an historic occasion, for " a frolic or a fight." While the marines who landed at Guantanamo were not drawn from the ships of Sampson's fleet, but were a special detachment which had been lying sweltering in the transport *Panther* at Key West, they were still marines, a branch of the naval service with naval traditions behind them and the whole fleet to back them up. When they landed, the landing was conducted with naval system. The *Marblehead* and the *Yankee*, lying off shore, shelled the woods which might possibly shelter a hostile Spanish force. The *Oregon*, *Yosemite* and *Scorpion*—the latter with a crew of naval reserves from Michigan—lay near by, prepared to send additional forces ashore in the event reënforcements were necessary. But they were not. The Spaniards, who fled while the fleet was doing the shelling, left a flagstaff standing upon which the Soldiers of the Sea ran up the Star-Spangled Banner, while the band played the battle hymn of the Spanish War, " There'll be a Hot Time in the Old Town To-night." This peaceful atmosphere did not long endure, for, as has been noted, the Spaniards came back to the attack; but by that time the marines had dug themselves in and were ready for defense.

One day, however, the defenders of Camp McCalla, as the post was called, after the commander of the *Marblehead,* were caught, if not exactly napping, at least very much unprepared for self-defense. The men had been getting the camp ready for a long stay and taking such sanitary precautions as burning all Cuban huts in the neighborhood which might be infected with yellow-fever germs. The work was arduous, the day sweltering. Toward night, no hostile sound having arisen from the dense woods, the officers posted scouts on the outskirts of the camp and allowed the men to go in bathing. Several hundred of them stripped and were joyously disporting themselves in the surf, when a Cuban came running into the camp, closely pursued by Mauser bullets. At the same time came shouts of warning from the scouts, and a spluttering fire from their rifles, while heavier volleys came from the thick brush on the hills. The enemy had seized this most untimely occasion for an attack. Naked men caught up rifles and cartridge belts and ran to where the officers were forming companies and sending company after company out to the firing line.

The steadiness and discipline of the marines on this occasion were peculiarly admirable because many of them were green men enlisted at the opening of the war, and the attack, as may be judged from the circumstances, was an absolute surprise. Nevertheless, they responded like veterans to the word of command, content with a cartridge belt for their entire clothing and shooting with the precision of men at the butts. The Spaniards soon drew off, but not until two marines had fallen, James McColgan and William Dunphy, privates both, and the first Americans to lose their lives on Cuban soil.

During the night the enemy returned to the attack, not attempting to carry the American post by assault but lurking in the thickets and sniping away at the tents on the chance of striking some one of their inmates, or at the dark figures of sentinels outlined against the sky. In this attack Surgeon John Gibbs was killed—the first United States officer to be killed in Cuba.

The next morning, Colonel Huntington moved the camp to lower ground in order that the men might not be such conspicuous targets. It was no easy task. Never had the tropic sun been hotter than when the marines painfully carried tents, boxes and bedding down the hillside, while the Spaniards in the bushes blazed away with their Mausers. Most of the enemy thus engaged were guerrillas used to irregular and forest warfare. They adopted long before the modern name was known a very effective species of camouflage by decking themselves in palm leaves and, as they were supplied with smokeless powder, their place in the edge of the jungle could hardly be detected. The ships searched the thickets with shells, but the foe would disappear from one place only to appear in another. Two raiding parties sent out from the camp only found their path blocked by the dense vegetation, and no one visible to fight. It was like fighting gnats. Two days and nights of this sort of hostilities was pressed by the enemy, and even when the marines sent out burial parties to lay away their dead the bullets rained as fiercely upon the men who drew up by the side of the chaplain at the grave as they did upon men at the guns.

Wearied by the persistence of the enemy, the marines landed three field guns, mounted them in the trenches, and with these probed the jungle incessantly. The *Marblehead* also searched the bushes by night with searchlight and shell, but still the nagging stream of bullets flew from the jungle. In the end, however, a Cuban brought in word that the Spaniards had a sort of base not far from the camp, where they had a tank full of drinking water, the only supply in that neighborhood, and a heliograph for communication with the Spanish fort at Caimanera at the head of the bay. Taking along a few Cubans, a detachment of marines marched against this base and destroyed it, smashing the water tank and capturing the heliograph. From the prisoners they took, the marines learned that the Spaniards had 2,000 armed and disciplined men in the neighborhood, and they wondered why, with such a force, they had not swooped down on the 600 marines encamped on the beach and annihilated them. The fact recalled the statement made by General Garcia, the Cuban leader, to the officers of the American army when they first arrived in Cuba. Said he, "The Spaniards never attack; remember that. They *never* attack."

It may be said in passing, however, that in defense they were most gallant, and that there was a time when if the Spanish General Linares, in command at Santiago, had led his troops out from behind his breastworks in a determined attack upon the

American lines the chances are that he would have driven Shafter into the sea.

For after the overwhelming defeat of the Spanish fleet, the story of which it is unnecessary to tell here, disease and death made their appearance in the American army. Yellow fever and malarial fever ran their fatal course, and General Shafter, himself, admitted that six weeks after landing 75 per cent of his troops were unfit for service. In the camp at El Caney, to which from 18,000 to 20,000 fugitives flocked before the surrender of Santiago, the very air was foul from unburied mules and horses, and even human victims of the battle. Food was scarce for the troops, and scarcer for the refugees. The rainy season was on and the troops were ill-equipped for that incident of a tropical summer. When General Miles visited Cuba he had the extraordinary experience of having a whole battalion of naked men turn out in due form to salute him. Upon inquiry it was found that these troops had no change of clothing nor any place to dry their clothes. Accordingly, at the first shower of rain, they stripped, stowed their clothes in the shelter tent and went in nature's garb until the rain had passed. The fact that the clothing, supplied to the troops campaigning in Cuba in summer, was intended for use in South Dakota in midwinter, had something to do with their readiness to discard it.

The rapid spread of malarial and other fevers in the army camps called especial attention to the efficient methods adopted in the marine camp at Guantanamo. The difference was due only and wholly to expert knowledge of methods of sanitation, and their rigid application in the daily life of the marines. Every soldier who went to Cuba was solemnly adjured to boil the water before using it, but not one was given anything to boil it in, and even matches for kindling fires soon became rare and precious possessions. Every gallon of water served in the marine camp was boiled at headquarters. Army officers, finding Cuban huts or houses conveniently located, moved into them as offices, or used them as camp kitchens, without giving a thought to the germs of pestilence that might be lurking in their walls. The marines burned every such hut within the borders of their camp and for hundreds of yards around it. The closest watch was kept on the health of the men. As much of the service of the navy has always been in the tropics, they were provided with white duck suits fitted for the climate, and their food supplies furnished through the navy department were of a sort to which they had long been accustomed, and which were suited to the conditions under which they were serving. As a result, when Shafter was cabling that 75 per cent of his men were unfit for service because of illness, the sick list at the camp at Guantanamo showed less than two per cent of the command laid up. Curiously enough, this superiority of the navy department in caring for its men was shown as much at home as abroad.

When Camp Wikoff, on Long Island, to which the troops were sent after the close of the war, was full of typhoid fever, the camp at Portsmouth, prepared and conducted by the navy department, and policed by marines, in which 1,100 Spanish prisoners were kept, was as healthful as a summer resort.

The defeat of Admiral Cervera and the surrender of Santiago virtually ended the Spanish War. Some of the marines were kept for a time in Cuba for the maintenance of order, and even after the erection of the Cuban republic the corps was twice called upon to give its aid to the maintenance of the established authority there. Of these occasions we shall have more to say later.

But far across the Pacific in the Philippine Islands, peace with Spain brought no cessation of the marines' warlike activities, for there, when we had duly thrashed the Spaniards and occupied Manila, the native Filipinos, or a large portion of them, under the leadership of Aguinaldo, demanded a more than proportionate share of the fruits of victory and speedily came into conflict with United States authority.

Aguinaldo, a leader of both political and military capacity, had long kept up a revolutionary movement against the power of Spain. He was encouraged, after the battle of Manila Bay, by Admiral Dewey, who had him brought from Hongkong, where he had been living in exile, and aided him to raise an army among the natives. With this encouragement, and as a result of his participation in the final battle of Manila, Aguinaldo conceived an exaggerated notion of his own share in the victory then won and, on being coldly suppressed by the American authorities, gradually drifted into a position of active rebellion against them. As early as March, 1899, Admiral Dewey thought it prudent to cable to Washington for the immediate dispatch of a battalion of marines. They arrived early in May, protesting that it was not their fault that they had not been there much earlier. Indeed, they were ready to start a few hours after the admiral's dispatch reached the barracks at New York. But their transport was found to be too small to hold them, and it was nearly a month before another vessel could be secured. The battalion was under the command of Colonel P. C. Pope, was quartered in Fort San Filipe and garrisoned Cavite. Repeated appeals for more marines were sent to the United States, and by 1901 five additional battalions were in the Philippines. Some of these, however, were moved down to China, where they took part in the punitive expedition against the Boxers. But at the end of 1901 there were ashore in the Philippines, and in addition to the members of the corps on the ships in those waters, a total of 58 officers and 1,547 enlisted men of the marine corps.

As fast as they arrived they were distributed to different posts, scattered throughout the island, only a few at each one. But they were efficient men all, and they administered the affairs of the districts to which they were assigned with a fine combination of political commonsense and military determination which proved highly effective in ultimately pacifying the islands. The fight for the ultimate subjugation of the revolutionists was a long one, extending over a period of years. To recount its full history would be impossible in a book of this compass, but one or two of the more striking actions fought by the marines may well have brief attention.

In March, 1899, a party of bluejackets and marines dragging a Colt automatic rapid-fire gun and under command of Ensign C. Davis, was advancing from La Loma church along two narrow roads through the forest. They were in hostile territory, and, indeed, were seeking the insurgents who they knew had built strong intrenchments from 10 to 25 feet thick at short intervals along the road on the river bank and along a railroad that paralleled the river. The country was admirably adapted for defense purposes. Dense forests or thickets of bamboo alternated with rice fields, partly submerged. A network of tidewater rivers penetrated the whole.

On March 25th the little detachment discovered a strong force of the enemy entrenched near Cabalahan on the further bank of a river. This force, however, had but little stomach for fighting against modern ordnance. The Colt gun was brought into action and its fire soon drove the Filipinos from their works and far into the dim distance. But a few

MARINES ARE AT HOME ANYWHERE,—IN A TREE AND
IN THE TROPICS

days later, at the Marialo River, the fighting was a little more vigorous. There again the enemy was dug in, but a dense bamboo thicket afforded the advancing marines cover to within about 75 yards of the enemy's trenches. The insurgents had some antiquated guns, but although they made a prodigious noise they did little execution. The American fire, however, was more effective. Under it the insurgents broke and ran, 23 of them throwing up their hands in token of surrender, although a deep river intervening prevented the American forces from seizing them. Some 20 more who tried to escape were mowed down by the Colt gun. The fire was both accurate and murderous. In the body of one of the unfortunate slain were found six holes from the bullets of the rapid-fire gun, all in a space that could be covered by a hand. This weapon, then rather novel, was the precursor of the rapid-fire gun now employed by the tens of thousands on the French battlefields. It was peculiarly effective against the half-armed Filipinos, and as operated by the practiced marines repeatedly silenced the insurgents' artillery at a range as great as 2,000 yards.

In October, 1899, the marines fought a pitched battle as a separate unit without either military or naval aid. A force of 356 of the Soldiers of the Sea, commanded by Lieutenant Colonel Elliott, were ordered to attack the town of Novaleta held by the insurgents. The Spaniards, before the overthrow of their power in the islands, had several times tried to take this place from the natives, but were invariably thwarted, on one occasion sacrificing a whole regiment in their attack. The enemy's work defending the town could only be reached by passing over a causeway raked by the hostile guns. This, however, the marines accomplished with their accustomed dash. But at the end of the causeway the narrow road plunged into a dense thicket of thorn bushes. The ground on either side was low and marshy and intersected by many tidewater streams. The only method of advance was by the road, and this the marines accomplished at a sharp run in the face of a very heavy fire until they reached an open field upon which to deploy. Before them they found a fort with flanking intrenchments running out on either side, and from this position the insurgents were pouring upon the assailants a fierce and effective fire. A separate body of the enemy on the left flank opened upon them with artillery, whereupon the attacking force hastily faced to the left, dropped to the ground and opened a rattling fusilade which soon silenced that attack.

Roused by their officers, they took up the advance again upon the fort, this time deploying through rice fields always knee deep and sometimes almost shoulder deep in mud and water. Struggling through this sort of country was very wearing upon the men, and, coming to a slight dyke which rose a few inches above the flooded field, they threw themselves to the ground for a brief rest. After a very few minutes for recuperation the bugles blew the charge; leaping to their feet, still too breathless to cheer, the marines plunged forward. The insurgents fired but one volley and fled. Novaleta, which had so long defied Spanish power, was in the hands of the Americans.

The insurgent Filipinos, however, were far from being pacified, and two years later, in October, 1901, a battalion of marines under Major Waller was sent from Cavite for the purpose of subduing the natives of the Island of Samar, who were in a state of active insurrection. This expedition was to coöperate with an army force under General T. H. Smith. The marines had the southern part of the island assigned to them for pacification. It was no slight job. The natives, known as Moros, were of the most savage disposition, and born fighters. The country which, of course, they knew well and the Americans not at all, was marvelously adapted for defensive warfare. The expedition had to pursue the foe up fortified cliffs and into caves in the mountains. At one point they had to climb a cliff rising 200 feet from the river and honeycombed with caves occupied by the enemy which could only be reached by means of bamboo scaling ladders. The Moros had provided tons of rocks, which they hurled down on the storming parties. The cliffs were of soft stone, in the nature of pumice, and cut away the men's shoes so that before the end of such a battle they were almost barefoot.

This march across Samar engaged an expedition

of 50 marines, six officers and a force of native scouts and bearers. The food early ran short, the country was waterlogged and the men were almost always soaked to the skin. Early in January, Major Waller, Lieutenant Halford and 13 men who were still in good physical condition, pushed on, seeking relief. But the relief force failing to find assistance returned after a few days. In all the command worked and fought its way through the thickets of Samar for almost two months. They accomplished in the end what they had set out to do, but at grievous cost to themselves. The irony of fate came in the trial by court-martial of Major Waller and other officers after they had performed this exacting duty. It appeared that General Smith had issued orders of a degree of severity not at that time recognized as legitimate in war. Among them was the command that the life of no Filipino male above the age of 12 should be spared. The marine officers were accused of having accepted and acted upon these orders. But as the court-martial found that they were simply obeying the behest of a superior officer no guilt was attached to them.

The marines remained in the Philippines for some time after this expedition. Their handiwork was apparent, not merely in suppressing later outbreaks among the natives, but in encouraging the latter to adopt more civilized forms of social and political life and make themselves fit subjects of the American nation.

CHAPTER XIII

What Peace Means to the Marines.—Fighting the Boxers
in China.—The Mission to King Menelik.—Service in
Cuba.—Nicaragua, Santo Domingo and Haiti.

PEACE between Spain and the United States left
many of the marines in Cuba and Porto Rico, many
in the Philippines and some in camp at Portsmouth,
N. H., where they guarded a large encampment of
Spanish prisoners. In October of 1898, at a peace
jubilee in Philadelphia, the famous Marine Band,
followed by 26 officers and 451 men, paraded, and
shortly thereafter the corps celebrated its first cen-
tennial anniversary—on which occasion Secretary
John D. Long issued a general order praising the
marine corps for its first 100 years of service.

In the following year it enjoyed unusual attention
at the hands of Congress and its permanent force
was fixed at 211 officers and 6,000 enlisted men. It
was a material increase in the peace establishment
of the marine corps, but occupation was soon found
for all. Trouble in Samoa, which was then administered under a vague sort of a joint protectorship
by the United States and Great Britain, called the
marines into action. Two native chiefs were struggling for the so-called throne. It became necessary

for the marines to land, and as usual to have the situation well in hand. They marched upon a native village not far from Apia, but fell into an ambush which necessitated some active fighting before they could keep back the hostiles. The ground was unfavorable for defense, as the marines were caught on a road descending through a defile to a ford, while their assailants were hidden in deep grass. They, however, fought their way out after a long and hard engagement. British marines had joined in the expedition, but were not involved in the actual combat.

The most important event in the history of the marine corps at this period was its participation in the military operations undertaken by a number of the Great Powers as a result of the disturbances caused by the " Boxer " uprising in China. Gradually growing enmity towards missionaries and other foreigners brought about extensive attacks upon Europeans in many parts of China, resulting in considerable loss of life and in the flight of many citizens of various countries to Pekin, where they hoped to find safety under the protection of their several embassies and legations. Unfortunately, however, as this movement spread, the Chinese government, then still of an imperial form, sided with the Boxers. The results of this were attacks on many of the foreign legations in Pekin, the murder of the German ambassador, the loss of a number of lives among the foreign residents and, finally, the siege of that part of Pekin which had been assigned to the foreign embassies.

It soon became apparent that considerable forces would be needed to rescue the Europeans and Americans whose lives were endangered in China. Austria-Hungary, France, Germany, Great Britain, Italy, Japan, Russia and the United States decided to combine their forces, both naval and military, as none of these countries had a sufficiently large force of its own in Chinese waters to permit separate operations with any hope of success. The general plan agreed upon was to capture the city of Tientsin, and then, as quickly as possible, advance from there to Pekin to the relief of the legations which were practically cut off from all communication with the outside world, excepting only occasional short reports which they managed to smuggle through the Chinese lines, and all of which urged the greatest possible speed if a general massacre in Pekin was to be averted.

The United States had a number of warships in Chinese waters, but the landing forces which they could supply were entirely insufficient for the work on hand. As usual, therefore, the marine corps was called upon to furnish additional forces. Fortunately a fairly powerful force of marines was stationed at that time in the Philippines. Of these six officers and 101 enlisted men, together with several companies of the Ninth U. S. Infantry embarked from Cavite, P. I., on June 14, 1900, for

Taku, China, where they were augmented by the addition of two officers and 30 men upon their arrival on June 18th. The marines were under the command of Major L. W. T. Waller, and landed on the 19th, immediately beginning their advance towards Tientsin and reaching without opposition Tong-Ku, about 12 miles from Taku. This was the terminus of a railway leading into the interior, but the track had been torn up and further advance was delayed until it had been repaired. Finally, on the 20th, 130 United States marines, together with 440 Russians, were sent forward by train. They were soon followed by British, German and additional Russian forces.

When within 12 miles of Tientsin it was decided to disembark and await further reënforcements and the marines, together with the Russians, bivouacked that night. The next day Major Waller yielded to the arguments of the Russian officers and joined in the immediate advance against Tientsin which they recommended. The small force was led by a detachment of marines with a Colt automatic gun, while the balance of the marines formed the rear guard. Early in the morning of June 21st they reached the Chinese part of the city. Soon afterwards, at a point almost opposite the imperial arsenal, they were met with a heavy and steadily increasing fire coming from the walls. For some time the marines' Colt gun succeeded in controlling this fire, but it finally jammed and became useless.

The Chinese were much superior in number and, of course, held strongly fortified positions. It, therefore, became necessary for the Americans and Russians to withdraw, the marines again forming the rear guard. The Chinese followed for four hours, but were unable to seriously disturb the orderly withdrawal of the American and Russian troops. Three marines were killed and seven wounded. Altogether this little handful of marines and soldiers had marched about 30 miles within 12 hours and fought for the best part of five hours. The retreat stopped at the same place from which the advance had been started the day before. There English, Russian and German reënforcements came up during the night and brought the total force up to about 2,000 men. The next day a new advance was started early in the morning. Major Waller had attached himself with his small force to the British troops, of which he formed the advance guard. Within a few hours the Chinese were encountered and for more than five hours were steadily driven back toward Tientsin, which was entered early that afternoon, June 24th, and all the foreigners besieged there by the Chinese were relieved.

Shortly thereafter the Russians attempted to capture the imperial arsenal in front of which Major Waller had been forced to begin his retreat on his first advance. A small detachment of marines was sent to their assistance and, together with a British company, were among the first to charge over the parapet and to assist in driving about 7,000 Chinese out of this strong position. In five days Major Waller's marines had marched almost 100 miles, fighting practically all the way, even though they hardly ever had more than one meal a day. In spite of these hardships, increased still more by intense heat, they were always willing and cheerful and the commanding officers of the various other detachments expressed their admiration of the marines' work in glowing terms.

It was during one of the halts in the advance that Major Waller showed the stuff the marines were made of. All of the troops were wearied with long and hard marching and with persistent fighting under heavy odds. A council of war was called at night to determine whether the march should be interrupted for a period of rest or whether it should be resumed the following morning. One after another, French, British, Japanese and other commanders voted for the period of rest. When it came to Major Waller's turn to vote, he said:

" Gentlemen, I have no desire to influence your judgment or to dictate your actions, but whether the rest of the expedition goes on or not, the United States marines will renew the march at sunrise."

The whole expedition was on the march at sunrise.

Another anecdote relative to this expedition is well known in the marine corps. After the expedition had reached Pekin it was still necessary to break its way into the walled city. Assaults were directed against several of the gates. Company D, Captain Long, was the first to reach the gates of the Forbidden City. The men had no artillery with which to batter down the barriers, but that did not stop them. " Wreck " Kelly was the thinnest man in the company. That qualified him to crawl under the gate, but halfway through he stuck.

" Give us a shove, boys! " he cried; and the men of Company D shoved to such effect that his blouse and trousers were almost torn from his body and considerable of his skin became mingled with the soil of China. But they got him through, and he opened the gate from the inside.

No one thought much about it until that night, when Kelly suddenly ejaculated:

" By jingo, boys, suppose there'd been a Chink with a knife on the other side of that gate! "

It had just occurred to him.

Tientsin, however, was entered, but not subdued. Chinese reënforcements had come up and had entered the Chinese part of the city. On the other hand, the allied forces, too, had received reënforcements, and on July 9th it was finally decided to make an assault against the Chinese right. In this action, which proved successful, the Americans participated. Two days later, July 11th, an additional force of Americans, amounting to 18 officers and 300 men, arrived at Tientsin from Cavite, just in time to take part in the assault on the walled city of Tientsin, which was begun on the 13th. The marines were ordered to advance along the mud wall in a northerly direction and arrived at the south gate two hours afterwards. Soon after that they joined the British in an attack on the extreme left of the Chinese. Across difficult territory, the marines advanced by rushes to a line of trenches about 800 yards from the enemy. There the Chinese attempted twice to drive back the Americans by flank attacks, but were unsuccessful both times. In the early part of the evening, it became necessary to withdraw from this position, an operation which was carried out in spite of its difficulties with entire success. Early the next morning, the allied forces entered the walled city through the south gate, which by then had been blown in. The city was found filled with the bodies of Chinamen. The survivors of the garrison fled and, apparently, were sufficiently cowed to leave the allied forces in undisputed possession of the entire city. During the battle of July 13th, in which 5,650 men took part on the allied side, 900 of whom were Americans, the American losses amounted to 24 killed, 98 wounded and 8 missing, out of total losses in killed and wounded of 750.

In the meantime, there had been going on a heroic struggle against tremendous odds in the city of Pekin. Early in 1900, two detachments of marines had been sent directly to Pekin to serve as a guard at the United States legation. There were only

54 men under Captain J. T. Myers and N. H. Hall. They arrived at Pekin on May 31st and were quartered next to the legation compound. For some days nothing happened. On June 6th, however, the railroad communications were interrupted, and from then on there was hardly a day that passed without attacks against one or the other foreign legations or some of the other buildings in which the foreign refugees from all parts of China had been quartered. Gradually it became more and more apparent that the Chinese authorities were supporting the Boxers, and on June 18th a demand was made upon the foreign ministers to leave the city within 24 hours and to retire to Tientsin. This demand was refused and indirectly resulted in the murder of the German minister on June 20th while on his way to the Tsungli Yamen to bear this refusal as the chosen representative of his colleagues. Day by day now the position of the besieged foreigners became more and more desperate. Incessant attacks during day and night necessitated practically continuous service on the part of every member of the small force defending the legations, growing smaller and smaller every day through losses in killed, wounded and sick. Ammunition gradually, but steadily, decreased, and so did the food supply. In spite of all these difficulties, however, the various legation guards held out. Barricades had been built and were held, not only against frequent assaults, but at times even formed the base for courageous

charges in the face of the enemy. One of the most notable of these was made by the American marines under Captain Myers on July 2nd. A number of rifles and some ammunition were captured, two of the marines losing their lives. On July 16th an armistice was made with the enemy, but firing soon began again.

To the United States marines fell the most difficult and dangerous portion of the defense by reason of the proximity of the United States legation to the great city wall and the main city gate over which the large guns of the Chinese had been planted. The American legation, together with the position held by the marines on the wall, was the key to the whole situation. Twice the marines were driven from the wall, and once they were forced to abandon the legation, but each time they immediately retook it and held it to the last against several hundred Chinese.

Relief, however, was in sight. After the battle of Tientsin reënforcements began to arrive from all parts of the world. Among these were another battalion of marines under Major Biddle, who now assumed command over all the marines, 482 strong, and on August 4th joined the advance upon Pekin. Two days later the American forces fought the only engagement in which they took part on the road to Pekin. Although the enemy's artillery fire was very accurate and they were greatly superior in numbers, they were promptly put to flight.

Finally, on August 14th and 15th the attack against Pekin began. Again the marines were in the lead. They took a position over the Chienmen gate, clearing the barricades to permit the artillery to come into action on the pagoda. After stubborn resistance the enemy was driven out. The west gate was taken on the 16th and the marines held these positions until the 19th, when they moved into a position in the Tartar City. Not until September 28th were the marines withdrawn from Pekin when they returned to Cavite, P. I.

But not all the life of the marines is made up of storming parties, punitive expeditions and policing barbaric lands. At the Pan-American Exposition in Buffalo in 1901 a detachment was encamped and gave exhibition drills daily for the entertainment of guests. Later, the same detachment acted as the guard of honor on the funeral train of President McKinley, who was assassinated in Buffalo. At the many expositions which followed, marines were always represented and the exhibition of their camps no doubt added greatly to the wide recognition of the character and service of the corps. Police service was rendered by American marines in two of the great earthquake disasters of the world, that at San Francisco in 1906 and one at Messina, Italy, in 1908.

A picturesque expedition, somewhat reminiscent of the one during our war with the Barbary powers already described, was that undertaken by a body of 18 marines commanded by Captain George C. Thorpe to the then unknown town of Addis Abeba in Abyssinia. The state department knew something about this locality, although that knowledge was and is denied to the average man, and, as it desired to negotiate a treaty with King Menelik, had asked for an escort to convoy a diplomatic agent to that monarch's court. A gunboat took the party to Somaliland, but thence the more primitive conveyance of camels and mules was necessary to take the party across a desert and over a mountain range. The trouble came when the native escorts, who acted as guides and dragomen, threatened to strike unless they should be allowed to dictate the route. Captain Thorpe was suspicious. The leaders of the natives wanted to go by an all-desert route or none, and the American officers conjectured that their purpose was to get the little force into the desert, there abandon them and return for plunder days later after heat and thirst had put an end to the expedition. He refused to acquiesce in their demand. At first they threatened, then gathering up their weapons, started to leave. Instantly, Captain Thorpe commanded his men to seize and bind the ringleader. It was done.

Calling an interpreter, the captain said:

" Tell that man he is going with us over the route we have selected, and going feet foremost at the end of that rope, the other end being made fast to a mule."

The prisoner raised a frantic yell. His fellow Dankalis at once made as if to charge upon the party, but the marines stood firm and on looking in the muzzles of their rifles the natives yielded. The expedition continued on its way with its now thoroughly subdued guides. Its leader said afterwards that it was fortunate that the bold demeanor of the marines had settled the controversy without bloodshed. Had one of the Dankalis been killed the tribesmen throughout the desert would have rallied to oppose the expedition at every step and its members ultimately would have been slaughtered.

In 1902 Congress increased the total enlisted strength of the corps to 6,812 men and conferred the rank of major general upon its commander. Only a year later the number went up to 7,502 enlisted men, and in 1908 the corps was allowed by Congress 8,771 enlisted men.

In 1906 the Latin-American tendency to come to blows over their elections manifested itself in Cuba. Open insurrection broke out against President Palma, who was a candidate for reëlection, and to maintain order and assure the continuance of democratic government the United States intervened in accordance with the Cuban treaty. As usual, the marine corps led the forces of occupation. At various times during that year five expeditionary battalions were sent to Cuba, and the ships of the squadron then in Caribbean waters were stripped of marines until 2,795 enlisted men and 97 officers were ashore. There was no fighting. The Cubans yielded readily to the display of force, and the troops were gradually withdrawn, with the exception of one provisional regiment that remained on the island until 1909. The success with which order was maintained without friction or armed collisions spoke highly for the diplomatic tact of the marine officers.

Guantanamo, on the south shore of Cuba where our marines had established their camp during the Spanish War, was ceded to the United States as a naval base by the treaty terminating that war. It has become the largest naval station in the West Indies, and detachments of marines are there at all times, sometimes preparing for expeditions to Central America or Mexican points. Central America, in fact, has received a very considerable share of marine attention. Nicaragua at various times has found it necessary to invite or to enjoy without invitation, the attention of this corps of trouble destroyers. In 1909 a regiment of 709 men and 32 officers occupied Corinto for several months. Bluefields engaged the attention of a smaller force in 1910. The largest and the most important of the Nicaragua expeditions, comprising a force of some 1,200 men, was landed in August, 1912, and remained six months. This last force was the only one of the three that came into actual armed conflict with the natives. The usual revolution was progressing, and, upon instructions from Washington, the marines supported the governmental forces against the insurrectos. Two considerable battles were fought in October. The first was the capture of the insurgent fortress, Massaya, in October. There the marines stormed Barranca and Cayotepe hills, both formidable positions, the latter being a steep elevation of about 300 feet, well protected by barbed wire and entrenchments. It had long defied the government forces and was considered impregnable. Even before reaching its base, the marines had encountered grave obstacles to their progress. The rebels had torn up the railroad and attempted to destroy the rolling stock, but both were repaired by the marines, who thereupon acted as engineers, firemen and brakemen. Reaching the scene of battle, they were for a while in a hollow exposed to the fire of the Nicaraguans who were intrenched on the heights above. After a period of rifle fire the marines started out in two columns on opposite sides of the hill. They followed the time-honored tactics of a brief rush forward, a drop, a period of firing at the enemy and then another advance. Their attack was irresistible, and with the loss of but a few men they carried the crest of Cayotepe. Thereupon, the guns mounted there were turned upon the works on the other hill, which in its turn was speedily evacuated. Four of our men were killed and eight wounded while two days later, in an attack on the city of Leon, three were killed and four wounded.

Nicaragua was not yet quieted when the black population of Santo Domingo broke out in bloody revolution. It was in 1912 that trouble first arose there, and a large expedition of marines made its way to the island and looked at the shore over the guards of their vessel. Apparently, their moral influence exerted at that distance was sufficient, for they returned to their post without landing. But in 1914 two companies from a force then serving in Haiti were sent ashore and policed the island, until in 1916 matters became so serious that a more considerable expedition was sent in. The American legation and consulate in Santo Domingo were occupied, and gradually all the principal ports of the island were taken under American control. The people fought savagely. A regiment commanded by Colonel Pendleton, finding it necessary to march some 75 miles inland to Santiago, had to fight every step of the way, finding all bridges destroyed and the road blocked by the retreating blacks. Not until the revolutionists laid down their arms, and agreed to the erection of a provisional government under the auspices of the marine corps were the hostilities abated.

When this was accomplished, however, the marines devoted their attention and energies to more peaceful undertakings. In Santo Domingo, and the adjoining republic of Haiti, they demonstrated that a body of men picked primarily for fighting purposes and acknowledged to be at the head of the military

A WINTER MORNING IN LORRAINE

profession could adapt themselves to the task of restoring peaceful institutions and bringing order and wise civil administration out of the chaos wrought by revolution.

They established sanitary and hygienic regulations, so necessary in the tropics, and enforced them. Wagon tracks were developed into real roads. Telephone and telegraph wires were strung and their proper management was taught to the natives. Railroads were put in order and perhaps for the first time in their history maintained real schedules. Schools were opened, children made to attend them, while the parents were taught the novel duty of keeping themselves and their progeny reasonably clean. Wandering bands of brigands were suppressed and property protected. Customs were collected and used for the benefit of the people, or the foreign creditors of the country, without deduction for graft. The finances of both countries were gradually put in order, and industry and trade took on new life. The marines were leaders in all this work, acting not merely as policemen, but guides, philosophers and friends to the people. After 1916 they had little need for the exercise of force, except for the suppression of isolated bands of bandits in the less accessible parts of the country.

The problems which confronted them in Haiti were much the same as those in Santo Domingo. There, too, rival factions of native politicians sought to substitute bullets for ballots and carry elections by force, or, failing that, by the more sinister method of assassination. The marines at first protected the American legation and American property at Port au Prince, the capital. In time, as the revolutionary activities spread, it became necessary to protect the people against themselves. Some 2,500 men in all were landed, under command of Colonel Waller, and for a time had their hands full with real fighting. The actual revolutionists were not hard to handle. But bands of brigands were many, and, as they had only plunder to live upon, fought savagely for the maintenance of their industry.

The Haitians called them the "Cacos," and against them the marines waged unrelenting warfare. The last band, some 120 strong, fortified themselves in a ruin dating back to the time of the English occupation on the crest of a high hill known as Fort Rivière. To this point they were followed by a mere handful of marines, 27 only, under the command of Major S. D. Butler. In his report of the action, Major Butler says:

"Rivière, on the top of Montagne Noire, about 4,000 feet above the sea, was an old French bastion fort, about 200 feet on a side, with thick walls of brick and stone, loopholed, and ranging from 15 to 25 feet high. The original entrance had been on the northern side, but had been blocked, a small breach in the southern wall being used in its stead. This breach in the wall, being the only entrance, was naturally covered by the defenders on the inside, making passage through it into the fort a very dangerous feat for at least the first man.

" Notwithstanding the fact that the fire of the defenders was constantly passing through this hole in the wall, Sergeant Ross L. Iams, of the Fifth Company, unhesitatingly jumped through, closely followed by Private Samuel Gross, of the Twenty-third Company, and the remainder of the Fifth Company in single file, the breach being too small to admit more than one man at a time. The action of these two men in entering the breach in the wall of Fort Rivière and the amount of courage required to do so are fully appreciated by me, who was close by at the time.

" I have been under fire several times myself and have never felt before such a keen desire to be somewhere—in fact, anywhere—else as I did when I realized that I might have to go through that hole first. While in this mood of indecision, my painful impressions were relieved by the action of Iams and Gross. I don't know whether I would have gotten up the courage to jump through that hole or not; but these two faithful friends of mine relieved me of all embarrassment, which embarrassment might have become so intense as to cause me to fall back upon my prerogative of a commanding officer with field rank and seek employment in some other part of the field of action."

In policing Haiti the marines were in constant danger of murderous and treacherous attack. Not infrequently, a few men would be established at some outpost and would have to beat off great mobs of natives who thought to rush them and overwhelm them by numbers. In one instance, one man alone was thus attacked by a considerable band, but fought with such desperation as to defeat their murderous purpose. This was Corporal Aubrey N. Haley, who was afterwards promoted to sergeant for his gallantry on this occasion. A brief condensation of his report will not be out of place here, it being noted

that the gendarmes referred to were native policemen:

"About three A. M. on the 29th I was suddenly awakened by the sound of rifle shots, the yells—*Cacos viva
Cacos!*—and a rush and stampede right into the gendarme
barracks. I thought at first it was a dream. In less than
a minute, and before I could get dressed, I could tell by
the yells from both sides that the gendarmes were taken by
surprise, scattered and running, leaving me at the bandits'
mercy. I was tempted to go out to aid the gendarmes; but
my gendarme cook grabbed me and said: 'You *pas sorter!*'
meaning 'You cannot go out!' It seemed like less than a
minute from the time I was awakened until the bandits were
trying to burst in on me through the windows and front
door. I had my shoes on, no socks, and shoes unlaced;
trousers on, fastened at the waist only; and shirt on, not
buttoned. If you could have seen a picture of me then—I
looked like a wild man. I was—almost.

"I had my rifle loaded and bayonet fixed; had chased
the cook to the rear door; and at that very instant they
seemed to pound on all the doors at once. Firing was fierce
from all sides. If you ever heard an old rifle bark mine did!

"I fired two shots through the door, which were successful, from the blood found there afterward. I immediately opened the window next to the door with the end of
my bayonet, and right in front of the window was a big
black 'buck' with a rifle. At the crack of my rifle he
tumbled like he was struck on the head with an ax.

"I rushed to the side window, which was almost broken
open, pushed it open as I had the other, and there was another
bandit right under the window, and two or three standing
off a few steps. At the crack of my rifle he tumbled also.
Fired the last shot in my rifle at another, but do not know
whether I hit him. I loaded my rifle again and fired three
shots at a lad about thirty yards away before he tumbled.

"By this time there was not a soul to be seen; I had
three lying in the yard groaning and struggling for life. I
kept the windows well guarded, while the cook kept the

rear door covered. I could tell by their horn that they were retreating toward Castellure. It was about an hour before I learned that the cook had killed a bandit from the rear door."

The marines are still in Haiti. They are administering it under the provisions of a treaty with the country, but conducting its affairs in association with civil representatives of the United States so well that the progressive men among the population are for the first time encouraged in the endeavor to bring the country up to civilized standards. As rapidly as possible authority is being reinvested in the natives. The Haitian constabulary made up in the main of native policemen, with a leaven of officers and men from the marines and the navy, is proving a useful force for the maintenance of law and order. For the work done in their behalf the Haitians have shown their gratitude by solemnly declaring war upon Germany when the United States entered upon that conflict. The opinion of the Kaiser concerning this defiance is not known.

What for a time seemed to be the beginning of a serious war with Mexico, which could only have ended in our annexation of large portions of that country, occurred early in 1914, when a large detachment of marines, followed by troops of the regular army, were landed at Vera Cruz. It was, in a sense, a punitive expedition. Our flag had been fired upon at Tampico, and the then president of the sorely racked and torn Mexican republic, Huerta, refused, or at any rate stubbornly neglected, to make due reparation. Moreover, a shipload of arms from Germany was reported to be approaching Vera Cruz, designed for the insurgents, and the United States professed its purpose of preventing their landing.

Both as a punitive expedition and as a check to the landing of the munitions of war this enterprise was a failure. The flag was never saluted. No apology was ever forthcoming. The arms were successfully landed at another port. But into the bickerings and political disputes that grew out of this expedition it is not my purpose to enter here. Enough to say that, after the fashion of the marines, the first regiment was landed on April 22nd under a heavy fire, wading ashore from their boats and fighting their way through the streets of the Mexican city, with snipers blazing away at them from every roof top and window. The custom house was seized, and while the Mexican army withdrew from the town the enraged citizens for two or three days maintained a harassing fire by which four marines were killed and 15 wounded. Once in full possession of the city, the marines compelled a surrender by its people of all their arms, and the sniping ceased. Friendly relations were soon reëstablished. The city was cleaned up. What a tremendous amount of cleaning up the marines have done in the medievally dirty towns of tropical America history will some day record in a book on hygiene given over to that topic. Sanitary rules were introduced and enforced, and, by way of finally capturing the volatile Latin-American heart, daily concerts were given in the plaza by the ships' bands.

The whole United States thought that the force thus established in Vera Cruz would not be withdrawn but would proceed to Mexico City, and finally subjugate the Mexicans whose turbulent and revolutionary activities had made the relations between the two countries exceedingly strained. In this expectation, however, the country was disappointed. Although an American army under General Funston was added to the marine force on shore, the invasion went no further than the occupation of Vera Cruz for some months. Perhaps it was as well, though sentiment in the United States was strongly in favor of pacifying Mexico by making it part of this nation. Had this been undertaken we should have been in the midst of a Mexican war at the moment when the aggressions of Germany compelled us most unwillingly to enter heart and soul into the colossal combat in Europe.

CHAPTER XIV

The United States Enters the European War.—Increase of
the Marine Corps.—Characteristics of the Corps.—Requirements for Enlistment.—The Marines in France.—
Battles of Château Thierry and Bois de Belleau.—Some
Personal Records.—The Flying Corps.

THE United States had ample warning that the
inexorable movement of events would compel its
participation in the great European war, yet when
the moment came for its entrance upon the conflict
it was, as always, utterly unprepared for the
struggle.

Though the storm had been raging in Europe for
nearly three years, gradually extending its borders
so as to take in, one after the other, nations that
had hoped to remain neutral, the government of the
United States clung to the hope that it might remain
immune. The battle-lightnings flashed and struck in
Asia and in Africa, but we continued to trust that
some omnipotent power would avert them from our
shores. Even when the Kaiser's murderous hand
tore the *Lusitania* apart, and sent scores of our
people to a cruel death, a powerful element among
our citizenship scouted the idea that we should
avenge them by force of arms.

The months upon months that were spent in the

interchange of diplomatic notes with Germany might have been most profitable to our country had preparations for war been pressed, while efforts to avert it were being earnestly urged. We might, in that time, have raised armies, created a store of munitions of war, strengthened our navy and prepared ourselves for the struggle which everyone, save politicians and pacifists, saw was inevitable. But we did nothing of the sort, and when, on April 7, 1917, the President declared war upon Germany we were just as unprepared as when in 1812 we declared war upon England, or upon Spain in 1898. We had sat often enough in the dear school of experience but had apparently learned nothing there.

At the moment of the declaration of war the United States Marine Corps possessed an actual strength of 344 officers and 10,896 enlisted men. Under the law of 1916 its authorized strength was 597 officers and 14,981 men, but it had never been recruited up to that number. The law wisely conferred upon the President emergency power to increase the authorized enlistment to 17,000 men, and this power he exercised a few days before the declaration of war.

A great part of the marine corps was, at the outbreak of the war, serving outside the borders of the United States, some of the men on stations whence they could not well be spared, as those in Haiti and Santo Domingo, and in the Philippines. Comparatively few were, at that time, stationed on ships—about 1,750 in all.

May 22, 1917, Congress enacted a law providing
for the increase of the numbers of the marine corps
during the war to a total of 1,197 officers and
30,000 enlisted men. Up to the present moment
(1918) all enlistments in the corps are purely voluntary. The draft has never yet been called on to
fill the ranks of the Soldiers of the Sea, and the
qualifications for enlistment have been, as will presently be shown, most rigid. How greatly the
thought of active service stimulated the ambition of
those fit for membership in this *corps d'élite* is
shown by the jump in the number of enlistments from
4,068 in 1915 to 17,748 in 1917. During the period
between April 7, 1917, the date of the declaration
of war, to June 30, 1917, the close of that fiscal
year, no less than 12,108 gallant young Americans
came forward and signified their desire to be among
those " First to Fight."

Membership in the marine corps, however, is
not lightly won. The requirements are high, much
higher than in any other branch of the service, and
the scrutiny of the applicants most rigid. It may
be worth while to depart here from the historical
narrative, and outline briefly what the youth who
seeks membership in the corps must bring to it, and
what will be his duties, emoluments and chances for
advancement if accepted. It must be kept in mind
that the conditions described existed in the fall of
1918, and were, of course, subject to change in the
exigencies of war.

To begin with, the applicant must be either native

born, or a naturalized citizen of the United States, and statistics show that those native born are in the great majority. The marine corps is American through and through. In height the applicant must be above five feet five inches, and in weight not less than 130 nor more than 245 pounds. The age limit is between 18 and 36. Candidates must be unmarried, of strong constitution, not addicted to drugs or liquor and able to read and write. After their physical examination, they are given a final test by an officer who judges of their moral and mental fitness for the corps. Even in the rush to fill the ranks during the great war, the percentage of rejections was extremely high, averaging nearly 90 per cent.

What does the man get if accepted? That question is all important to the man who, for the first time, appears before the recruiting officer. The rate of pay, the nature of the service expected of him and the opportunities for advancement are the great factors in determining him to join the corps. Particularly the last, for to form an élite corps such as the marines aspire to maintain, ambitious youths must be appealed to, and the first thought of an ambitious man is for promotion.

Let us consider these subjects in order. The pay of a newly enlisted marine is $30 a month. Board and lodging, clothing, medical attendance, practically all of what are termed the necessities of life, are furnished him without charge. His pay goes up with his period of service and promotions won until it may reach $75 a month. By individual effort he can win still higher pay. Expertness with the rifle is rewarded by an increase of $2, $3 or $5 a month as he becomes a " Marksman," " Sharp-shooter " or " Expert Rifleman." Honest and faithful service wins a good-conduct medal for each period of enlistment—four years—and upon reën-listment each such medal adds 83 cents a month to his regular pay. While serving on ship or outside the United States, except in Hawaii or Porto Rico, he gets a 20 per cent increase, and if, on ship, he is assigned to duty with the great guns, his pay is increased from $2 to $10 per month, according to his expertness and the class of gun he serves.

Marine corps officials declare that very few men, and those only newcomers in the service, draw the minimum pay.

If the marine is thrifty, any savings he may deposit with the government are held for him and repaid with four per cent interest when he leaves the service. If he is prudent and desires to make provision for his dependents, or for himself in case of disabling injury, he can take out insurance with the government at the rate of 67 cents a month for each thousand dollars. This insurance is paid to his dependents in the form of an endowment. That is to say, in the case of a marine carrying $10,000 in insurance, his dependent relatives, after his death, would receive $57.50 a month for 20 years, or should he be disabled he would receive a like amount from the government for that period.

But this is purely voluntary insurance. The marine need not take it unless he so desires. The government, however, insures him without action, or payment on his part. Should he be killed in action, and leave a widow, she will be cared for as long as she remains unmarried, with payments ranging from $25 to $57.50 a month according to the number of children. Should the man be totally disabled he will receive from the government from $30 to $75 a month.

It will be seen, therefore, that if a marine prudently takes out voluntary insurance that, with the government guarantee, assures him a comfortable income in case of disabling injuries.

Once enlisted the recruits are sent to the marine barracks at Mare Island, California, and at Paris Island, South Carolina. There for two months, five hours a day, he studies and practices the following subjects:

Care of Clothing and Person.
School of the Recruit.
Physical Drill with and without Arms.
Manual of Arms.
Packing Knapsacks and Blanket Rolls.
Patrolling.
Signaling.
Artillery Drill.
Pitching and Striking Tents.
Extended Order, Advance and Rear Guard.
Boxing.

Individual Cooking.
Military Courtesies.
Carrying Messages.
Nomenclature of the Rifle.
Squad and Company Drill.
Bayonet Exercise.
Guard Duty.
Street Riot Drill.
Wall Scaling.
Field Fortifications.
Athletics.
Swimming.
First Aid to the Injured.
Handling Boats.

Thereafter, during the continuance of the present war, he will probably be transferred to the big training camp at Quantico, Virginia, where he will be taught trench-digging, hand-to-hand fighting, liquid fire defense, gas attacking, etc.

Thus perfected in the art of war, he is sent to the front. Then begins a richly variegated life. At this moment of writing, marines are fighting with Pershing in France, serving on our battleships in the cold gray waters of the North Sea, guarding our legation at Pekin, China, protecting American interests in Nicaragua and Cuba and doing really constructive work in Haiti and Santo Domingo. They are on ships in all quarters of the globe, and on guard at all our navy yards at home. In the past they have served in Egypt, Algiers, Tripoli, Mexico, China, Japan, Korea, Cuba, Porto Rico, Panama, Nicaragua, Santo Domingo, Formosa, Sumatra, Hawaii, Samoa, Guam, Alaska, the Philippine Islands and Haiti.

A poet of the marine corps—they are a tuneful lot—has described in verse this highly varied and exciting life thus:

> "They've fought with Tripolitan pirates,
> They've handed the English a few,
> They've bowed the proud necks of the Spanish and Mex,
> And they've walloped the Chinaman too.
> They've reasoned with Zulu and Malay,
> They've fought in our own Civil War,
> And they've had a few scraps with the little brown Japs
> And with Gu-gus way out in Samar."

Most of these activities have taken place in times of peace. In fact, the marine gives a new reading to the ancient adage, " In time of peace prepare for war."

Ambition always beats high in the American heart. The marine corps would never have secured the high order of men it possesses if the opportunities for advancement were not plentiful. What these opportunities are is best set forth in the following extract from an official handbook issued by the recruiting bureau:

During the period of the war all commissions in the marine corps will go to worthy enlisted men. If you would be a commissioned officer in the corps you must first enter the ranks. The Napoleonic idea that every private soldier carries a marshal's baton in his knapsack is literally true in the marine corps and all the higher ranks are open to worthy young men of character and ability. Vacancies are constantly occurring in the noncommissioned grades, and men are selected to fill them in accordance with their records, individual merits and ability to perform the duties of the higher positions. Encouragement and opportunity are given to young men of good character and ability to remain in the service and climb to the higher positions of trust and honor.

One hundred enlisted men are picked from the marine corps and navy each year, by competitive examination, to be sent to the Naval Academy at Annapolis, Md., there to be educated and trained as officers, and, upon graduation, they will be commissioned in the marine corps or navy.

The law also provides for the promotion of noncommissioned officers to the warrant rank in the grades of marine gunner and quartermaster clerk. Such officers receive from approximately $1,125 to $2,500 a year and are entitled to the same privileges of retirement as warrant officers of the navy. The number of warrant officers of the marine corps is not very large and appointment to warrant rank is restricted to competent and worthy noncommissioned officers.

After the declaration of war, the first transport to leave American shores was loaded to the guards with United States marines. During these early stages of American participation in the war, it is not permissible to give either the numbers of the detachments or the place to which they were destined. Enough for the moment to say that they were ordered to prepare the way for the great American army that presently thereafter came pouring overseas, sometimes as many as 350,000 in a month, to the ports and camps which had been prepared for them by the marines. The latter form but a small body of men in comparison with the hundreds of thousands of soldiers, but they are recognized as a picked corps—in fact, what the Germans have taught us to call shock troops. There were, indeed, in the late summer of 1918 only about 14,000 marines in all upon the other side, while at the time when Ludendorff bade fair to overwhelm France, and pounce upon Paris in his great drive of March 21, 1918, there were but 6,000 marines in all in France.

But Frenchmen, and particularly French officers, say that handful of United States marines saved Paris.

It is early yet to write the history of a conflict the latter phases of which are still raging. But let me try to put into some consecutive form the story of this fight of the marines which saved Paris, as it may be gleaned from the letters of eyewitnesses who told all the censor at that time would permit.

It was June in Picardy. The great drive which Ludendorff had started on the 21st of March had reached its zenith. The German wave had rushed forward, halted, pushed forward again, recoiled and, gathering new strength, plunged onward irresistibly. The world, outside the Teutonic alliance, looked on aghast. The crime, the calamity of a Boche occupation of Paris seemed inevitable. The foe swept on past all the allied defenses. He reached Château Thierry. He crossed to the south bank of the Marne.

And then the unexpected, the incredible, the miraculous happened.

At Château Thierry was a division—the Second— of American troops. They had just reached the front from Paris after a hard journey of 30 consecutive hours in motor trucks. Some of the trucks broke down and the men had to hike it. They hiked cheerfully, rather than risk losing the impending battle.

At the front, the marines were ordered to act as supports to the French, who were opposing the advancing foe in a series of rear-guard actions. You see, these "leathernecks," as the marines call themselves, were still new to European warfare, and the masters of strategy were a trifle shy about putting them in the first rank of the defense. The plan was that the French should hold out as long as possible against the advancing foe, then fall back, passing through the lines of the Americans, who would then take up the defensive fight. The marines somewhat questioned the wisdom of going into a fight all prepared to fall back. It was not their way. But they figured that after the French had retired they could fight the battle their own way.

According to programme, the French held the enemy on June 1st and on the 2nd came dropping wearily back by twos and threes. The Americans—three battalions of marines, a regiment of infantry and a detachment of engineers—deployed out along a line of about seven kilometers long and awaited the attack. It came on the evening of the 4th. Floyd Gibbons, a correspondent of the Chicago *Tribune*, who was desperately wounded in the course of the fighting, describes that action thus:

" About five o'clock in the evening of June 4th the enemy attacked anew toward the American left, where it joined on with the French. They advanced through a wheat field in platoon columns, in perfect order, flushed with many successes, confident of victory.

" And then the Americans opened up. They showered the oncoming waves with shrapnel until the fields seemed to be sprouting thousands of magnificent white daisies. Machine guns and rifle fire raked the German ranks. The leathernecks took careful aim before every shot. Unhurried, unflustered, they worked their weapons as though on the target range. French observers were amazed; they had never seen such rifle shooting. That soldiers should sight carefully in the heat of battle was something new in European warfare, where the rifle has grown to be something on which to stick a bayonet.

"No troops could stand against that fire. The Boches wavered—came on again. Why lie about the enemy? In mass formation they fight like brave men—none better. Twice they hesitated, stopped: twice they resumed the advance.

"Then they broke. They broke and started to crawl off through the standing grain. The Americans could see the wheat sway as though stirred by a stiff breeze, and they whipped those areas with bullets.

"A French airman came swooping down from the blue. Wildly exultant, he signaled to our troops 'Bravo!' and darted back to give a new range to the artillery. The latter caught a German battery moving into position and annihilated it."

The navy department, shortly after the battle, gave out with justifiable pride a letter from an eye-witness of the fighting, evidently a marine, or one who stood with the marines. For some cautious purpose the department concealed the name of the writer, but the style suggests Mr. Gibbons once more. We quote the description of the opening of the battle:

"We had installed ourselves in a house in La Voie Chatel, a little village between Champillon and Lucy-le-Bocage. From one side we had observation of the north and northeast. They came out on a wonderfully clear day in two columns across a wheat field. We could see the two twin brown columns advancing in perfect order until two-thirds of the columns, we judged, were in sight.

"The rifle and machine gun fire was incessant, and over-head shrapnel was bursting. Then the shrapnel came on the target at each shot. The white patches would roll away, and we could see that some of the columns were still there, slowed up, and it seemed perfect suicide for them to try. You couldn't begrudge a tribute to their pluck, at that.

" Then, under that deadly fire and a barrage of rifle and machine-gun fire, the Boche stopped. It was too much for any men. They burrowed in or broke to the cover of the woods, and you could follow them by the ripples of the green wheat as they raced for cover."

The writer declared the rifle fire of the marines amazed the French who saw it.

" That men should fire deliberately, and use their sights, and adjust their range," he says, " was beyond their experience. It must have had a telling effect on the morale of the Boche, for it was something they had not counted on. As a matter of fact, after pushing back the weakened French and then running up against a stone-wall defense, they were literally ' up in the air ' and more than stopped. We found that out later from prisoners, for the Germans never knew we were in the front line when they made that attack. They were absolutely mystified at the manner in which the defense stiffened up, until they found that our troops were in line."

After the first day's success the marines moved forward to assault the Bois de Belleau, and the town of Bouresche. The former was a dense wood, cut up with gullies and littered with bowlders. In it were about 1,000 of the Boches plentifully supplied with machine guns, which they planted behind protecting rocks, hid in the gullies, or ensconced in the protecting thickets. North of the Bois the foe had about 20 machine guns on an elevated plateau. In all, the position was, if not impregnable, at least a very formidable one, as the marines found to their cost when they attacked it without due artillery preparation. They were driven back both from the

AS THEY LOOKED ON THEIR WAY TO CHATEAU-THIERRY, WHERE THEY
STOPPED THE GERMAN RUSH ON PARIS

wood and from the plateau. The former position was indeed reached by one platoon under Lieutenant Timmerman, which captured two guns and 17 prisoners, but in the main the Americans were held up. For 48 hours they persevered. One company had every officer killed or wounded. Finally, it was determined to withhold further assaults until the artillery had tried its hand. Fifty batteries were put on the job.

Meanwhile, the battalions which had been sent against Bouresches were having their own troubles. The town had been treated to a heavy fire of artillery until it was believed that the Boches had been driven out. The supposition was unfounded. The Germans fairly fed on shells and shrapnel, and when the marines charged the old town across the crimson fields of glowing poppies—every eyewitness expatiates on the glory of those poppies—the defenders were right there with machine guns and rifles.

The advance was in the good old American style which our soldiers have been taught for generations —a swift rush for 50 or 60 yards, then down flat on their bellies, working their rifles and machine guns for all they were worth. Then up and on again. The marines held the center, with companies of infantry on the flanks. The men advanced, five yards apart, in waves separated by about 60 feet. In the first and third waves were automatic riflemen and hand grenadiers, in the second and fourth rifle grenadiers and riflemen.

They tell of one of their officers, Captain Duncan, that he accompanied this advance, smoking a pipe and jauntily swinging a swagger stick. "All right, men," he said quietly. "The guide is left, remember. Hit the line together, boys." One wishes it were possible to chronicle his escape, but he was first wounded, then killed by a shell in the dressing station where he was being treated.

Bouresches was a hard nut to crack. Behind every ruined wall, in the second stories of houses, behind piles of débris, on the roofs of houses were planted machine guns and snipers. Hard fighting with hand grenades and the bayonet gradually cleaned up the town. But to hold it was no easy task. The Boches wanted that town. Moreover, they did not want to be driven out by Americans, of all troops. Their leaders had assured them that there were not enough Americans in France to count for much, and that they would not fight, any way. So they stood manfully to their guns, and most of them died there. In the end, the town was held by the marines, but only after several hundred fresh men had been sent in to replace those fallen.

But Belleau Wood had yet to be taken. It was an acid test of the marines' grit and dash. The French name means "Wood of the Beautiful Waters," but the marines, from the wealth of a cruel experience, called it Hellwood, with the accent on the first syllable. Later the French renamed it " The Wood of the Marines," in honor of those who shed their blood in driving the Boches out.

That task was accomplished by a battalion of 958 men and 26 officers. At least that was the number of men who went in. Seven officers and 340 men remained when the rattle of the machine guns died away. Hours of bombardment by 50 batteries had destroyed all semblance of a wood, but in the tangled meshes of the débris the Germans still hid their machine guns and worked them murderously. They were driven out by hand-to-hand fighting, in which the officers joined. Commands were impossible. It was every man for himself.

It was one thing to take the wood; another to hold it. At night German airplanes flew over the battlefield, dropping bombs on the men below. By day their artillery searched the wood with shells, and their machine guns sprayed it with bullets. But the marines stayed there five days. It was necessary sometimes to send out for provisions or more munitions. No easy detail that. Once 45 men started out on such an errand. Three returned. Machine guns, gas and shells did for the rest. Of a party of 30 sent for ammunition six came back. There grew up the precarious profession of runners. Individuals, instead of parties, were sent for needed supplies and all were volunteers. "Never once," said the commanding officer in a later report, "was there the slightest hesitation shown about carrying out these hazardous messages, and it was a miracle how they got through."

Not long after the end of this battle a shipload of the marines wounded there were brought to New York and taken to local hospitals. An official of the marine corps secured from many of these sorely wounded men some description of their experiences. Just one of these, the story of a mere private, just twenty years old, whom " fate tried to conceal by naming him Smith," may well be quoted here as illustrative of the ordinary fighting man's view of his job:

" We had just finished our second period in the trenches and were retiring for a rest when orders to move came. My company, the Forty-ninth of the Fifth Regiment, was packed into auto trucks and we rode for 24 hours and stopped back of the lines at Château Thierry, where we were held in reserve five days until the morning of June 6th.

" At four A.M. we went over, or rather charged forward, since there were no trenches to speak of and the fighting was all in the open or in woods.

" There wasn't a bit of hesitation from any man. All went forward in an even line. You had no heart for fear at all. Fight—fight and get the Germans was your only thought. Personal danger didn't concern you in the least and you didn't care.

" There were about 60 of us who got ahead of the rest of the company. We just couldn't stop, despite the orders of our leaders. We reached the edge of the small wooded area and there encountered some of the Hun infantry.

" Then it became a matter of shooting at near human targets. We fixed our rifle sights at 300 yards, and aiming through the peep, kept picking off the Germans. And a man went down at nearly every shot.

" But the Germans soon detected us and we became the

objects of their heavy fire. We received emphatic orders at this time to come back and made the half-mile through the woods without hardly losing a man on the way.

"German machine guns were everywhere. In the trees and in small ground holes. And camouflaged at other places so that they couldn't be spotted.

"We stayed for the most part in one-man pits that had been dug and which gave us just a little protection.

"We saw one German a short distance before us, who had two dead ones lying across him. He was in a sitting posture and was shouting 'Kamerad, Kamerad.' We soon learned the reason. He was serving as a lure and wanted a group of marines to come to his rescue so that the kind-hearted Americans would be in direct line of fire from machine guns that were in readiness.

"Now isn't that a dirty trick? Say, it made me sore. Before I knew what I was doing and before I realized that everyone was shouting at me to stay back I bobbed up out of my hole and with bayonet ready beat it out and got that Kamerad bird. It seemed but a minute or so before I was back. But, believe me, there were some bullets whizzing around. They came so close at times I could almost feel their touch. My pack was shot up pretty much, but they didn't get me.

"After that I thought I was bullet proof, and didn't care a damn for all the Germans and their machine guns.

"Soon we charged forward again. I saw one Dutchman stick his head out of a hole and then duck. I ran to the hole. The next time his head came up it was good-night Fritz.

"We were running along when a German pops up right up from the weeds on the roadside and shot at a sergeant with me. The bullet got the sergeant in the right wrist. I got the German before he dropped back into the weeds.

"Every blamed tree must have had a machine gunner. As soon as we spied them we'd drop down and pick them off with our rifles. Potting the Germans became great sport. Even the officers would seize rifles from wounded marines and go to it.

"On the second day of our advance my captain and two

others besides myself were lying prone and cracking away at 'em. I was second in line. Before I knew what had happened a machine gun got me in the right arm just at the elbow. Five shots hit right in succession. The elbow was torn into shreds but the hits didn't hurt. It seemed just like getting five little stings with electricity.

"The captain ordered two men to help me back. I said I could make it alone. I picked up the part of the arm that was hanging loosely and walked.

"It was a two-mile hike to the dressing station. I got nearly up to it when everything began to go black and wobbly. I guess it was loss of blood. But I played in luck, for some stretcher bearers were right near when I went down."

Both the Wood and Bouresches were permanently held by the Americans. Moreover, the success of the marines in stopping the Germans at this point, and in actually beating them back marked the turning point of the great German drive planned on March 21st by Ludendorff. It may fairly be said to have been the beginning of the victorious advance of the Allies under the brilliant command of General Foch, which began on the 6th of July. The marines, many of whom were still unused to warfare, had met the very flower of the German army and defeated it. They made six attacks and repulsed nine counter-attacks. Their single division was opposed at all times by two German divisions and sometimes by three. Among these was the crack Fifth Guards Division, which had been first to cross the Marne in 1914 and had always been reckoned the invincible command of the Kaiser's magnificent army. They with the rest were beaten by the marines.

Our own people were ill-informed as to the measure of this victory and the amount of glory won by our Soldiers of the Sea. The cable dispatches were rigidly censored, and such praise as was given to the marines was but grudgingly measured out. But the French, who were on the ground, and particularly the civilians who appreciated the magnitude of the danger from which the marines had saved them, were ungrudging in their praise. The mayors of Meaux and neighboring towns and villages on the Marne, in a letter to the commanding officer of the American forces in that district, said:

"The civilian population will never forget that, beginning in the month of June, when their homes were threatened by the invader, the —— Division victoriously stepped forth and succeeded in saving them from the impending danger. The mayors who were eye witnesses of the generous and efficacious deeds of the American army in stopping · the enemy advance send this heartfelt expression of their admiration and gratitude."

A body of soldiers that can win such a tribute from the people whose country they defended certainly deserve all the applause and all the glory which their own nation may vouchsafe.

"Devil-dogs" the Germans have come to call our marines. Not a complimentary epithet, perhaps, but one indicative of at least some respect for their prowess. As the size of our armies on the other side increases, we may expect to hear less of the participation of marines in such battles as that of Château Thierry, Cantigny or Bouresches. Gallant as their service there was it was not action of the sort for which the corps was designed. A body of less than 100,000 picked men is not the variety of troops which should be thrown into a general assault, or brigaded with 10 times their number in a general campaign. Picked men deserve picked service. It was natural that marines should be sent, for example, to the Murman peninsula, where conditions demanded rather a small and highly efficient body of troops than a great army. It may be expected that they will be used largely in Russia, where diplomacy and the military arm must go together if the Allies are to save anything out of the wreck.

Be sure that whatever the service may be to which the marines are called, it will be well done. Moreover, it will in most cases be picturesque. Somehow the fates for a hundred years or more seem to have thrown into the way of this corps precisely the sort of service that an adventurous youth would seek. Stories? Why, the life of such a veteran marine officer as, for example, Major General W. T. Waller has been one long romance. He was appointed to the corps in 1880. Since that time we have taken part in but one war—until the present one—and that war neither long nor hotly contested. But Waller looks back upon heading a landing party at Alexandria during its bombardment by the British fleet, moving more than 20,000 rounds of ammunition from one burning building and saving the lives of a score of Greek women trapped in another. He commanded a battery on the *Indiana* when Cervera came out of Santiago and made the record of 1,744 shots in 65 minutes. He was in command of the marines on Dewey's flagship, *Olympia,* at the Battle of Manila Bay. He headed a detachment of marines in China in a successful attack on a fort during the Boxer rebellion. He helped to add Panama to the list of American republics, and brought order into the turbulent republic of Haiti. And General Waller's experiences are but typical of those of the men who have spent their lifetimes in the marines.

And then there was Sergeant Dan Daly—I say " was," for he may be there no longer, for the losses of the marines have been running so high that General Pershing insists that the remplacement camps shall hold one hundred per cent of the force in the field. A much decorated, and withal a somewhat *blasé* hero, is Sergeant Daly. Two Congressional Medals of Honor decorate his breast. One was awarded for gallantry in Pekin during the Boxer outbreak, when alone and single-handed he held a bastion all night under heavy fire. The second he won at Fort Dipitie, in Haiti, where against odds of ten to one he led a storming party at daybreak, captured the fort, and burned it. Recommended for a third medal for valor at Vera Cruz, Sergeant Daly sailed for France before Congress had time to act. Gazing meditatively over the side as his transport steamed into St. Nazaire, Daly was overheard to say softly:

" I've got two of them gadjets now. I wonder if I'll get another over here."

If he lasts he probably will, for the records of the commanding officer cite him for two instances of valor—one when he extinguished a fire in the ammunition dump, and again when, alone, he rushed upon an enemy machine gun emplacement and captured it.

China, Haiti, Mexico and now Belleau Wood, in France! But to the marines such little changes of scene are all in a day's work.

The reader will recall Stephen Crane's description of the imperturbable marine who signaled the ships at Guantanamo. His name was Quick—Sergeant Quick. The correspondents saw him again in 1914 at Vera Cruz, where he was hoisting Rear Admiral Fletcher's flag over the newly established headquarters. We encounter Quick again at the battle of Belleau Wood—Sergeant-Major now, and the holder of a medal of honor, for it is almost 20 years since he did that job of wigwagging amid the storm of Spanish bullets. This time he is one of the men who went for fresh ammunition under the German guns, and led into the wood a detachment of replacement men to take the places of the dead and wounded, and taught them the ways of the Boche.

But the marines also taught the Boches something

of their ways. A captured report of Lieutenant von Bey, a German intelligence officer, after the battle of Belleau Wood, has this to say of our men:

"The Second American Division may be classified as a very good division, perhaps even as assault troops. The various attacks of both regiments on Belleau Wood were carried out with dash and recklessness. The moral effect of our firearms did not materially check the advance of the infantry. The nerves of the Americans are still unshaken.

"The individual soldiers are very good. They are healthy, vigorous and physically well developed men of ages ranging from 18 to 28, who at present lack only necessary training to make them redoubtable opponents. The troops are fresh and full of straightforward confidence. A remark of one of the prisoners is indicative of their spirit: 'We kill or get killed.'"

A statistician, testing the truth of that last phrase in the light of the reports of the killed and wounded in France, showed that the casualties among the marines in France to July 14 were about 11 per cent.; for the army as a whole less than one per cent. Among the marines, for each man killed 1.85 were wounded; in the remainder of the army, 3.27.

The latest development of the Marine Corps is its newly established Flying Section. Not content with ships of the sea, and ships of the desert, the "leathernecks" must needs take to the ships of the air as well. At the moment of writing this book the authorities are reticent as to the size of the aerial section or the plans for its development. But they cannot wholly conceal what individual airmen have been doing.

There, for example, was Lieutenant Edmund G. Chamberlain, a " devil-dog " that flew, if you can imagine such a strange zoölogical combination. Chamberlain was on a furlough in July, 1918. Men's ideas of cheerful furloughs differ. Some seek London's music halls. Chamberlain went out to an English aviation camp to look it over. He found a bombing squadron about to go out, and persuaded the British commander to lend him a machine and let him go along as a volunteer. Indeed, most of us will admit that that was a more thrilling way of spending a " day off " than in the best of the music halls. On this trip he downed two German airplanes, and, as the sport seemed good, he volunteered for a second day. The story of his later exploits I quote from the *Recruiters' Bulletin,* published by the Marine Corps:

" The next day came Lieutenant Chamberlain's wonderful exploit. He was one of the detachment of thirty aviators who went out over the battlefield through which the Germans were being driven by the Allies. As the thirty machines circled about over the fleeing Teutons, they were attacked by an equal number of German machines. It was a hurricane battle from the first, and almost at the inception of the combat the British lost three planes.

" In the tempest of machine gun bullets that roared about his machine, Lieutenant Chamberlain's engine was damaged. One of his machine guns became jammed, and he seemed to be out of the action. But instead of starting for home, he remained to offer assistance to two other airplanes which had been attacked by twelve German machines.

" His machine had lost altitude, owing to engine trouble, but, when he was attacked by a German, he opened such a hot fire that the enemy went into a dive toward the earth. His two companions were now engaged in a life and death struggle, and Lieutenant Chamberlain went to their assistance. His action probably saved the lives of the two Englishmen.

"His engine was now working better. He climbed up toward the enemy, and, with a burst of fire, sent one of them crashing to the earth. A second was shattered with another volley from his machine gun. Then Lieutenant Chamberlain looped out of a cordon of enemy machines which had gathered to finish him, and, as he sailed away, he shot the wing off another German machine.

"The leader of the German squadron came straight at him, but was met with such a torrent of bullets that his airplane joined the others sent to earth by the American.

"The lieutenant then turned for the British lines. His engine had 'gone dead' and he was forced to volplane, carefully picking his way through the smoke clouds of shells fired at him by the enemy's anti-aircraft cannon.

"As he made a wide sweep toward his destination, he saw beneath him a column of German troops and into it he poured a gust of machine gun bullets from the gun which had been jammed, but which he had succeeded in putting into action again. The Germans scattered and Lieutenant Chamberlain flew on for an eighth of a mile and came to earth.

"The American found that he could not carry off the equipment in his machine so he took his compass and started running across the fields. As he did so he encountered a patrol of three Germans. He shouted to them to surrender, waving his compass above his head, like a bomb. Two of the enemy ran, but the third surrendered.

"The lieutenant started again for the British lines, but came upon a wounded French officer, whom he picked up and carried, driving his prisoner before him. He waded a brook under heavy fire and finally arrived within the British lines in safety with the French officer and the German prisoner.

"Chamberlain then reported 'ready for duty,' asked the major in command of the British airmen not to make any report of the affair and refused to give his name. The major was unable to keep the affair quiet and the full details were made a part of his official report of the day's fighting."

Well! Perhaps that will do for a final example of the spirit which animates the United States Marines, the Soldiers of the Sea, the " Devil Dogs " as the Huns have learned to call them, or the " leathernecks " as they prefer to call themselves. The imagination balks at the effort to forecast the deeds that they will do, the records they will make in this war. In the past, though the neglect of recording officials has enveloped much of their gallantry in obscurity, they performed deeds of valor which rival those of the premier corps of romance, the French Foreign Legion. To-day they are stronger in numbers, better in personnel than ever in their history, and they are embarked upon the greatest conflict at arms that men have ever known. Before it is ended they will be able to add many new and thrilling stanzas to the Marines' Hymn which has been sung in every clime and under every condition of hardship and of triumph:

THE MARINES' HYMN

From the Halls of Montezuma,
  To the shores of Tripoli,
We fight our country's battles
  On the land as on the sea.
First to fight for right and freedom
  And to keep our honor clean
We are proud to claim the title
  Of United States Marine.

Our flag's unfurled to every breeze
  From dawn to setting sun,
We have fought in every clime or place
  Where we could take a gun;
In the snow of far-off Northern lands
  And in sunny tropic scenes,
You will find us always on the job—
  THE UNITED STATES MARINES.

Here's health to you and to our Corps
  Which we are proud to serve,
In many a strife we have fought for life
  And never lost our nerve;
If the Army and the Navy
  Ever look on Heaven's scenes,
They will find the streets are guarded by
  THE UNITED STATES MARINES.

THE END

MILITARY AND COLONIAL HISTORY CLASSICS
Reprinted By

The Scholar's Bookshelf
THE AMERICAN REVOLUTION

THE AMERICAN REVOLUTION AND THE BRITISH EMPIRE,
By R. Coupland

This 1930 work presented studies of the impact on the British Empire and the roots of British imperialism of the defeat suffered in the American Revolution. The author discusses, in a series of studies, how the British leaders and George III analyzed and faced up to the consequences of the loss of the American colonies, the subsequent loss to France of several Caribbean possessions, the reawakening of Irish revolutionary restlessness, and the necessity for new directions in mercantilist and imperialist policy, the new importance of Canada, and the emergence of the idea of Commonwealth. 2005: 331 pages, softcover. ISBN: 0-945726-71-6.

BORDER WARS OF THE AMERICAN REVOLUTION,
By William L. Stone

One of the most complete histories ever published of the place of Canadians and Native Americans in the American Revolution, starting with an account of Joseph Brant and moving right into the events on the frontier, especially in New York, the divisions among the Loyalists, the role of natives in the Hudson campaigns and Saratoga, the mounting of expeditions against the natives by the Continentals, and the hostilities, especially those involving Brant, that extended well past the end of the war. 2 Volumes in 1. 2005: 766 pages. Softcover. ISBN: 0-945726-61-9.

A BRIEF NARRATIVE OF THE RAVAGES OF THE BRITISH AND HESSIANS AT PRINCETON IN 1776-1777, *Varnum Lansing Collins, Editor*

"A Brief Narrative" of these two battles, originally unsigned, but written by an eye-witness at Princeton, and invaluable for its account of the "twenty-six days tyranny" of the British and Hessian occupation of Princeton as well as its comments on the causes leading to the Revolution and the brutal methods adopted by the British in attempting to suppress it. 2005: 64 pages, softcover. ISBN: 0-945726-81-2.

DEFENCES OF PHILADELPHIA IN 1777, *Worthington Chauncey Ford, Editor*

An essential documentary history of the defense of Philadelphia as organized and carried out by Washington and his generals. The work consists of more than 220 letters to and from all involved during the year, all recording in detail how Washington, Greene, Wayne, and many others assessed the situation, preparing for a British naval invasion and evaluating how the city might be fortified. Reprint of the 1897 publication. 2005: 300 pages, softcover. ISBN: 0-945726-56-2.

THE DELAWARE CONTINENTALS, 1776-1783, *By Christopher Ward*

The landmark study in the military history of the American Revolution written by the author of "The War of the Revolution." The work is an exhaustive study of the organization of this regiment and its action throughout the war, especially at Long Island, Brooklyn, Trenton, Princeton, and the middle Atlantic states and its later service at Camden, King's Mountain, Guilford Court House, and Yorktown. Unabridged reprint of the original 1941 edition. 2005: 620 pages, illustrated. Softcover. ISBN: 0-945726-65-1

THE DIARIES OF GEORGE WASHINGTON, 1748-1799, *John C. Fitzpatrick, Editor*
A complete and unabridged reprint edition of the famed, standard Fitzpatrick edition of Washington's diaries as first published by Houghton Mifflin in 1925, including reproductions of the original frontispieces. 2005: 1862 pages, softcover. Set of 4 Volumes. ISBN: 0-945726-78-3.

THE FIRST AMERICAN CIVIL WAR; FIRST PERIOD, *By Henry Belcher*
Belcher's 1911 study presented a re-assessment, from the British point of view (the author was a Fellow of King's College), of the American Revolution, viewing it as a British civil war, examining the politics common to both sides of the Atlantic, and inquiring into the moral and social background of the struggle, the positions of leaders like Washington, Howe, Burgoyne, Gage, Samuel Adams, Benjamin Franklin, and others, the critical role of Boston, and the campaigns at Boston, New York, and Philadelphia. Rich in detail and unusual interpretations, this outspoken work sheds a great deal of light on the British in the revolutionary struggle. 2005: 838 pages, softcover. 2 Volumes in 1. ISBN: 0-945726-62-7.

GENERAL ISRAEL PUTNAM ("OLD PUT.") A Biography, *By George Canning Hill*
Hill's 1865 book was the first book-length biography of the American general who served in both the French and Indian War and the American Revolution, and presented a colorful account of the man and his activities as well as of the military life and history in which he figured. 2005: 282 pages, illustrated. Softcover. ISBN: 0-945726-80-5.

HENRY KNOX; A Soldier of the Revolution, *By Noah Brooks*
Reprint of the first (1900) and still indispensable biographical study of Washington's Chief of Artillery and the first Secretary of War. The work drew on the Knox manuscripts and remains and essential work in the early military history of the United States. 2005: 368 pages. Softcover. ISBN: 0-945726-76-7.

A HISTORY OF THE CAMPAIGNS OF 1780 AND 1781 IN THE SOUTHERN PROVINCES OF NORTH AMERICA,
By Lt. Col. Banastre Tarleton Universally hated by the Continentals for his combat brutalities, Tarleton wrote this account of the last years of the Revolution and published it in London in 1787. Filled with documentation, statistics, and quotations from important letters as well as several unique maps, the work presented an exhaustive, extensively documented chronological history of the shifting of the war from New England and New York to the south, the arrival of Cornwallis, the state of the royal armies, and the battles at Catawba, "Guildford," "York town," and the end. 2005: 530 pages. ISBN: 0-945726-82-1.

HORATIO GATES; Defender of American Liberties, *By Samuel White Patterson*
Still the essential biography of the victor at Saratoga and the work that cleared up generations of misinformation about Gates and the mistakes he made in his career. The book presents an invaluable assessment of the Saratoga campaigns, Gates's relief of command and its circumstances, his many struggles to rehabilitate himself, and his subsequent career. 2005: 488 pages. ISBN: 0-945726-83-X.

LETTERS OF BRUNSWICK AND HESSIAN OFFICERS DURING THE AMERICAN REVOLUTION, *Translated by William L. Stone*
Stone's 1891 publication was the first to present an English translation of a group of private letters written by German officers serving as mercenaries in the American Revolution, and gathered nineteen valuable letters shedding a great deal of light on the personalities and events surrounding Burgoyne's campaign, their experiences after his defeat, and their later journeys to Philadelphia and elsewhere. 2005: 276 pages, softcover. ISBN: 0-945726-84-8

THE LIFE OF ARTEMAS WARD;The First Commander-in-Chief of the American Revolution, by Charles Martyn
The basic biographical study of the man who commanded the Americans at the Battle of Bunker Hill and later figured in military operations around Boston, eventually becoming the commander of the Eastern Department. The work presents a highly detailed account of the war in Boston from 1775 to 1777, and also covers Ward's post war career as a Federalist Congressman. 2005: 334 pages, illustrated. ISBN: 0-945726-52-X.

THE LIFE AND LETTERS OF JAMES WOLFE, *By Beckles Willson*
The first and still the most complete biography of the British general who fell on the Plains of Abraham, presents his entire personal and military life from his early service in Scotland at Culloden and Inverness and on to Louisbourg, Quebec, and the St. Lawrence. Includes many letters and documents found only in this volume. 2005: 540 pages. ISBN: 0-945726-85-6

GENERAL WOLFE'S INSTRUCTIONS TO YOUNG OFFICERS, *By James Wolfe*
Facsimile reprint of Wolfe of Quebec's 1780 publication, a basic text for the military man of his time, covering with great logic and actual event illustrations such topics as drill, clean living, the deployment of troops, transport, and materiel, and the role of adjutants and quartermasters. Includes the texts of many of his orders intended to properly organize and command an army. 2005: 106 pages, softcover. ISBN: 0-945726-49-X

LIFE OF GENERAL PHILIP SCHUYLER, 1733-1804, *By Bayard Tuckerman*
The first biographical study of Schuyler, originally published in 1903, and still essential for the study of his role in the American Revolution, especially the invasion of Canada, Ticonderoga, and his subsequent political career. 2004: 288 pages. Softcover. ISBN: 0-945726-86-4.

THE LIFE OF BENEDICT ARNOLD; HIS PATRIOTISM AND TREASON, *By Isaac N. Arnold*
The author, not a relative of the Revolutionary War general and traitor, published this book in 1879 in an attempt to "ask a fair hearing and justice," though not a defense for Arnold's treason. The book was the first substantial study of Arnold's services in the war at Ticonderoga, in Canada, at Saratoga, Valcour Island, and in other Hudson Valley campaigns, detailing his services to the Revolutionary cause, his wounding, good relations with Washington, and then his downfall, with chapters on his wife, Major Andre, his trail, and his later services with the British army. Remains the most complete study of Arnold's career. 2005: 444 pages. Softcover. ISBN: 0-945726-55-4.

ARNOLD'S EXPEDITION TO QUEBEC, *By John Codman*
The first and still the most thorough study of Arnold's 1775 attempt to capture Quebec, with a full account of its planning and execution, the tremendous difficulties imposed by the terrain and the weather, the assault, the death of Montgomery, and the ultimate failure of the expedition. Includes the 2 original oversize foldout maps, 14 1/2" x 5 1/2" and 11" x 14". 2005: 340 pages, illustrated. Softcover. ISBN:0-945726-61-9.

THE LOYALISTS IN NORTH CAROLINA DURING THE REVOLUTION
By Robert O. DeMond
The definitive study of the state which contained a greater number of Loyalists in proportion to its population than any other colony, and was home to Col. John Hamilton, the most important Tory leader of the Revolution. The book details the operations of the dissenters, including their military and political activities, their gradual defeat and sufferings, and eventual confiscation of their property and their exodus from the state. 2005: 292 pages. Softcover. ISBN: 0-94572687-2.

MAJOR-GENERAL ANTHONY WAYNE AND THE PENNSYLVANIA LINE IN THE CONTINENTAL ARMY, *By Charles J. Stillé*
First published in 1893, this was the first full-length study of Wayne and his role in Washington's army at Valley Forge, the campaigns in New York, New Jersey, and Pennsylvania, the role of the Pennsylvania Line at the time of Arnold's treason, the closing battles in Virginia and Georgia, and Wayne's service after the war. Exhaustive in detail and filled with documentary material, the book remains essential for studies of Wayne and how the Continental Army was formed and operated. 2005: 441 pages, many illustrations. Softcover. ISBN: 0-945726-46-

MILITARY JOURNAL DURING THE AMERICAN REVOLUTIONARY WAR FROM 1775 TO 1783, *By James Thacher*
First published in 1854, and known as "Thacher's American Revolution," this highly detailed record of the author's experiences as a medical officer between January 1775 and January 1783 presented a remarkable military history of the war and especially the sufferings of the American army and the actions of the American officers and generals who Thacher observed and sometimes cared for. The volume also remans invaluable for its extensive appendixes which include substantial biographical sketches of American generals and several documents including Burgoyne's "Observations" respecting the Battle of Saratoga. 2005: 552 pages, softcover. ISBN: 0-945726-88-0.

NATHAN HALE 1776; Biography and Memorials, *By Henry Phelps Johnston*
Johnston's 1901 publication was based on the large amount of new information about Hale that was discovered since the earliest biography of him, published in 1856, including much of Hale's correspondence and other material. The book presents an essentially complete account of Hales' four years at Yale, his career as a schoolmaster, his joining the Continental Army shortly after Lexington, his participation in the Battles around New York, his capture, and execution. Documentary appendix includes many letters and Hale's army diary, and many other notes. 2005: 246 pages. Illustrated. Softcover. ISBN: 0-945726-90-2.

OBSERVATIONS ON SOME PARTS OF THE ANSWER OF EARL CORNWALLIS TO SIR HENRY CLINTON'S NARRATIVE, *By Lt. General Sir Henry Clinton*
Clinton's 1783 defense against Cornwallis's many accusations and publications, especially the "Answer to That Narrative," which complained about the mishandling of military support for the Yorktown campaign. The book contains the texts of several important letters and orders essential to studying the British operations in the south and 1 original map. 2005: 116 pages, softcover. ISBN: 0-945726-91-0.

OCCUPATION OF NEW YORK CITY BY THE BRITISH, *By Ewald Gustav Schaukirk*
Reprints this German clergyman's day-by-day account of what he saw as a missionary in New York City, noting the movements of troops, rumors of battles in New Jersey and around New York, activities of Hessian troops, right through to the surrender at Yorktown. 2005: 32 pages, softcover. ISBN: 0945726-92-9

OUR STRUGGLE FOR THE FOURTEENTH COLONY; CANADA AND THE AMERICAN REVOLUTION, *By Justin H. Smith*
The still-definitive study of the effort of the thirteen colonies to bring Canada into the American Revolution from the earliest efforts of the Boston Committee of Correspondence on through the carrying of military operations up through the Hudson Valley and on to Quebec, Canadian defenses under Carleton, and concluding with the failure of Arnold's expedition and the ultimate abandonment of the efforts of the American revolutionaries. Unabridged reprint of the New York: 1907 edition. 2005: 638 + 635 pages. Softcover. Set of 2 Volumes. ISBN: 0-945726-68-6.

THE SIEGE OF CHARLSTON BY THE BRITISH FLEET, *Edited by Franklin B. Hough*
An important 1867 documentary history of the siege and surrender of Charleston in May, 1780 which gathered and arranged many central orders, letters, and other documents illustrating the events and personailties involved, especially the roles of Admiral Arbuthnot and Sir Henry Clinton, the position of the Charleston Loyalists, and the light of the revolutionary inhabitants of the city who were declared "the Abettors of the American Rebellion" by the British. 2005: 228 pages, softcover. ISBN: 0-945726-95-3.

SIMCOE'S MILITARY JOURNAL; A History of the Operaions of a Partisan Corps Called the Queen's Rangers, *By Lt. Col. J.G. Simcoe*
The basic history of the famed "Simcoe's Rangers," and their activities between Simcoe's accession to command on October 15, 1777 and the end of the war, written by their commanding officer in 1787 but not published until 1844. The work is invaluable for its material on the occupation of New York and the fighting in the South, with many detailed accounts of battles supported by unique maps. Includes the original substantial documentary appendix of letters and papers as well as the ten original maps. 2005: 334 pages. softcover. ISBN: 0-945726-96-1

THE STRUGGLE FOR AMERICAN INDEPENDENCE, *By Sydney George Fisher*
Reprint edition of Fisher's massive history of the American Revolution, a major history which debated many points with the earlier works of Fiske and Trevelyan, pioneered the study of many aspects of the military history of the war, including its political background and the actions of important British generals and politicians, and presented what remains one of the most comprehensive histories of the war. 2005: 574 + 585 pages, illustrated. Softcover. Set of 2 Volumes. ISBN: 0-945726-54-6.

TORCHBEARER OF THE REVOLUTION, *By Thomas Jefferson Wertenbaker*
Still the basic and essential history of Bacon's 1676 rebellion in Virginia, tracing the background of the events, the place of the Native Americans in the picture, his role in settling and colony-building, the significance of the events for the American Revolution, and Bacon's place as "the greatest figure of the first century of American history." 2005: 248 pages, softcover. ISBN: 0-945726-98-8.

THE VIRGINIA CAMPAIGN AND THE BLOCKADE AND SIEGE OF YORKTOWN 1781, By Col. H.L. Landers
An invaluable, highly detailed history of the closing campaign of the American Revolution, with extensive material on the French-American alliance and the roles played both in the diplomatic background and the military history of the campaign by Louis XVI, Franklin, Vergennes, D'Estaing, Rochambeau, and Lafayette. The work includes special chapters on Clinton and Cornwallis, the sea battle off the capes of Virginia, and the siege and surrender of the British. Originally published in 1931 by the U.S. Government Printing Office to commemorate the 150th anniversary of the events. 2005:219 pages, illustrated. Softcover. ISBN: 0-945726-43-0.

WAR OUT OF NIAGARA; Walter Butler and the Tory Rangers, *By Howard Swiggett*
The only full-length study of the American Revolution in northern New York presents a full account of the Loyalist issues of the area, the role of the Mohawk Indians, battle actions in 1778-1780 involving many diverse issues and forces, and the controversial role of Walter Butler's Rangers and the battle at Cherry Valley.. 2005: 309 pages, illustrated. Softcover. ISBN: 0-945726-53-8.

THE BRITISH NAVY IN ADVERSITY; A Study of the War of American Independence, *By W.M. James*
A remarkably comprehensive and well informed study originally published in 1926 and written by a Royal Navy captain who focused on the challenge presented to British seapower by the American Revolution with its issues of international maritime warfare, challenges to the Admiralty which had let the Royal Navy fall behind its rivals, neutrality, commerce, and other questions. The author presents a narrative history of British naval operations around the world during this time, the military and civilian leaders, strategies, and overall results. Extensive documentary material includes lists of commissioned ships. Many illustrations and maps. 2005: 459 pages, softcover. ISBN: 0-945726-10-4.

FRANCE IN THE AMERICAN REVOLUTION, *By James Breck Perkins*
The still indispensable, most fully documented study of the pivotal role of France in the world politics of the American Revolution, tracing France's new world situation as the Revolution neared, American diplomatic efforts to ally with an enemy of Britain, the role of such individuals as Silas Deane, Benjamin Franklin, Lafayette, and Rochambeau, and the decisive French military intervention at the end of the war. Reprint of the original 1911 Houghton Mifflin publication. 2005: 544 pages. Softcover. ISBN: 0-945726-18-X.

GENERAL WASHINGTON'S SPIES ON LONG ISLAND AND IN NEW YORK, *By Morton Pennypacker*
One of the very few works on Washington's secret service, this book remains the central study of espionage activities centering around New York during the American Revolution, identifying some twenty prominent families and family members under the leadership of Robert Townsend of Oyster Bay and Abraham Woodhull of Setauket, and including Anna Strong, William Floyd, Caleb Brewster, and others. The book includes the first major studies of Nathan Hale and the Benedict Arnold treason. Reprint of the original 1939 publication of the Long Island Historical Society. 2005: 302 pages, illustrated. Softcover. ISBN: 0-945726-18-X

THE MAJOR OPERATIONS OF THE NAVIES IN THE WAR OF AMERICAN INDEPENDENCE, *By Alfred Thayer Mahan* Mahan's uniquely informed perspectives pioneered the study of the naval aspects of the American Revolution, and presented detailed and carefully organized chapters on the naval campaigns on Lake Champlain, Boston, Charleston, Narragansett Bay, the reaction to British invasions in New York, Philadelphia, and the Hudson Valley, the repercussions of naval wars abroad, the operations at Yorktown, and subsequent battles in the West Indies. Reprint of the original London: 1913 edition. 2005: 280 pages, illustrated. Softcover. ISBN: 0-945726-14-7.

THE NINETEENTH OF APRIL, 1775, *By Harold Murdock*
First published in the early 1920s, this study by a professional historian was the first to present a complete reconstruction of the day which saw the beginning of the American Revolution, and remains unparalleled for its record of the events, large and small, that took place. The work drew on both British and American sources and offered some favorable reflections on the British conduct of the encounter as well as the retreat to Charlestown. Includes several period illustrations and maps. 2005: 134 pages, softcover. ISBN: 0-945726-15-5.

THE CAMPAIGN OF 1776 AROUND NEW YORK AND BROOKLYN, *By Henry P. Johnston*
This work, from which all other military historians of the American Revolution
have drawn, presents an exhaustive account of the American Revolution battles of
Brooklyn, Long Island, Kip's Bay, Harlem Heights, and on to Trenton and
Princeton and the closing of the 1776 campaign. The work is supplemented by
more than 60 letters and reports describing the events by participants. Reprint of
the original 1878 publication of the Long Island Historical Society. Includes the
original 36" x 15 3/4" foldout map. "Indispensable." *David McCullough.* 2005:
509 pages. Softcover. ISBN: 0-945726-12-0.

THE COMMAND OF THE HOWE BROTHERS DURING THE AMERICAN REVOLUTION, *By Troyer Steele Anderson*
A classic study which offers essential perspectives on nearly every aspect of the
American Revolution during the first two years, with a great deal of valuable mate-
rial on the British estimate of the crisis, preparations, the battles at Boston, Long
Island, New Jersey, and Pennsylvania, all focused on the roles of Richard and
William Howe. "In no book has Sir William Howe been more fairly treated and, by
consequence, in none has his inadequacy been more completely laid are."
American Historical Review. Reprint of the original 1936 Oxford University
Press edition. 2005: 368 pages. Softcover. ISBN: 0-945726-02-3.

GENERAL GAGE'S INFORMERS; New Material Upon Lexington and Concord: Benjamin Thompson as Loyalist and the Treachery of Benjamin Church, Jr., *By Allen French*
Reprint edition of this 1932 work by the most important historian of the events of
April, 1775, the first work to draw on the Gage MSS. The work showed how Gage
kept informed about American sentiments and plans and gathered sixteen basic
documents and accounts detailing the events of the day as well as a chapter on the
story of Benjamin Thompson, later Count Rumford. The author also presented evidence that the Americans fired first at Lexington. 2005: 207 pages, illustrated.
Softcover. ISBN: 0-945726-07-4.

HISTORY OF THE SIEGE OF BOSTON AND THE BATTLES OF LEX-INGTON, CONCORD, AND BUNKER HILL, *By Richard Frothingham*
Originally published in 1849, this was both a celebration of American independence
as represented in the creation of the Bunker Hill Monument, and a surprisingly comprehensive history of the 1775 military operations that started the American
Revolution and the siege of Boston that followed the Battle of Bunker Hill, with
detailed accounts of British rule of the city, their evacuation of the city, many original documents, and the celebration of the victory. This is a reprint of the 4th, 1873
edition which included many revisions, additions, additional documents and illustrations. Includes the two original oversize foldout maps. Map sizes 12" x 18" and 17"
x 19 3/4". 2005: 422 pages, illus. Softcover. ISBN: 0-945726-09-0.

A NAVAL HISTORY OF THE AMERICAN REVOLUTION, *By Gardner W. Allen*
Still in many ways the most comprehensive work of its kind, this massive study
presented highly detailed accounts of battles at Lake Champlain, off Boston and
Maine, Charleston, Delaware Bay, and year-by-year histories of all other significant engagements both along the American coast and at sea. The work also presents extensive coverage of the ships of the revolutionary navy, its commanders,
foreign alliances, diplomacy, prisoners, and naval conditions during this era.
Reprint of the original 1913 edition. 2005: 752 pages, 2 Vols in 1. Softcover.
ISBN: 0-945726-00-7.

THE ORGANIZATION OF THE BRITISH ARMY IN THE AMERICAN REVOLUTION, *By Edward E. Curtis* A fully detailed study of the British Army focused on its operations in the American Revolution, with separate chapters on its administrative machinery, recruiting, provisioning, and transportation. The book remains unique for its gathering of contemporary documents illuminating aspects of these topics. Reprint of the original 1926 Yale University Press edition. 2005: 223 pages. Softcover. ISBN: 0-945726-06-6.

OUR FRENCH ALLIES; Rochambeau and His Army, Lafayette and His Devotion, D'Estaing, DeTernay, Barras, DeGrasse, and Their Fleets in the Great War of the American Revolution from 1778 to 1782, *By Edwin Martin Stone*
An exhaustive account of virtually every aspect of the role of the French in the American Revolution, covering not only the actions of the French but also of the American forces as they engaged in various campaigns with French support. The work identifies hundreds of military and naval figures on both sides, reprints many of their first-hand accounts of events, and details the ways in which figures on both sides contributed to the cause and welcomed each other. First published in Providence, Rhode Island in 1884, the work also includes a great deal of unique material on military operations there. Includes much unique documentation of individual units and leaders as well as many contemporary illustrations. Also includes the original 22" x 17" foldout map. 2005: 632 pages. Softcover. ISBN: 0-945726-19-8.

THE PRIVATE SOLDIER UNDER WASHINGTON, *By Charles Knowles Bolton*
Still the standard work on how Washington's army was formed and maintained; the varieties and sources of food and equipment; relations between officers and the ranks; camp duties and diversions; hospitals and prison ships; army maneuvers; and the attitudes of the ordinary foot soldier as expressed in diaries, letters, journals, and other writings. Reprint of the original 1902 Scribner's publication. Illustrated. 2005: 258 pages, softcover. ISBN: 0945726-05-8.

THE TAKING OF TICONDEROGA; The British Story, *By Allen French*
The author used several first-hand accounts by British officers and soldiers to provide an excellent chronological history of British planning and operations in the Hudson Valley campaigns and also established in this book for the first time the roles of Benedict Arnold and Ethan Allen in the American defense. Reprint of the original 1928 Harvard University Press ISBN: 0-945726-07-4.

THE TURNING POINT OF THE REVOLUTION; Or, Burgoyne in America, *By Hoffman Nickerson*
Still the standard and unmatched study of Burgoyne's campaigns intended to split the American colonies. Shows how the strategy was worked out and prepared, how Burgoyne was selected, and how the battles at Bennington, Ticonderoga, Stanwix, and the Highlands went against the British, brought about their retreat and surrender, and opened the way for the French alliance. Reprint of the 1928 edition. 2005: 500 pages, illustrated. 2 Vols in 1. Softcover. ISBN: 0-945726-16-3

NAVAL AND OTHER MILITARY HISTORY

SOLDIERS OF THE SEA; The Story of the United States Marine Corps, *By Willis J. Abbot*
Reprint edition of the first comprehensive history of the U.S. Marines, first published in 1918 when their role in World War I was beginning to be noticed and applauded. The work covers the Marines from their establishment through the War of 1812, and in service throughout the world. 2005: 358 pages, softcover. ISBN: 0-945725-97-X

SEA-POWER IN THE PACIFIC; A Study of the American-Japanese Naval Problem, *By Hector C. Bywater*
Noting that tensions in political relations between Japan and the United States were expected in some quarters to lead to war, the author published this perceptive book in 1921, studying the naval outlook in the Pacific and the strategic situation of the naval powers,"the full significance of which does not appear to be realised either in Japan or the United States." The book presents an indispensable summary of the state of the Japanese Navy at the time, its ships, men, material, administration, shipbuilding resources, submarines and aircraft, strategy, and a concluding chapter, "Possible Features of a War in the Pacific." 2005: 342 pages + 4 maps. Softcover. ISBN: 0-945726-94-5.

THE WAR WITH MEXICO, *By R.S. Ripley*
Reprints the basic and still unreplaced history of the Mexican War, written by a Brevet Major in the U.S. Army, and first published in 1849. Well aware of the "novelty and importance of the struggle," Ripley gave an impartial and comprehensive view of the war based on his personal observations of the country and his acquaintance with many of the American officers and some Mexicans. Reprint edition. 2005: 522 + 674 pages. Softcover. 2 Volumes. ISBN: 0-945726-99-6.

THE SCOUTING EXPEDITIONS OF McCULLOUCH'S TEXAS RANGERS, *By Samuel C. Reid, Jr*.
An important work on the Mexican War, first published in 1847 and detailing the 1846 campaign of the American army, especially at Monterey and Buena Vista. Written by an active member of the Texas Rangers, the book includes a great deal of detail about their organization and lives, leaders and adventures, and the battles in which they were involved. 2005: 251 pages. Softcover. ISBN: 0-945726-93-7.

COMMODORE JOHN BARRY; Father of the American Navy, *By Joseph Gurn*
The first full-length biographical study of Barry remains fundamental not only to the study of his career but also the foundation of the American navy. The work presents unmatched, detailed accounts of his career spanning the era from the American Revolution to the first diplomatic and military challenges posed by France to the Adams administration, tracing in detail his rise to high rank, his and George Washington's cooperation and military thought, the construction of early naval ships, including the "Constitution," and his legacy for American naval history. Reprint of the 1933 edition. 2005: 318 pages, softcover. ISBN: 0-945726-72-4.

THE CRIMEA IN 1854 AND 1894, *By Gen. Sir Evelyn Wood*
A participant's highly detailed first-hand account of the Crimean War and the battles of the Alma, Sevastopol, Balaklava, Inkerman, and the conclusion of the war and death of Lord Raglan. The book was first published in 1895 and was occasioned by the author's return to the areas in which he fought, and he expresses severe criticism of the British government's mismanagement of the war. 2005: 400 pages, illustrated. Softcover. ISBN: 0-945726-51-1

A HISTORY OF AMERICAN PRIVATEERS, *By Edgar Stanton Maclay*
A still unreplaced work in American naval history, this 1899 study (dedicated to Theodore Roosevelt, "Pioneer of the Modern School of Naval Writers") remains the most comprehensive study of the role of the early privateers in the establishment of the American navy and their support of naval operations against Britain. The work traces the history of colonial privateering, its special dangers, and the roles of such figures as Truxtun, Porter, Biddle, Decatur, Perry, as well as such leading privateers as Silas Talbot, Jonathan Haraden, Solon Drowne, Thomas Boyle, and many others in early national privateering and navy building. 2005: 519 pages, illustrated. Softcover. ISBN: 0-945726-63-5.

THE MONITOR AND THE NAVY UNDER STEAM, *By Frank M. Bennett*
A pioneering history, first published in 1900, focusing on the origin, career, and influence of the "Monitor" and how that ironclad occupies a pivotal place in the gradual transformation of ships of war from the wooden sailing ship to the steel armored steam battleship. Many illustrations depict these ships and the actions in which they were involved. 2005: 430 pages, softcover. ISBN: 0-945726-89-9

OUR NAVAL WAR WITH FRANCE, *By Gardner W. Allen*
The basic study of the spoliation of American commerce by the French in the years 1799-1801, describing the events, their economic costs to the new nation, and how the United States faced up to its first international crisis through diplomatic efforts and through laying the foundations for a navy. 2005: 323 pages, illustrated. Softcover. ISBN: 0-945726-58-9.

OUR NAVY AND THE BARBARY CORSAIRS, *By Gardner W. Allen*
The first full study of the events of a forty-year period from 1778 to 1818, showing how the United States managed to build a navy with such ships as the "George Washington, Philadelphia, Constellation, Constitution," and others, and eventually defeat the depredations of the Barbary pirates in battles at Tripoli and Algiers under Bainbridge, Prebel, Porter and Decatur. Reprint of the original 1905 edition. 2005: 354 pages, illustrated. Softcover. ISBN: 0-945726-01-5.

JACKSON AND NEW ORLEANS; An Authentic Narrative of the Achievements of the American Army under Andrew Jackson Befire New Orleans, *By Alexander Walker* An exhaustively detailed, chronological account of Jackson's defense of New Orleans, originally published in 1856, vividly written, and exploring, among many other things, Jackson's strategies and tactics, the roles of Packenham and Lafitte, and how the opposing forces planned, organized, and executed their offensive and defensive moves, all the actions along the way, and the reasons for the ultimate American victory. 2005: 411 pages, softcover. ISBN: 0-945726-70-8.

THE WAR OF 1812 ON THE NIAGARA FRONTIERS, *By Louis L. Babcock*
Still the most detailed account of the campaigns and battles on the Niagara, with detailed accounts of the skirmishes and battles at Queenston Heights, York, Fort George, Lundy's Lane, Izard's campaign down the Niagara, and all the intervening events. The book includes valuable documentary data on war losses as well as many maps. Reprint of the original 1927 edition. Includes all the original oversize foldout maps. 2005: 385 pages, illus. Map size 14"x7 1/2". Softcover. ISBN: 0-945726-04-X.

THE FALL OF CANADA; A Chapter in the History of The Seven Years' War, *By George M. Wrong*
Still the definitive study of the events of 1759-1760 surrounding the British campaign under Amherst to take Montreal and Quebec, with detailed studies of the strategies and tactics involved, the French defense, and the worldwide implications of the fall of New France. Reprint of the original 1914 Oxford University Press edition, complete with the original oversize foldout map. 2005: 272 pages. Map size 21" x 13 1/2". Softcover. 0-945726-21-X.

DRAKE AND THE TUDOR NAVY; With a History of the Rise of England as a Maritime Power, *by Julian S. Corbett*
Reprint of the second edition (1899) of this classic study of a critical period in the evolution of the British Navy focusing on Hawkins, Drake, the struggles in the Spanish Main, Drake's circumnavigation, the defense against the Armada, and Drake's subsequent expeditions and eventual disgrace. Presents unique information about Drake, the evolution of the British Navy, its political background, and the international conflicts of the Elizabethan world. 2005: 415 + 461 pages, foldout maps. Softcover. Set of 2 Volumes. ISBN: 0-945726-67-8.

THE SIEGE OF HAVANA 1762, *By Francis Russell Hart*
Still the definitive account of this operation which occurred during the war
between England and Spain declared in early 1762, the diplomatic background,
and the naval conflict between the two Caribbean powers, why the capture of
Cuba was a primary concern of England, the relative strengths of the naval forces
involved, the roles of Admirals George Keppel and George Pocock, the details of
the siege operations, and the outcome. Reprint of the 1931 edition. 2005: 54
pages, softcover. ISBN: 0-045726-59-7.

THE EVOLUTION OF NAVAL ARMAMENT, *By Frederick Leslie
Robertson*
Traces the evolution of the smooth-bore gun, carronade, truck carriage, shell gun,
rifle gun, and their propelling machinery during the age of fighting sail and up to
the coming of the ironclad. The work is highly detailed and includes expert
appraisals of various developments over the decades in an accessible writings style.
2005: 307 pages, illustrated. Softcover. ISBN: 0-945726-64-3.

**A HISTORY OF THE ROYAL NAVY FROM THE EARLIEST TIMES TO
THE WARS OF THE FRENCH REVOLUTION,** *By Nicholas Harris
Nicolas*
First published at London in 1847, this remarkable and irreplaceable work was
intended to fill the lack, at that time, of an adequate history of the foundation,
rise, and establishment of "that mighty Navy to which [England] owes alike her
security and her pre-eminence among Nations." Includes many documentary
appendixes. 2005: 469 + 534 pages. Softcover. Set of 2 Volumes. ISBN: 0-
945726-66-X. .

FIGHTING INSTRUCTIONS, 1530-1816, *Edited by Julian S. Corbett*
This 1905 publication pioneered the study of British naval tactics by making available a substantial group of chronologically arranged writings which document the
process of thought and lines of argument by which the classic tacticians arrived at
their theories and recommendations about tactics, weapons, movement, the management of ships and men, and managing the challenges of evolving naval technology both in England and abroad. The writers include Lord Lisle, Sir Walter
Ralegh, Lord Wimbledon, the Duke of York, Prince Rupert, Lord Anson, Sir
Alexander Cochrane, and many others. Reprint edition. 2005: 366 pages.
Softcover. ISBN: 0-945726-60-0.

A TREATISE OF ARTILLERY, *By John Muller*
Facsimile reprint of the third, London: 1780 edition of this eighteenth-century
British treatise on the construction of guns, their measurements and capabilities,
movement, ammunition, stores, and use aboard ships. This edition included special material on the use of gunpowder. Includes all the original detailed illustrations
and reference material. 2005: 216 pages, softcover. ISBN: 945726-47-3.

AMERICAN COLONIAL HISTORY

**HISTORY OF THE CITY OF NEW YORK IN THE SEVENTEENTH CEN-
TURY,** *By Mrs. Schuyler van Rensselaer*
Exceptional for its comprehensive coverage of the discovery, settlement, and political, social, cultural, and economic life of New York City under the Dutch and the
Stuarts, this work remains the foundation stone for historical studies of the city
and also early colonial Amrerica. The author also treats in detail relations with the
Indians, the administrations of the various Dutch and English governors, discon-
tents and rebellions, the evolution of political organization. The work closes with a
full account of the Jacob Leisler episode. Unabridged reprint of the original New
York: 1909 edition. 2005: 533 + 640 pages. Softcover. Set of 2 Volumes. ISBN:
0-945726-48-1.

THE AMERICAN COLONIES IN THE SEVENTEENTH CENTURY, *By Herbert L. Osgood*

Complete reprint edition of Osgood's pioneering, still-indispensable, and exhaustive history of the American colonies, and virtually every aspect of their establishment, evolution of governmental and financial systems, and the problems of imperial control, especially during the interregnum. Substantial chapters on each colony from Massachusetts Bay to the Carolinas constitute the starting point for the study of the American colonies. Unabridged reprint of the original London: 1904-1907 edition. 2005: 1619 pages, softcover. Set of 3 Volumes. ISBN: 0945726-76-7.

Vol I.The Chartered Colonies. Beginnings of Self Government. 2005:578 pages.ISBN:0-945726-7.
Vol II.The Chartered Colonies.Beginnings of Self Government. 2005: 490 pages.ISBN: 0-945726-74-0.
Vol III. Imperial Control. Beginnings of the System of Royal Provinces. 2005: 551 pages. ISBN: 0-945726-75-9.

KING PHILIP'S WAR, *By George W. Ellis and John E. Morris*

First published in 1906, this work remains the central, indispensable, and most comprehensive study of New England in the years 1675 and 1676 and how the new colonists were forced into cooperative union in the face of the challenges of the Indians. The book was the first to draw on contemporary correspondence between the governors and military, religious, and other leaders of the time in order to identify the principal participants, especially the Indian leaders, and present a chronological history of the events and their outcome. 2005: 326 pages, softcover. ISBN: 0-945726-69-4.

NARRATIVES OF THE INSURRECTIONS, 1675-1690, *Edited by Charles M. Andrews*

The basic documentary source for the significant insurrections and rebellions in the American colonies, including Bacon's, the Carolina proprietors of 1680, the events of 1689-1691, and other events of the 1690s. Reprint of this volume from the "Original Narratives of Early American History" originally published in 1915 by Scribner's. 2005: 414 pages, softcover.ISBN: 0-945726-03-1.

NARRATIVES OF THE INDIAN WARS, 1675-1699, *Edited by Charles H. Lincoln*

A basic source for the New England Indian Wars of the late 1600s, documenting the wars of 1675, the captivity of Mary Rowlandson, and the "Decennium Luctuosum" of Cotton Mather (1699), an account of the 10-year struggle with the Indians in the last decade of the 17th century. Much of the material reflects the international aspects of these struggles in the light of events abroad. Reprint of this volume from the "Original Narratives of Early American History" of the 1913 edition. Includes the original 14" x 12" map. 2005: 316 pages. Softcover. ISBN: 0-945726-12-0.

WORLD WAR I

GALLIPOLI DIARY, *By General Sir Ian Hamilton*

An exceptionally direct, detailed, and outspoken diary of the author's experiences between March and October, 1915. Written in retirement by a career British soldier, the most decorated general in the British Army at the time, and veteran of the colonial wars in Africa, the book is rich in invaluable first-hand material on the strategic situation, the landing, the technology of armaments, ammunition, and equipment, the planning, and the roles of Kitchener, Churchill, and others. The author's frequently withering, close-up verbal portraits of the leaders and their shortcomings make this an indispensable source for the British role in the campaign. Includes three substantial appendixes on armament and strategy as well as illustrations. Unabridged reprint of the New York: 1920 Doran edition. 2005: 798 pages, softcover. 2 Volumes in 1. ISBN: 0-045726-44-9.

WHEN THE U-BOATS CAME TO AMERICA, *By William Bell Clark*
Originally published in 1929, this important study of U-boat warfare remains the
most complete study of German submarine operations on the East Coast of the
United States in 1918, when 200,000 tons of shipping and 421 lives were lost in
actions that were quickly forgotten. The author, a U.S. Navy Rear Admiral, traced
the operations of 3 U-boats between June and August, their results and the public
commotion they caused, how the U-boats made their 3,000-mile voyages from
Europe, and their fate. 2005: 359 pages, softcover. ISBN: 0-945726-60-0.

AS THEY SAW US; *Foch, Ludendorff, and Other Leaders Write Our
War History, By George Sylvester Viereck*
Viereck's 1928 publication gathered texts such as "The American Soldier in the
World War as Seen by a Friend," by Marshal Ferdinand Foch, "The American
Soldier in the World War as Seen by a Foe," by General Erich Ludendorff, and
seven other essays on the A.E.F. and its operations at the Aisne-Marne Triangle,
St. Mihiel, and the Meuse-Argonne in the Fall of 1918, all written by German or
French officers. The book provides not only unique material on the military history
of the war but also on how the opponents viewed each other a decade later and
what the prospects were at that time for "universal brotherhood." 2005: 386
pages. Softcover. (Scholar's Bookshelf)

A.E.F.; Ten Years Ago in France, *By Major Gen. Hunter Liggett*
One of the first reliable and comprehensive histories of the American participation
in WWI. First published in 1927, the seven chapters by the Commander of the
First Army of the A.E.F. presented separate studies of the background of U.S.
entry, and detailed descriptions of the campaigns at Chateau-Thierry, Belleau
Wood, the Marne, St. Mihiel, and the Meuse-Argonne. Includes documentary
records of the staffs of the Third Army and other units. 2005: 335 pages, softcover, illustrated. ISBN: 0-945726-13-9.